LIVINGSTONE

DAVID LIVINGSTONE
By courtesy of the National Portrait Gallery

LIVINGSTONE

By

R. J. CAMPBELL, D. D.

With Illustrations

GREENWOOD PRESS, PUBLISHERS
WESTPORT, CONNECTICUT

The Library of Congress has catalogued this publication as follows:

Library of Congress Cataloging in Publication Data

Campbell, Reginald John, 1867-1956.
  Livingstone.

    Bibliography: p.
    1. Livingstone, David, 1813-1873.
DT731.L8C3 1972   916'.04'20924 [B]   77-138212
ISBN 0-8371-5567-3

Originally published in 1930
by Dodd, Mead and Company, Inc., New York

Reprinted with the permission
of Dodd, Mead and Company

First Greenwood Reprinting 1972

Library of Congress Catalogue Card Number 77-138212

ISBN 0-8371-5567-3

Printed in the United States of America

1644083

PREFACE

WHEN Messrs. Dodd, Mead & Company did me the honour of asking me to undertake the preparation of a new biography of David Livingstone, bringing up to date our knowledge of the great missionary explorer's life and the permanent effects of his work, I suggested that it might be better to assign the commission to some one more closely associated with the London Missionary Society by whose authority Livingstone had been originally trained and sent to Africa, and under whose supervision the first fifteen years of his career both as a missionary and a traveller had been spent. For various reasons into which there is no need to enter here the suggestion was not acted upon, but on my ultimately consenting to write the book, the London Missionary Society most generously placed the whole of its unpublished archives relating to Livingstone at my disposal. Not only so, but the managing editor of the Society, Mr. David Chamberlin, assumed the heavy and responsible task of sifting the great mass of material thus available and passing on to me whatever might prove to be of value. In addition to this, Mr. Chamberlin has kept in close touch with me throughout, reading through the successive chapters as they were written and making important suggestions. He has also prepared the map which accompanies the book, and furnished some of the illustrations from the sources at his command. My debt to him and the great Society he so worthily represents is thus very considerable, and I gratefully acknowledge it.

I am also under obligation to the Rev. J. I. Macnair and the members of the Livingstone Memorial Committee at Blantyre for their kindly offer to allow me to consult the Livingstone MSS. in their possession. Unfortunately, the offer came too late for me to be able to make as full use of it as I could wish, but, as will be seen from the following pages, it has been helpful, particularly in regard to Livingstone's relations with his family in the latter part of his life. Nor must

I omit to mention the courtesy of Dr. Hubert Wilson, Livingstone's grandson, in furnishing to me through Mr. Chamberlin some interesting facts bearing upon the family origins and still more for lending and permitting me to examine at leisure the manuscript Journal and small diaries covering the period of the Zambesi expedition. The Journal of over eight hundred pages was locked, as all Livingstone's larger Journals were, and the services of an expert had to be requisitioned before it could be opened and read. It is this bulky volume which is referred to occasionally herein as the locked Journal, to distinguish it from the smaller note-books which have no fastening; the lock appears to have been fixed by Livingstone rather for the sake of preserving the contents from damage than for privacy; there is less of a piquant character in the Journal than in the small diaries.

Warm thanks are also due to Lady Hunt of Sudborough House, Northants, daughter of the Rev. Horace Waller, who edited Livingstone's *Last Journals,* for allowing me to work through the letters written by Livingstone to her father, together with the latter's private memoranda of his relations with the great explorer from 1862 onward. These have been to me a most interesting find, and have served to light up Livingstone's personality for me as no published record of his work has ever done. To see the man through Horace Waller's eyes is, I think, to see him as he was in his maturity, and to obtain a clearer insight into the greatness of his mind; the pardonable human foibles disclosed in the process but serve to make his personality the more real, and in some ways more attractive. Blaikie's *Life of David Livingstone,* the fullest and most accurate account of its subject's career which has yet appeared, is defective in one important respect: it ignores everything which might suggest that the great man had any of the faults and weaknesses of ordinary humanity; it inferentially represents him as flawlessly wise and good, never making a mistake, never descending from the loftiest pedestal of motive and conduct. Livingstone's character can take care of itself; it needs no whitewashing. The massiveness of his personality stands out the plainer and nobler from the acerbity and unreasonableness into which he occasionally breaks in the Waller correspondence, and his sharp denunciations of conduct of which he believes himself justified in complaining are not exactly models of Christian meekness; he has fixed prejudices, too, which nothing can overcome.

To the Rev. Andrew Forson of Motherwell, editor of the *Scottish Congregationalist,* I am indebted for some particulars of Livingstone's early life, and for putting me on the track of others. At Mr. Forson's request the Rev. J. A. Lees, formerly minister of St. James's Church, Hamilton, most kindly wrote out for me in his own hand the reminiscences of the connection of the Livingstone family with this church in the explorer's boyhood, which are briefly referred to in the second chapter. These reminiscences constituted the bulk of an article by Mr. Lees which appeared in the *Chronicle* of the London Missionary Society for August, 1925.

Obviously in a work like the present it has been impossible to cover all the ground of Livingstone's varied activities; a delimitation had to be made and adhered to. What has been aimed at is to give a clear, connected narrative of the events of Livingstone's life in their more specifically personal aspects, to portray him as a man with a sense of vocation and describe his method of discharging it, to show how his mind unfolded and his purpose correspondingly, to exhibit him as a Christian philanthropist even more than as a traveller with a quenchless passion for discovery. Necessarily, therefore, no attempt could be made herein to describe other than cursorily the important additions made by Livingstone to natural science in any or all of the several main departments to which he contributed. His own reports in this field are extant, and make fascinating reading; they are enough in themselves to establish their author's reputation as a brilliant and patient observer, but any summary of them that would be worth the making would far exceed the space at my disposal. The same applies to the various sidelines Livingstone touched as his work developed—political, sociological, ecclesiastical, commercial. To deal with any one of them adequately would take us too far from our main track; they can but be mentioned severally as they impinge upon or deflect the course of the narrative without being traced further. Little that is new and nothing vital to an understanding of Livingstone's policy in regard to them has been omitted; the bibliography contains the sources in which they can be more exhaustively studied by those wishful to do so.

The spelling of names is somewhat of a difficulty. Rarely has Livingstone's phonetic reproduction of a native appellation been adopted by writers of the present day. He took no notice of such philological distinctions as "Ba" and "Ma" for a people prefixed to the real name of their tribe—Ba-Rotse or Ma-Rotse, Ma-Kololo, Ba-Mangwato, Ma-Tebele. Bechuana for a people and Sechuana or Sichuana for the language they spoke he did pay attention to, because he found it already marked at Kuruman, but he did not trouble much about consistency in his spelling of the names of individuals or localities. Still, on the whole, it has been deemed advisable to adhere to Livingstone's usual spelling unless there is clear reason for discarding it in favour of another form in any given instance. It should be remarked that even his spelling of his own tongue is not always accurate, as his private correspondence sometimes surprisingly reveals—*e.g.,* "seperate," "watershead," "revalation." Such slips are not infrequent.

It will be seen that the new material included in this book from original sources and not hitherto made public is fairly large in amount and of considerable value. If it adds little to what is already generally known of the facts of Livingstone's life and labours, it enhances its human interest and our understanding of the man himself.

The references to passages in Livingstone's works are to the London editions.

CONTENTS

ILLUSTRATIONS

MAPS

AT THE VICTORIA FALLS

"WHERE goes the river?" Livingstone enquired.
  Then did a dusky Solomon declare,
    With naked dignity and learned air:
"White Chief, the knowledge many have desired
We give to you. It is a lion tired
  By a great leap, who seeks afar his lair,
    Sleeps, and by sand is covered; none know where."
Thus the witch-doctor, confident, inspired.

Th' intrepid Traveller thought otherwise.
  Ever he journeyed on undauntedly.
Not years of loneliness; nor nightly cries—
  Perils of man and beast; not agony
Of burning days of fever and of flies
  Deterring; till, at last—"The sea, the sea!"

ARTHUR VINE HALL: *Poems of a South African.*

LIVINGSTONE

CHAPTER I

AFRICA AND LIVINGSTONE

THE Dark Continent, as it is so often termed, is at once the oldest and the newest great division of the earth's surface in point of civilization. If the claim of Professor Elliot Smith and the experts who hold with him, that Egypt is the cradle of human culture, can be sustained, the world is Africa's debtor to a greater extent than has ever yet been computed, and we are confronted with the paradoxical fact that Europe is returning to the centre and south of that vast area some of the stream of cultural development that originally proceeded from the north. W. J. Roome[1] draws attention to the strikingly suggestive fact that in A.D. 598 an appeal was addressed to Christian Africa on behalf of Pagan England. Pope Gregory wrote to Eubogius of Alexandria: "The English race, situated in the far corner of the world, has hitherto been in unbelief, worshipping stocks and stones. But, aided by your prayers, I sent a monk. Now letters have arrived telling me of his work. They show that he and those sent out with him shine amongst that nation with such miracles that they seem to imitate the mighty works of the apostles. At Christmas last more than ten thousand English people were baptized. I tell you this that you may know . . . what your prayers are doing at the world's end; for your prayers are where you are not: your holy works are evident where you are."

The fertilizing flow of thought and energy which, passing from Egypt through Greece, brought into being the entire civilization of the West, dried up on the northern shores of Africa itself, and never at any time succeeded in thrusting through the great natural barrier of the Sahara or penetrating below the sources of the Nile. Under Roman imperial rule, it is true, great things were done in the development of the resources of the vast stretch of territory lying between the Red Sea

[1] *Can Africa be Won?* p. 6.

I

and the Atlantic, and including the principal part of modern Egypt, Tripoli, Algeria, and Morocco, as the ruins of Timgad and Constantine remain to testify to this day. The Christian church of northern Africa, with its metropolitan centres in Alexandria and Carthage, was in the plenitude of its vigour no unworthy peer of the other ancient patriarchates of Christendom, and there is no more mysterious or melancholy fatality recorded in the annals of the rise and fall of religious movements than the disappearance of this great church before the hordes of Islam. The contrast between the obstinate barbaric fanaticism of the Mohammedan inhabitants of northern Africa to-day and the brilliance and splendour of the past is very painful. The church of Tertullian, Cyprian, and Augustine conferred benefits on mankind which will never be forgotten; but the efforts of Cardinal Lavigerie and the numerous Protestant missionary agencies of our time to recover the lost ground have not greatly prospered.

The Africa of the centre and south remained untouched by the dramatic vicissitudes of the north. Ethnologically, the continent falls naturally into three main divisions. The mixed white and brown races bordering on the Mediterranean and extending southwards to the desert represent the Africa that has played an important part in human history. The Bantu races, which cover the whole of tropical Africa and are found in considerable numbers well down into Cape Colony may hardly perhaps be classified as the indigenous Africans, but it is they who have the best title to be considered the typical Africans and the most fecund occupiers of its soil. On the southernmost fringe and the desert spaces adjoining are the Hottentot and Bushman strains, which are yielding to the pressure of the whites on the one side and their stronger black-skinned neighbours on the other. Of these three great sections, the various Bantu tribes are at the present moment, and will be for long to come, the portion of Africa's inhabitants that presents to statesmanship and Christian evangelization the most serious problems and the most promising field for ameliorative endeavour. The Hottentot-Bushman type gave great concern to the white settlers at the Cape and to the British administration in the first half of the nineteenth century, but of the far more vigorous Bantu stocks little was known until David Livingstone came on the scene. This is a generalization which requires to be qualified to the extent of saying that the slave trade had made us acquainted with the Bantu African as represented by the negroes of the west coast, who for centuries had been forcibly drawn upon by Europeans to furnish slave labour, especially for the plantations of northern and central America.

Farther inland the inhabitants remained in their original state of savagery right through the period of recorded history. That they should have been able to do so may seem strange to modern observers —stranger still, perhaps, now that the truth is established of the spontaneous burgeoning of civilization in different portions of the globe and at different periods, apparently without stimulus from outside. This certainly appears to have been the case with the comparatively advanced cultures of the American continent before Europeans landed there. Recent excavations in Nevada and cognate archæological discoveries in Central America have virtually placed beyond doubt the fact that the aborigines of the western hemisphere are of Mongolian origin, and migrated from Asia from twenty-five to thirty thousand years ago, bringing with them nothing above the level of primitive barbarism; the truly surprising heights of artistic and social development to which they attained with the lapse of time, and which are now proved to have been much greater than we have hitherto known, were entirely of native growth, and owed nothing to the example and influence of any superior race or social order. Why Bantu Africa should not have made similar progress no one can say with certitude, but the most probable explanation is twofold: The conformation of the continent cut off the people dwelling in the interior from intercourse with the rest of the world, and the tribal system permitted no excellence in anyone but the chief and kept the population divided into comparatively unstable warring communities of small size Wide desert spaces to the north and south, high mountain ranges to east and west, combined with a dearth of water communications, kept the dwellers in this enormous region segregated from all other races, and in a state of ignorance little better than animalism. We have to remember, too, that if the central African knew nothing of the outer world, neither did the outer world know anything of him. Ignorance of what central Africa was really like, topographically and otherwise, was general up to the middle of the nineteenth century. Until Livingstone revealed the truth, the most fantastic notions were entertained concerning it, as a glance at the map of Africa previous to 1856 would prove.

Nor had Europe's contact with Africa hitherto been in the main a beneficent one; on the contrary, it had been more of a curse than a blessing. The slave trade, begun by the Portuguese in the fifteenth century, was carried on and increased by the English from the sixteenth to the eighteenth. It has been estimated by competent authorities that the traffic cost Africa no less than a hundred million lives, not to mention the appalling total of suffering and degradation associated therewith, and which have done more than anything else to keep Africa in a backward state. The African has unjustly been looked down upon by his white masters as an inferior type incapable of the advancement made by the nations that have subdued and exploited him. This mistaken view, against which Livingstone was among the first to protest, is at length giving way before the evidence of sociological facts. The educated negro is showing himself able to do most that his white contemporary can do both intellectually and physically. As the present writer has frequently had occasion to observe in the United States and elsewhere, the very features of the coloured man tend to approximate to those of the European under the same cultural influences as are enjoyed by the latter.[2] There is no more groundless misapprehension than the common one that the descendant of negro slaves must speak pidgin English and behave like a child. It is sometimes startling to one unprepared for the phenomenon to see a European face and expression combined with a coal-black complexion, and to hear a refined and beautiful voice proceeding from the lips of the same person and discoursing intelligently on vital topics of the hour. Truly a miracle, when the generations of induced slave mentality that preceded it are taken into account.

[2] Some sociologists question if this is necessarily to the advantage of either race.

The four centuries during which Africa was regarded as a quarry for the supply of cheap labour inflicted immeasurable injury both upon the native races and their oppressors, for no one will deny that slavery as an institution reacts unfavourably upon the whole population of any country where it prevails. In 1813, the year in which Livingstone was born, Great Britain and the United States took a joint stand against the traffic in human flesh which, until then, had been the staple of commercial intercourse between the African coast and the English-speaking communities of the new world, most of the human freight being carried in British ships for the enrichment of British mercantile houses. Six years earlier the traffic had been declared illegal in the British Empire, but it was not until 1833 that slavery as an institution ceased in British dominions. From that date onward British policy was directed to the suppression of the evil trade it had done so much to foster, but the comparative ill success attending the policy did not become generally known until Livingstone's revelations broadcast it to the world. He set a mark upon Africa deeper than any empire builder has ever done; indeed, it may with truth be said that it was chiefly he who made possible the moral trusteeship of the advanced over the backward races which is now a principle of the League of Nations. Article twenty-two of the Covenant of the League is the explicit recognition of this principle and of the obligation that rests upon the stronger powers to conform to it. No nation has any longer an absolutely free hand in disposing of the lives and property of subject peoples; there is a court of international public opinion to which every mandatory power is in some sort responsible, and this is a newly created authority whose effective exercise is bound to increase. The British imperial Government has frankly admitted and applied the principle of trusteeship to all its dealings with the populations and resources of the extensive territories under its rule in Africa. As will be seen in the following pages, this was Livingstone's vision; for this he wrought, and hoped, and suffered for the greater part of his mature life, and for this in the end he died.

He gave to the world a new view of the African—of his educability, industry, and capacity for moral improvement. This is a fact which, as Professor Sedgwick said a generation ago,[3] should be classed amongst the most valuable of Livingstone's contributions to the world's knowledge and moral health. Earlier missionaries, like Philip and Moffat, on African soil, and others among the African slave stocks of the West Indies, had proclaimed that the African was endowed with potentialities of intelligence and character far beyond what he was usually given credit for; but Livingstone forced the fact upon universal attention because of the greater scale upon which his work was done, and the multitudes of hitherto untouched independent populations he was the means of introducing to civilization. "Let no one say that Africa labours under a natural incapacity for civilization," cried William Pitt in his speech in support of the abolition of slavery in 1792. ". . . *We* were once . . . as savage in our manners, as degraded in our understandings. Some of us may live to behold the natives of Africa engaged in the calm occupations of industry, in the pursuit of a just and legitimate commerce. We may behold the beams of science and philosophy breaking in upon their land . . . and joining their influence with that of pure religion. . . . Then may we hope that even Africa, though last of all the quarters of the globe, shall enjoy at length, in the evening of her days, those blessings which have descended so plentifully upon us." This notable utterance exactly expresses what Livingstone believed and unweariedly preached both by example and testimony, and he succeeded in doing what neither statesman nor philanthropist had succeeded in doing before him: he broke down stubborn barriers of prejudice and stupidity, and let in a flood of new light upon a problem of a magnitude hitherto unguessed by the leaders of mankind.

He was but just in time. As G. M. Trevelyan penetratingly points out,[4] had slavery not been abolished as detrimental to the physical and moral welfare of civilized peoples—or at least solemnly repudiated as inconsistent with the *jus gentium*—before the rush for the partition of Africa among the great European powers in the latter part of the nine-

[3] *Cambridge Lectures*, p. 125.
[4] *History of the Nineteenth Century.*

teenth century, there might have been established a number of new slave states on the African continent with inconceivably evil reactions upon ordered human society everywhere. It is not too much to say that the intensity of the moral ardour aroused by Livingstone made such a sinister eventuality impossible. Africa would have been thrown open by someone else sooner or later if he had not done it; but on the character of that someone else would have depended the nature of the results to follow. Is it likely that the mere head of a military expedition or even the members of a company engaged in scientific exploration would have produced the effect that Livingstone did by going alone and unsupported except by natives through strange and turbulent lands? To this day the path he took is marked by a greater respect for the white man than other routes; he was the first representative of the white race that the inhabitants of inner Africa had seen, and the impression he made remains. Commissioner Unsworth, of the Salvation Army, who has crossed and recrossed Africa at various points in the discharge of his duty, remarked to the present writer that it was his experience that wherever Livingstone had gone the natives had learnt to look for good at the hands of the European and be receptive to it, but that where others had fought their way through it was not so; in the latter case the white man's motives were suspect and aloofness was maintained. Obviously the atmosphere that Livingstone carried with him and the new sympathy and respect for the African that he awakened in Europe and America, a sympathy and respect whose tokens were quickly apparent in the kind of help they furnished to Africa, did much to counteract beforehand the mischiefs that were certain to accrue from the sudden mingling of entirely different ethnic strains at widely different stages of historic and cultural development.

The chief reason for Livingstone's lasting influence on the unsophisticated African soul was his character. This he knew, and frequently took occasion to warn other travellers that they would be judged by their behaviour. Primitive and rude the native might be, irrational and at times loathsome in his ways, but he possessed an unerring eye for what was better than himself; in fact there was no surer sign that he was worth helping than his instinctive capacity for distinguishing between good and evil in the examples presented to his observation; and when he saw, as he could not avoid seeing, the inconsistency between precept and practice, only too apt to prevail where the white man set his foot, he would be repelled instead of attracted thereby. Subsequent history has only too fully justified the reiterated warning. It was so with the Portuguese and the Boers, and when the tide of French, Belgian, German, and British enterprise began to flow strongly over the newly opened territories it gained in force. The greatest asset that the reputation of Great Britain has ever possessed in Africa is the respect felt by natives of every grade for the manhood of David Livingstone. No less important and abiding has been the same influence upon the minds and hearts of his own countrymen and upon millions of others to the remotest corners of the globe.

That influence is not lessening; rather it grows with the years. Everyone now admits that the work which Livingstone accomplished for the benefit of Africa deserved all the laudation it received from contemporaries, but with the lapse of time its proportions expand. The greatness of the man stands out in clearer perspective. What he advocated and what he did are seen to have been more significant and fruitful than even he could have anticipated. The tale of his achievements increases day by day, and the desire to know more of the manner of man he was and of the way in which his life was spent is as keen and general as when, fifty years ago, the news of his passing in the African wild caused universal sorrow. It is in the endeavour to meet this desire and to estimate the worth of the direct outcome of deeds which thrilled an earlier generation, when performed unaided by a humble missionary of the Christian Gospel, that the following story is told.

CHAPTER II

LIVINGSTONE'S ORIGIN AND EARLY YEARS

DAVID LIVINGSTONE came of Scottish Highland stock on the father's side. On the mother's he derived from a no less virile but widely different race, that of the Lowlanders of Strathclyde, with their tenacious democratic traditions and stern Calvinistic faith. It was to the blend of these two that he owed the qualities that chiefly distinguished him throughout life. This is a fact which needs emphasis, for it has not always received due recognition. Mrs. K. W. Grant, an authority of deservedly high reputation on the subject of Gaelic lore, says in her *Myth, Tradition, and Story from Western Argyll:* "There were traits in the character of David Livingstone that puzzled his biographers—Lowland Scot, Englishman, and American alike—and that they could not account for. There are no enigma to his Highland countrymen. He has been held up to admiration as an example of 'the highest type of Anglo-Saxon race' by those who persistently ignore the old race to which the British Empire to-day owes so much. Yet so typically Scottish Highland was he, even in personal appearance, that on one occasion a Livingstone of Bachuill and on another a member of the Achnacree family was greeted as 'Dr. Livingstone' by visitors from London who had seen the great explorer. One lady caused much amusement to the bystanders by insisting on kissing the hand of the plain, honest farmer whom she mistook for his illustrious relative, whom she had seen and spoken to." The point thus tellingly made is one of considerable interest, but fails to take account of the fact that the Lowland strain in Livingstone was at least equally marked —the patience, doggedness, perseverance, and strength of will that carried him through so many difficulties and dangers. Heredity does not explain everything in a great man; certainly it does not do so in Livingstone's case. But it explains much, and in any estimate we make

9

of the factors that went to the forming of one of the most notable personages of the nineteenth century we must allow full weight, both to the keen imagination and high spirit of his Gaelic ancestry, and to the moral strength of the Covenanting stock of his maternal grandsire.

Livingstone's own brief sketch of his family history, prefixed to his *Missionary Travels and Researches in South Africa,* hardly takes us back far enough, and the information it supplies is but meagre. It is said to have been written at the request of the publishers in order to satisfy public curiosity in regard to his antecedents. We are told therein that his paternal great-grandfather fell at Culloden fighting on the side of the Young Pretender; that his grandfather, Neil Livingstone, a small farmer in Ulva, was compelled by poverty to move to Blantyre, near Glasgow, where he and his sons became employees in the cotton factory of Monteith and Co.; that all these sons but one, David's father, subsequently took service either in the army or navy. The son who remained at home, Neil Livingstone the younger, became a small tea dealer, married in the same modest social rank to which he himself belonged, and brought up his children in the fear of God. The picture painted by Livingstone of his early home life is an attractive one. He pays reverent tribute to the influence and example of both his parents, comparing his father with the description given by Robert Burns of the head of a poor respectable family in *The Cotter's Saturday Night.* Upon his own youthful experiences he dwells with cheerful retrospect. Not only did he count it no disadvantage to have had to undergo the discipline of privation and struggle, but testifies: "Looking back now on that life of toil, I cannot but feel thankful that it formed such a material part of my early education; and, were it possible, I should like to begin life over again in the same lowly style, and to pass through the same hardy training."

This manly and simple statement of facts within the knowledge of the great missionary himself has since been added to in various ways, partly based on conjecture, but full of human interest. Dr. Alexander Carmichael has given in the *Celtic Review* (vol. v., pp. 356 *ff.*) some dramatic details which appear to link the family of David Livingstone with memorable events in Scottish history. He differs from Livingstone in his account of the fate of the aforementioned great-grand-father, and assigns to the family a more impressive pedigree by deriving it from the Barons of Bachuill. The original Baron of Bachuill was an ecclesiastical functionary, and the title dates from the beginning of the thirteenth century, when the bishopric of Argyll and the Isles was established by papal authority. The custodian of the "baculum" or pastoral staff of the bishop had to be a layman of good standing and repute. The position carried with it certain duties and privileges of an important character, the former including the administration of diocesan revenues, and the latter the holding of a grant of land. The office was vested in a branch of the sept now known by the name of Livingstone, though whether David Livingstone's line had any connection with it is not so clear. Dr. Carmichael's version of the facts is as follows:

The Barons of Bachuill are of interest to all who are interested—and who is not?—in Dr. David Livingstone. The great missionary explorer was descended from these Livingstone Barons of Bachuill in Lismore. Neil Livingstone, the young son of the old Baron, joined the army of Prince Charlie, and was in the rising of 1745. He escaped, but not scatheless, the disasters of Culloden, and made his way home to Bachuill. But Lismore was not a safe asylum, being the country of the Campbells, and the parish of the Rev. John MacAulay. This John MacAulay, who had been minister of South Uist, was the grandfather of Lord MacAulay, and like his father in Harris, the Rev. Aulay MacAulay, he made himself obnoxious by trying to secure the Prince.

Neil Livingstone crossed from Lismore to Morven, and after a time from Morven to Mull, and finally from Mull to Ulva, adjoining.

Donald Livingstone, the son of Neil Livingstone, was in the local Fencibles of his day. During the annual drills at Oban and Stirling he made the acquaintance of his namesake and distant kinswoman, Catherine Livingstone, whose father was a farmer at Bailemore in Kerrara, opposite Oban. When his regiment was finally disbanded, Donald Livingstone married Catherine Livingstone and brought her home with him to Ulva. Things, however, did not prosper in Ulva with the young people, and after a time they removed to Blantyre on the Clyde. Donald Livingstone had a son, Neil, the father of David Livingstone, whose name will live while courage, honesty, and humanity are admired among men.

The divergence from Livingstone's own account of the identity and history of his not very remote ancestors is sufficiently apparent, and has been commented upon by the Rev. A. MacLean Sinclair in an article in the *Celtic Monthly* of June, 1909. Admitting that Livingstone may have been mistaken in stating that his great-grandfather was killed at Culloden, argues Mr. Sinclair, he can hardly have been mistaken in regard to other matters on which his grandfather must have been his informant; he would at least know his grandfather's name and the maiden name of the grandfather's wife, which were not Donald and Catherine Livingstone, but Neil Livingstone and Mary Morrison. The point is placed beyond doubt by a letter written to Mr. Sinclair by David Livingstone's elder brother John on April 8th, 1891, in reply to a direct inquiry, the salient paragraph reading:

> My grandfather, Neil Livingstone, and his wife, Mary Morrison, with their family, left Mull or Ulva about the end of last century and settled at Blantyre, near Glasgow, and remained there till they died. The names of their children were John, Charles, Duncan, Donald, and Neil, with two daughters, Kate and Margaret; but they are all dead now. Neil was my father.

The family name at this period appears to have been spelt, or at least registered, without the final "e," and continued to be so until about the middle of the nineteenth century, when for some reason the longer form was adopted, probably as being more in harmony with the usage of other Scottish Livingstones. The managing editor of the London Missionary Society, in a note to the present writer, says: "The earliest letter I can find in our archives with the signature 'David Livingstone' instead of 'Livingston,' as previously, is dated September 22nd, 1855."

Unwilling to leave names and dates unverified, Mr. Sinclair caused a search to be instituted in the Register House, Edinburgh, in 1906, and was rewarded by finding the entries relating to the marriage of Neil Livingston and Mary Morrison, together with a record of the baptism of their children successively. The pivotal registrations are these:

1774, December 27th.—Neil Livingston in Letermore and Mary Morrison were married.

1788, November 30th.—Neil Livingston and Mary Morrison in Ferininardory had their lawful son Neil baptized.

The names of the other children appear as stated by John Livingstone, one only being omitted.

Where Ferininardory may be no one seems to know, though there have been many guesses. Whether it was situate on the mainland or in Ulva it is impossible to say with certainty. What chiefly concerns us is that the Neil Livingston born there in 1788 was David Livingstone's father.

The elder Neil Livingstone (for so the name is spelt in the subjoined certificate) left Ulva for Blantyre in 1792. Of this migration Mrs. Grant has a different story to tell from that which David Livingstone gives in the preface to *Missionary Travels,* though not necessarily inconsistent therewith. It is to the effect that an unscrupulous neighbour managed to have the crofter dispossessed of his holding by bringing a false accusation against him. The truth was discovered before the evicted household left the island, and the factor or landlord's agent wished to restore the holding, but to this Neil Livingstone would not consent. He could not, he said, remain in a position where he had been treated so unjustly on the mere word of a covetous third party; his self-respect was too deeply wounded to be soothed by reinstatement and acknowledgment of a mistake. Here the Highland pride peeps out, and the Highland mistrust of friendly professions made after an act of injury. The incident is not unlikely to be true, though the source of information is not stated.

The following is a copy of the letter of recommendation which Neil Livingstone the elder took with him on his departure:

The bearer, Neil Livingstone, a married man in Ulva, part of the parish of Kilninian, has always maintained an unblemished moral character, and is known for a man of piety and religion. He has a family of four sons, the youngest of which is three years, and three daughters, of which the youngest is six years of age. As he proposes to offer his services at some of the cotton-spinning manufactories, he and his wife, Mary Morrison, and their family of children are hereby recommended for suitable encouragement. Given at Ulva, this eighth day of January, 1792, by

> ARCH. M'ARTHUR, *Minister*.
> LACH. M'LEAN, *Elder*.
> R. S. STEWART, J.P., *Elder*.

Dr. Hubert Wilson, grandson of David Livingstone, being the son of the missionary's youngest daughter Anna Mary, has furnished the following traditional particulars of the family origin for inclusion in the present volume:

When St. Columba came to the island of Iona in the year 565, there came with him one Betan, whose descendants became physicians to the Columbian Church. Of these, in course of time were three families, the Beatons or Bethunes of Mull, of Skye, and of Islay. It is probable that from the first of these was descended the ancient and renowned family known in the Western Highlands as Mac-an-Leigh, or "Sons of the Physician." The Mac-an-Leighs, or as they came later to be known when the Gaelic name was anglicized, the "Livingstones," are found in Appin, Benderloch, and Loch Etive, on the mainland, also in the Peninsula of Morven and in the islands of Lismore and Mull.

If the Gaelic meaning attributed to the name be correct, the fact would have given satisfaction to David Livingstone had he known of it, which apparently he did not, despite the inquiries he made in Ulva after his second return from abroad, being desirous at that period to learn anything he could relating to his kindred antecedent to his grandfather's removal to Blantyre. That his name should have affinities with the healing art would have seemed to him felicitous.

Dr. Wilson accepts Carmichael's identification of the Livingstone stock in one or more of its several branches with that of the Barons of Bachuill, and further, though cautiously, its association with one of the most thrilling exploits in the stormy history of mid-eighteenth century Scotland. In the latter case he goes so far as to admit the possibility that his forbears in the direct line should be credited with having borne a part in a daring feat still fresh in Highland memory. The story is best told in his own words:

> The task of unravelling the tangled skein of a Highland descent in the troubled period of the Jacobite rising of the eighteenth century is a perplexing one. Accurate records are few and meagre, and tradition weaves its ample net round historical incident, confusing with its wealth of detail and its poetic bridging of the gaps the simple tale. Some of these old tales are highly romantic; among such the following explanation of the presence of the Livingstones in Ulva might be selected.
>
> Readers of R. L. Stevenson's historical romances, *Kidnapped* and *Catriona*, will readily recall the unfortunate murder near Ballachulish of Campbell of Glenure, the factor who was responsible to the Campbell of Argyll for collecting rents which had already been smuggled out of the country to the rightful landlord, who was an exiled Chieftain in France. Retribution followed this crime, taking the form of the judicial murder of "James Stewart of the Glens." James was condemned by a packed jury in Inverary, where feeling ran high and where everyone was a blind partisan of the offended Chief MacCullen Mhor. The body was condemned to be hung in chains on the rocky knoll—"Cnoch-a-Chaolais," above Ballachulish ferry on the south side. There it remained guarded by soldiers for three years—an object of shame to the local people, who were strongly anti-Campbell and pro-Stewart in their sympathies. A man, John Livingston of Ballachulish—the last of a long race of John Livingstons, who had been shepherds in Glen Etive—called to him his sons and suggested that they should redeem the good name of the neighbourhood by stealing the remains of the unfortunate James Stewart and burying them. The lads took the hint, and on a stormy November evening one of them invited the soldiers who

were on guard over the body to dine with them in the inn below.
The soldiers agreed, explaining that no one ever came near the place
—and no wonder, for who would want to inspect such gruesome
relics? While Tony Livingston and the soldiers were making their
way down the western side of the knoll, the other two brothers, who
had been in hiding on the Ballachulish side, sprang up, cut the body
down, and hurriedly carried it to a boat which was moored below.
The tide was on the turn, and it required but few strokes of the oars
to bring them across to the island called Eileannah-Juraich, where
they buried their burden.

In such troubled times it was deemed unsafe to return to their
father's house, so they profited by the now ebbing tide and the
darkness of the wild night and slipped through the narrows, and
before morning were on the Morven side of Loch Linnhe, where
they disposed of their boat and were heard of no more. It is conjectured that they crossed to Mull and found in Ulva a secure hiding-
place, where their descendants were the worthy couple whose
emigration in 1792 to Blantyre has been described.

Unfortunately David Livingstone, who tells us of his grandfather's
recollection of the six generations preceding his own, and of his own
interest in such a never-ending stock of stories, makes no reference
to an incident which, even in those less romantic days, must have
appealed to him on account of its daring and resource.

The reason why David Livingstone did not mention an occurrence
so memorable, and of which he could scarcely have been ignorant,
since it was well known to every Highlander, is more likely to have
been that he never thought of associating it with his own family
Either the ancestor actually concerned in it observed strict reticenc
on the subject out of regard for his own safety or the deed was pe
formed by other Livingstones. In either case, the sequence of even
is difficult to square with the dates on record. The body of Jame
Stewart was rescued from the gallows at a date not more than te
years after Culloden. If the Neil Livingstone whom Carmichael
describes as the son of the then Baron of Bachuill fought at Culloden,
and was in hiding in the isles in consequence, who was the John
Livingstone whose sons did what is here told of them, and who also

fled to the isles to avoid reprisals? How, again, are we to explain the presence of David's grandfather, Neil Livingstone, at Letermore in 1774, a sojourn anterior to his residence in Ulva? If it were this Neil's father who fought at Culloden, as David says it was, and if the latter were mistaken in believing that he was killed there, it is possible that he was the man alluded to as having shared with his brothers in the hazardous achievement narrated; but if proscribed, as he would be sure to be, and already in Ulva, how did he come to be on the scene? That his son Neil, David's grandfather, should be living in Letermore in 1774, and, as the Edinburgh register shows, have still been living there in 1777 when his second child was born, is not easily consistent with an earlier and later domicile in Ulva, though such a passing to and fro is not absolutely incredible.[1]

David Livingstone's recollections of his paternal grandfather were keen and vivid. "As a boy," he says, "I remember listening to him with delight, for his memory was stored with a never-ending stock of stories, many of which were wonderfully like those I have since heard while sitting by the African evening fires."[2] These stories consisted mostly of the Highland legends and traditions upon which Sir Walter Scott drew at a little later date in his *Tales of a Grandfather.* The grandmother contributed a share to these happy occasions by her accomplishment of singing Gaelic songs for the children's entertainment. She appears to have known the Gaelic tongue better than English, for we are informed that her son Neil, David's father, refurbished his Gaelic in later life in order to read the Bible to his mother in the language of her youth. Quite in keeping with what is stated above of the circumstances in which the Livingstones left Ulva is the grandfather's recital of the charge said to have been given by one of his own lineal ancestors to his sons on his deathbed. "In my lifetime," said this unnamed worthy, "I have searched most carefully through all the traditions I could find of our family, and I never could discover

---

[1] Since the above was written and in type, Mr. David Chamberlin writes to the author: "I have just visited the places in which the Ballachulish incidents of 1750 occurred—the murder of Campbell and execution of Stewart. I find there is a strong local belief that one of the rescuers of Stewart's body was David Livingstone's great-grandfather."

[2] Introduction to *Missionary Travels.*

that there was a dishonest man among our forefathers. If, therefore, any of you or any of your children should take to dishonest ways, it will not be because it runs in our blood: it does not belong to you. I leave this precept with you: Be honest."

Dr. Carmichael's researches have succeeded in unearthing a story which has some bearing on the claim here made.[3] As usual when the misfortunes of the Livingstones or the Stewarts of Appin are in question, a Campbell is the villain of the piece. A certain Sir Donald Campbell of Airds, an ecclesiastic of Reformation times, played the part of a northern Vicar of Bray, adhering to Rome or the tenets of Calvin as his interests dictated. He was a great thorn in the side of the contemporary Baron of Bachuill, and ultimately robbed him of his estate by means of an unscrupulous trick. Having suborned one of the Baron's dependents to kill and place the skin of a sheep belonging to himself on the Baron's premises, he took measures to have the latter falsely accused of the act.

On the following day it was reported that the black sheep of Alasrath was stolen. The people were alarmed, sheep stealing being a capital crime and Sir Donald implacable. The houses were searched, and that there might be no remissness of duty, Campbell himself accompanied the search party. The house of the Baron was searched like the rest, and there on the rafters was found the skin— lug-marks and all—of the black sheep of Alasrath. The people were astonished, and, apparently, none more than Sir Donald Campbell. Sir Donald gave the Baron the alternative of losing his head or losing his lands.

"Well," said the honest Baron, "I am not a thief; there has n̄ been a thief of my family as far back as I can trace. But so minded man has done this evil thing to me to bring mys grace and my children to ruin. I am not afraid to die—the guiltless die but once, the guilty many times; but rather than that posterity should cast up to my children that their father was hanged for stealing a sheep, I leave my land with you, Sir Donald, and my integrity with my children as their only legacy."

[3] *Missionary Travels*, p. 364.

THE BIRTHPLACE OF DAVID LIVINGSTONE AT BLANTYRE

From a pencil drawing by Robert Eadie, R.S.W.

Campbell immediately seized nearly the whole of the possessions of Livingstone of Bachuill, and left the victim in such poverty that his descendants never recovered their forfeited status. What foundation there may be for the story beyond that of oft-repeated oral tradition there is nothing to prove, but it is not without interest as accordant with the testimony of David Livingstone's ancestor. The special virtue emphasized by the latter as characteristic of the successive generations of his name and race is not exactly typical of the Gael. A scrupulous fidelity to one's own, together with a readiness to plunder the outsider, is commonly supposed to be a better description of the trend of Highland morality. Commenting on his grandfather's story, Livingstone mentions Macaulay's dictum that the Highlanders of the eighteenth and earlier centuries obeyed a rule of conduct similar to that of the Cape Kaffres, who were notorious cattle thieves. Highlander and Kaffre alike would be careful to share their booty with their chief after a successful foray, and so long as this custom was dutifully observed no punishment had to be feared, and presumably no sense of guilt was felt; there would be no belief that such brigandage was wrong. Livingstone himself half-humorously notes this in his dealings with the Makololo during his journey to the east coast in 1855. "In tribes which have been accustomed to cattle stealing, the act is not considered immoral in the way that theft is. Before I knew the language well, I said to a chief, 'You stole the cattle of so and so.' 'No, I did not steal them,' was the reply, 'I only *lifted* them.' The word 'gapa' is identical with the Highland term for the same deed." [4]

The words remembered and repeated by Livingstone's grandfather give expression to what is a Lowland rather than a Highland ideal if construed to mean literally what a modern Anglo-Saxon would mean by them. That Livingstone believed them in the latter sense we cannot doubt, for no man ever lived who was more minutely conscientious both in his statement of facts and his handling of property, and none more generous or self-forgetful. That he was able to take for granted as he did that the same was true of his ancestry for at least six generations before his grandfather's time is no small thing.

[4] *Op. cit.*, p. 526.

His indebtedness to the sturdy integrity of his humble progenitors who bore his name was great, and he knew it. He could not have wished to inherit a sounder moral tradition.

The strict honesty ascribed to and enjoined upon his branch of the Livingstone family, as stated above, was well exemplified in Neil Livingstone's own case, for we have his grandson's authority for the statement that part of the old man's regular duty was that of carrying large sums of money from Glasgow to the works at Blantyre. It is also said, and still repeated in the neighbourhood, that one of his most earnest desires was that of giving his children the best education possible to a man in his circumstances, and that to this end he grudged no expenditure he was able to afford, with the result that his sons obtained employment with the firm as clerks instead of ordinary operatives. One of them, Charles, rose to be head clerk in the firm's Glasgow office, but, to the father's great grief, was seized by a press gang and forcibly enrolled on a man-of-war, dying not long afterwards in the Mediterranean. The Highland fighting instincts must have developed in the others also, David's father excepted, for, as already noted, they successively forsook their secure civilian avocations to engage in war against the French. Dr. Wilson says they all fought at Waterloo.

The adventurous and roving spirit which made David Livingstone the man he was thus found expression in his uncles before him, and not only in them, but in the earlier generations of his line. Enough in the way of authentic tradition concerning the Livingstones of all branches is now accessible to prove that they were an intrepid, dauntless, questing breed. It detracts not at all from the reputation of David Livingstone to say that with him the wanderlust was bred in the bone along with an heroic temper that nothing could repress; but in his unique career these characteristics of his Gaelic kindred took a new and loftier form that has made them a permanent blessing to the world.

David's father exhibited none of the restlessness and love of change so conspicuous in his forbears and near relatives, unless his resignation of his clerkship to become an itinerant tea vendor and voluntary colporteur may be deemed such. He it was who in the divine order was the means of inspiring his now famous son with the missionary spirit, for in his modest way the younger Neil Livingstone was a missionary himself. As he went from door to door with the commodity in which he dealt he was accustomed to distribute religious literature and exert his personal influence for the spiritual good of those with whom he came in contact; young men especially were the objects of his earnest solicitude, and some of them owned in after days that he had helped them greatly in the formation of their ideals and the shaping of their conduct. Here again we have an anticipation of a method which David Livingstone spontaneously employed with African natives in his missionary journeys. He was never a preacher in the conventional sense, but, like his father before him, a persuasive and convincing conversationalist. His father-in-law, the veteran missionary, Dr. Robert Moffat, has given explicit testimony to Livingstone's effective exercise of this gift; it was more suitable to the kind of work to which he devoted his life than any amount of oratory would have been.

It was from his father, too, that he derived what was even of more value in his chosen vocation, his deep personal piety and strong Christian principle. Neil Livingstone the younger was that rare being at the beginning of the nineteenth century, a total abstainer, and in this his son David followed his example; the latter has recorded in his *Missionary Travels* that it was only when he had been brought very low by fever after his journey across the African continent that he submitted to drinking a little wine on the strong recommendation of his kind hosts, and found it of some benefit; he had never tasted alcohol before. As the sequel of this experience he carried a little brandy with him on later journeys for medicinal purposes, but made little use of it, and never changed his lifelong habit of abstaining from intoxicants; he notes in his Journal the devastating effects of indulgence in alcoholic beverages in tropical latitudes, both upon white men and native tribes. He never learned to smoke tobacco.

Close sympathy and affection always subsisted between David Livingstone and his father. Neil had something of the Gaelic readiness to flame up on slight provocation, but these ebullitions never lasted

long and were comparatively harmless. In an age when children were
treated sternly and kept in close subjection to parental control there
was no harshness in the discipline of the little home at Blantyre. David
Livingstone states that his father's "kindliness of manner and winning
ways caused the heart-strings of his children to twine around him." [5]
He could, and did, use the rod occasionally, but its applications were
rare, and never for what was deemed slight cause. It is in accordance
with what we have learned of the character of father and son respec-
tively that on the last occasion when David was given a touch of the
birch the cause of offence was his firm refusal to abandon scientific
reading and books of travel, and confine himself to dry treatises on
orthodox religious doctrine such as Wilberforce's *Practical Christianity*. The future missionary frankly acknowledges that he never
took kindly to the study of what were esteemed edifying religious
works in those days, and that one direct consequence of the thrashing
alluded to was to engender in him for several years afterwards a strong
prejudice, not only against these, but against religious reading of every
sort. His father's well-meant efforts to train him by force in the way
he should go might thus have had the effect of depriving the Church
of Christ of one of its brightest ornaments, and the foreign mission
field of the most stimulating personal force of modern times. Happily
the danger was averted through the seeming accident of the youth
himself happening to make acquaintance with the writings of Dr.
Thomas Dick—*The Philosophy of Religion* and *The Philosophy of a
Future State*. That this was no accident, but one of the earliest
instances of that special divine guidance which was to accompany him
until his life-work was done, is now clear to all who believe in an
overruling Providence. It was through the reading of these two books
that David Livingstone became established in the conviction he ever
afterwards held, that science and religion are not opposed to each
other, but mutually necessary and helpful revelations of the mind and
will of God. This, be it remembered, was long anterior to the publication of Darwin's *Origin of Species,* and the problem of harmonizing
the accepted findings of science with traditional Christian dogma is

[5] Introduction to *Missionary Travels.*

perhaps not so simple as Dr. Dick and his young follower imagined. But they were on the right line for solving it, and if Livingstone had not been assured of this he could never have attempted, much less accomplished, the colossal task in which he became a pioneer and waymaker for other men in several different fields.

When the Livingstone family settled in Blantyre after leaving Ulva, they made the acquaintance of a neighbouring family named Hunter, whose members occupied much the same station in life as their own and cherished similar religious and moral principles. The head of this family, David Hunter, like the elder Neil Livingstone, had been formerly a crofter; he had owned his own small home and agricultural holding at Airdrie, near Glasgow. His father, Gavin Hunter, belonged to the parish of Shotts, and was a strong Covenanter somewhat of the type described in Scott's *Old Mortality*. David Hunter—after whom David Livingstone was named—was a man of as profound religious convictions, but inclining perhaps towards a somewhat greater taciturnity than his Gaelic friends. He had been converted when only seventeen at an open-air service conducted by one of the notable Erskines—probably a son of Ralph Erskine. So great was the spiritual fervour displayed on the occasion that the people present stood ankle-deep in the midst of falling snow to listen to the fiery words of the preacher, and David Hunter used to say in after years that he had been so absorbed in what was being said that he had not been conscious of the inclement weather while the devotions lasted. If the service were like most others of the same sort during that period of earnest spiritual stirring, it would not be a short one; it might continue throughout the greater part of the day and succeeding days.

David Hunter's wife was named Janet Moffat, so David Livingstone's connection with bearers of the name of Moffat both by inheritance and marriage was destined to be close. The Hunters came to Blantyre for the same reason that the Livingstones did—namely, poverty; croft cultivation had ceased to pay. It is said that David Hunter had assisted needy neighbours at a cost which ultimately proved to be more than his slender resources could sustain, the result being that he had to abandon his holding and make a fresh start in life elsewhere. He succeeded in obtaining a position as tailor to the orphan children whom, according to a custom of the time, the firm of Monteith and Co. took over from the parochial authorities and boarded out in suitable homes.

These children were indentured to the firm for a specified number of years, the employers standing to them *in loco parentis,* maintaining them and teaching them their trade, and giving them a modicum of education in return for their services. The system was not as hard as has been represented, though the hours of toil were long and the fare plain. The nature of its operation depended to a great extent upon the character of the employer in every case, and in this respect Messrs. Monteith and Co. had earned a deservedly high reputation. David Livingstone records that the village schoolmaster of Blantyre was paid in part by Messrs. Monteith in order that their young employees should receive instruction at his hands along with his other pupils. The education thus made available for those who wanted it was far superior to anything of the kind provided under the factory system in England at the same period and for long after. It included some acquaintance with the Greek and Latin classics in addition to the obligatory reading, writing, and arithmetic which then, as now, formed the foundation of the curriculum of a primary school. Livingstone tells us that in consequence of the opportunities thus afforded and for which Scotland has been distinguished ever since the Reformation, some of his schoolfellows rose later to positions in the world which would otherwise have been totally inaccessible to persons of humble origin, and he rightly remarks that if such a system could have been established in England it would have proved a never-ending blessing to the children of the poor.

David Livingstone's father, while still a lad, was bound apprentice to David Hunter to learn tailoring. This was the decision of Neil Livingstone the elder, and does not seem to have been agreeable to the wishes of the subject thereof. Probably the alternative of spending the rest of his life on a clerk's stool in a cotton-spinner's office was equally objectionable to him and accounts for his exchanging both as soon as he was free to do so for an occupation which gave him more time out of doors and the privilege of greater mobility and variety of scene.

That there was something of the rover latent in his disposition is indicated by his liking for literature about foreign countries and missionary reports. He was a regular subscriber to these for many years, and shared with his children in the enjoyment of them, as his son reveals. Have we here another source of David Livingstone's predilection for a life of Christian adventure? His father evidently felt the same hunger without being able to satisfy it, except in the very minor degree possible to one in his circumstances.

The apprenticeship of Neil Livingstone to David Hunter, short as it was, had the consequence of bringing him into intimate contact with Hunter's daughter Agnes, and the two were married in 1810. In furtherance of the young husband's business they made their home in Glasgow for a time, and there their eldest son, John, was born. David was their second child. In preparation for his birth Agnes Livingstone returned for a time to her father's house in Shuttle Row, Blantyre, and here in the lowly abode that is now a place of pilgrimage to all who revere his name the great missionary explorer came into the world on March 19th, 1813. Five other children—three sons, two of whom died in infancy, and two daughters—were subsequently born to Neil Livingstone and his wife. For some reason the couple had elected to retransfer their home from Glasgow to Blantyre, residing at first in a tenement in Fore Row, and later going to live in the little house in which Agnes had been brought up; it is the house in Shuttle Row, Blantyre, which will be for ever associated with the childhood and youth of David Livingstone. Here he dwelt with his parents and brothers and sisters from infancy to manhood, and hither he came from his studies in Glasgow and London and from each of his first two African journeys to meet and mingle with those dear to him, and renew intercourse with the friends and neighbours among whom his formative years had been spent, and some of whom he held in undying affection.

David Hunter lived to an advanced age, a respected and honoured figure in the village community, dying in 1834, when he had passed his eighty-seventh birthday. His wife had predeceased him by almost half an ordinary lifetime. She passed away after a weary and lingering illness, when their daughter Agnes was still but a child of fifteen. Young as the latter was, she had been her mother's devoted nurse during that sad period, and acted as her father's housekeeper from then onwards, with the exception of the interval covered by the comparatively short earlier portion of her own married life. Her children loved their maternal grandfather as much as they loved old Neil Livingstone, though he had none of the Highlander's gift of dramatic story-telling. David Livingstone says of his mother that the picture that most vividly remained in his mind when looking back upon his early years was typical of the respectable Scottish poor, the anxious housewife striving to make both ends meet. She was the centre and light of the home, a gracious soul, tender, wise, and serene in spirit. She had the inestimable gift of being able to breathe cheerfulness and hope into the hearts of her little circle when skies were clouded and prospects drear. She, too, was something of a story-teller, and had her own particular budget of family reminiscences to draw upon for the benefit of her children and grandchildren, some of them as charged with terror and pathos as those of the Livingstones. She would tell how her grandfather, Gavin Hunter, narrowly escaped transportation for trying to get a poor woman's parish allowance of sixpence a week augmented, how he had feigned idiocy in the hope of deceiving his judges, and was saved at the last moment by a compassionate military officer and sent home to his wife and children. She retained the power of vivid narration almost to the very end of her long life.

She had all the characteristic independence of the Scottish people of her class and upbringing. The family at first attended the established church in Blantyre, but at a later date, about 1830 or shortly after, joined the Independent church at Hamilton, a building which still exists, but is now in use as a dwelling house. The Livingstones had to walk three miles every Sunday to reach this place of worship, and it was the friendly custom of the church members who resided near to entertain them and others who came from a distance. The late William Naismith, of the *Hamilton Advertiser,* a young contemporary of David Livingstone, used to relate that Mrs. Livingstone never would accept more hospitality than a kettle of boiling water for tea and seats at table for her family group; lunch for the hungry mouths she brought with her.[6] This native independence was balanced by a frugality and thrift that wasted nothing and made the utmost of a scanty store; it was a well-managed household over which this good woman ruled, and which she more than any other member contributed to keeping bright and happy. It is pleasant to know that she lived not only to see one son famous to the ends of the earth as the opener of new highways for the Gospel of Christ among the heathen, but to see another associated with him in that work, and the third and eldest doing well in a new land. She died in June, 1865, in her eighty-third year, eleven months after David Livingstone's second return from Africa. The conclusion of his first book,[7] published in November, 1857, contains this passage: "I have done something for the heathen, but for an aged mother, who has still more sacred claims than they, I have been able to do nothing, and a continuance of the connection (with the London Missionary Society) would be a perpetuation of my inability to make any provision for her declining years." It was from a small proportion of the profits of his writings and his modest salary as a British Consul from March, 1858, that he was enabled to add a little to what was being done by the others for their mother's maintenance and comfort.

Her husband died eight and a half years earlier, only a few weeks before David's first triumphal visit home, at the moment when the son's name was being acclaimed by the public for the tremendous feat of being the first white man to traverse from west to east a vast continent whose interior had been hitherto unknown. Those present at the deathbed relate that the dying man earnestly hoped to be spared long enough to greet once more the son of whom he was so proud. "You wished so much to see David," said one of the daughters as the end drew near. "Aye, very much, very much; but the will of the Lord be done," was the reply. Then after an interval of silence: "But

[6] Rev. J. A. Lees in London Missionary Society's *Chronicle,* August, 1925.
[7] *Missionary Travels.*

I think I'll know whatever is worth knowing about him. When you see him, tell him I think so." [8]

This touching incident is illustrative of the harmony that ever characterized the family life of Neil and Agnes Livingstone. Parents and children were accustomed after temporary separations to draw round the fire together in the evenings and recount to each other all their individual doings and expectations; the experiences of each were shared with all. When David was old enough to attend classes in Glasgow, he regularly came home at week-ends, and the Saturday evening chats were always looked forward to by everyone concerned and were apt to be prolonged to a late hour. On his final departure from home to take up his life-work, the loving family session was so difficult to break off that David proposed they should sit up all night. Motherly Agnes Livingstone would not permit this, however, in view of the long journey that had to be faced on the morrow. But at five in the morning they rose again; mother and sisters had hot coffee ready; then David at his father's request read a portion of Scripture and offered prayer for his dear ones whom he was leaving, and for himself in the untried field of service upon which he was about to enter. How simple and gracious it all is, and how charming a sidelight upon the kind of intimacy to which the inmates of the little home were habituated! That the head of the family, whose priestly function it was to lead the devotions of the rest, as illustrated in *The Cotter's Saturday Night,* should on this occasion have delegated the duty to his son has a certain solemn significance. It was like the laying on of hands; it was Neil Livingstone's reverent way of recognizing that David was now a minister of the Gospel, and in the act there was also something of a father's joy in listening to the son's voice leading in the exercises of worship at a moment so memorable and so charged with deep feeling. The farewells spoken, the older man set forth to walk to Glasgow with the younger and see him on board the ship that was to bear him away to Liverpool and foreign parts. The two never met again.

---

[8] Blaikie, *Life of David Livingstone,* p. 165.

David Livingstone states in his own account of his early life that in his struggle to obtain an education and qualify to become a medical missionary he never received a farthing of aid from anyone. This must mean that he was enabled to pay his way through University and medical training without financial assistance from any society or individual outside of his own family, otherwise the answer that he gave in writing to one of the questions put to him by the directors of the London Missionary Society before his acceptance is difficult to explain.[9] Asked what his occupation had been and what bearing it had had upon his academical career, he said he had supported himself at college by his earnings as a cotton spinner, and added: "A brother similarly employed gives a little assistance in college fees. The brother has a family to support." Here we have a fact worth noting. John is the brother alluded to; it could be no one else. A fine tradition of Scottish family life is that elder brothers help younger ones in poor circumstances to meet the cost of a college course. Such generous loyalty is neither so common nor so necessary nowadays as it used to be, but there are men still living and eminent in various walks of life who owe their start on the ladder of success to the timely support they received from the hard-won earnings of brothers and sisters a little older than themselves. As we see from the explicit testimony just quoted, David Livingstone was helped to some extent in this way. The help was small, no doubt; he had to rely mainly upon his own resources, but that any help was given at all is in the circumstances a fact that calls for appreciation. Like David, John was in the employ of Messrs. Monteith and Co., but severed his connection with that firm and emigrated some years after David left home. The latter gives some interesting information on this point in a letter addressed to the Rev. William Thompson, L.M.S. agent at Cape Town, and dated August 27th, 1850. One paragraph runs: "My brother Charles is settled as pastor of a church in Lakeville, Livingstone County, New York. He was educated at Oberlin and Andover. Indeed, he is a naturalized citizen of the United States. I have another brother settled in Lanark,

9 L.M.S. archives.

Canada W. My parents are also in that country, and having so many
relatives there I begin to feel anxious to have a more direct means of
communication than that which I have hitherto availed myself of—
viz., by way of England." [10]

Is it hazardous to suggest that John may have helped Charles a little
as he had previously helped his other brother? David was warmly in
favour of emigration for the whole family,[11] and this may have had
some influence upon the decision of John as well as Charles to seek
a habitation in the new world. Charles went on David's advice in the
hope of obtaining in the United States an education on easier terms
than in his native land, David furnishing him with part of the passage
money.[12] That John was still in Scotland in the earlier part of 1850
is attested by a reference in one of David's letters home in July of that
year, but he ultimately settled in Listowel, Ontario.

David Livingstone is usually represented as a self-educated man.
This is only true in the sense that every educated man is to a large
extent self-educated. The story which he himself relates, that at the
age of ten he began work in the cotton factory as a piecer, and with
part of his first week's wages purchased Ruddiman's *Rudiments of
Latin,* and studied it by placing the book open on the spinning jenny
and passing to and fro in front of it as he worked, has misled many
readers into imagining that he acquired his knowledge of the language
by his own unaided efforts. This was not so. The excellent preceptor,
to whom reference has already been made guided the sedulous young
learner over the stony places in the Latin grammar, and introduced
him to the more congenial task of construing Virgil and Horace.
Livingstone always spoke gratefully of the stimulus thus imparted to
his own youthful aspirations. The master, he said, was attentive and
kind, and taught him so well that at sixteen he could read Latin au-
thors better than at forty-six. It must have been hard work toiling
in a cotton factory from six in the morning till eight at night, with
intervals for meals, and it seems scarcely credible that he should have

[10] It is improbable that the parents actually went. The project appears to have been dropped.
[11] He sent money home to help in paying the passages.
[12] He sent Charles £5 for the purpose specified.

attended school in the evenings after such an exhausting day; yet so it was; we have his own definite assurance on the point. Furthermore, he was accustomed to go on studying till after midnight, a practice that his mother rightly objected to, and sometimes broke in upon by snatching the book out of his hands and packing him off to bed. This was a strenuous period in his history—up at five or soon after, toiling all day, pursuing self-appointed tasks into the small hours by candle-light. Only a robust constitution could stand it for long.

It came to an end with David's decision to enroll himself as a student at Glasgow University. Like many of his fellow-students, he worked in the summer to earn enough to pay his college fees and maintain himself at the University in the winter. It was needful to practise the utmost frugality and self-denial in order to make both ends meet under these conditions. Neil Livingstone and his son tramped Glasgow to-gether from morn till eve all through one wintry day, in the latter part of 1836, in search of lodgings for the young man, till at length they found an apartment at the low rental of two shillings a week. During his first two sessions David attended the Greek classes at the Univer-sity and the divinity lectures of Dr. Wardlaw. But by now he had decided to seek a medical degree with the object of offering himself for service in the foreign mission field; so from the beginning of his University course he put himself under the instruction of the Professor of Chemistry, Dr. Thomas Graham, and of the head of the medical faculty, Professor Andrew Buchanan. Through attending Professor Graham's demonstrations he made the acquaintance of the Professor's assistant, James Young, thus initiating a friendship which was to last throughout his life and be of great value to both men. It was chiefly owing to Young that he acquired the facility and precision in scientific observation which characterized his work in Africa in years to come; indeed, it is no exaggeration to say that it was Young who awakened in him the love of science and the consciousness of a special aptitude for it.[13]

[13] Young rose to high distinction in the scientific world, and his various discoveries and patents made him a man of wealth. During both of Livingstone's later expeditions he gave permission to the explorer to draw upon him for means to any extent, a generous facility which Livingstone did not abuse; any monetary promise given in pursuance thereof to a Portu-

A theologian Livingstone never became, though the teaching of Dr. Wardlaw set a deep mark upon his mind and determined his doctrinal convictions for the rest of his career. Never at any time did he consciously revise these convictions in any marked degree, though unconsciously through his experience of the different levels of mental and moral capacity in the heathen with whom he came in contact he gradually became more liberal in outlook. But he never exhibited any sympathy with advanced opinions either in Biblical scholarship or in the troubled controversies relating to human origins which were soon to shake to its foundations the accepted dogmatic system of the Christian Church. He objected to having his name coupled with the supposed heresies of Bishop Colenso at the British Association meetings at Bath in 1864, though the Bishop at the time was giving vigorous support to his protest against the exploitation of native races. Nor was he any more favourable to what is commonly called Darwinism when it was first sprung upon an astonished world. There is no evidence that he ever examined it carefully, and his own researches in the subject matter of ethnology did not lead him to formulate conclusions at all approximating to those of the champions of the theory of evolution; on the contrary, he makes the casual remark in his correspondence that he has seen nothing in his travels to encourage the view that man is descended from an ape-like stock.[14] From first to last Livingstone retained the evangelical faith in which he had been brought up, a faith necessarily broadened and rendered more sympathetic and tolerant by his growing knowledge of life in its manifold aspects, but remaining fundamentally unchanged. As a child of twelve he had for a time shown anxiety about his soul's salvation, which was only what was expected in the environment whence his earliest religious impressions were derived. As we have seen, this phase of his spiritual development passed for a time, and it was not till he entered his twentieth year that

guese trader or Arab slave dealer, written on an old piece of leather or a piece of the bark of a tree, was duly honoured by Young. He gave £2,000 towards a search expedition for his friend which proved too late to find Livingstone alive. He had Livingstone's body servants, Susi and Chuma, brought over to England and taken care of that they might help in giving information respecting the travels covered by the *Last Journals*. (*Cf.* the biographical articles in the *Dictionary of National Biography* and *Encyclopaedia Britannica*.)

[14] To the Royal Geographical Society of Vienna (Blaikie, *Life of David Livingstone*, p. 219).

he underwent what was regarded as true conversion. Even then the grave and cautious elders of the Independent church at Hamilton, to whom he applied for communicant membership, "dooted if Dauvit was soun'," and appointed two of their number to give him further instruction "in the doctrines." [15] David humbly underwent the required probation, and was ultimately received into the fellowship of the little church. His father held office in this church, but doubtless from considerations of propriety left to his colleagues the responsibility of judging of David's fitness for membership. The man who actually had most to do with preparing him for membership was a veteran named Arthur Anderson, a man of thoughtful mind and strong Christian character, between whom and young Livingstone a close personal attachment and mutual respect ever afterwards existed. That Livingstone took the decision of the elders very seriously is demonstrated by the fact that for five months he tramped regularly from Blantyre to Hamilton to be taught and prayed with by Arthur Anderson, ere the latter left justified in recommending him for solemn public reception as a communicant; church membership was not lightly entered upon at that time and place.

The first fruit of the spiritual experience brought to maturity under Arthur Anderson's influence was the decision Livingstone now took to consecrate himself to the service of Christ in some form of outpost service. That this was more than agreeable to his father we have already seen reason to believe, but we must not too hastily conclude that his vocation was as yet clear to him. He writes: "Great pains had been taken by my parents to instill the doctrines of Christianity into my mind, and I had no difficulty in understanding the theory of our free salvation by the atonement of our Saviour, but it was only about this time that I really began to feel the necessity and value of a personal application of the provisions of that atonement to my own case. . . . In the glow of love which Christianity inspires, I soon resolved to devote my life to the alleviation of human misery. Turning this idea over in my mind, I felt that to be a pioneer of Christianity in China might lead to the material benefit of some portions of that immense

[15] Rev. J. Brand Crombie in the *Scottish Congregationalist*, March, 1927.

empire; and therefore set myself to obtain a medical education, in order
to be qualified for that enterprise." [16]   It should be noted that Livingstone was thoroughly orthodox in the sense understood by his evangelical preceptors then and later, and in offering himself for the work of
the ministry abroad he had no more definite idea at first than that of
making converts on the approved evangelical pattern. Arthur Anderson helped him in this also. It was on Anderson's advice that he applied to the London Missionary Society, which had the distinction of
being entirely unsectarian. [17]

The directors invited him to London for a personal interview, but
Livingstone did not possess the means to pay the expenses of the journey. Thereupon Anderson applied to his own employer, Mr. Fergus
Ferguson, a member of the same church, and to Mr. Henry Drum-
mond, a lace manufacturer in the town of Hamilton, and these two
gentlemen jointly advanced the sum required. Little did any of the
parties to this friendly arrangement dream of the fateful nature of the
action they were taking and its stupendous outcome. On Livingstone's
first return from Africa, a figure of renown, in December, 1856, he
found time to pay a special visit to the humble church of which he
still counted himself a member. There in the autumn of 1857 he was
presented with a quaintly phrased address expressing the pride and
joy felt by his old friends and neighbours in the knowledge of his
achievements, both as a discoverer of hitherto unknown territories and
as a messenger of Christ to populations sunk in the darkness of savagery and superstition. [18]

It was in September, 1838, that Livingstone met the directors of the
London Missionary Society, and after being subjected to a preliminary

[16] Introduction to *Missionary Travels*.

[17] The first approach to the Society on his behalf was made by the Rev. John Moir, pastor
of Hamilton Independent Church, strongly recommending him. This was August 12th, 1837.
Livingstone's direct application was despatched on September 5th of the same year.

[18] One passage in this document reads: "Those of our number who were contemporary with
you cherish the remembrance of your early connection with us: the rest of us, though not
conjoined with them by recollection, are one with them by sympathy. . . . The effect of your
example we cannot pretend adequately to estimate. But if our youth have inherited the nature
of our fathers, shall they not imbibe some of your spirit as they read and hear of your deeds;
and shall fathers not seek to emulate the lofty devotion of yours, and offer their sons, too,
for humanity, to God? May not the contagion of such large-heartedness spread till every
Mammon be overpowered by generosity and truth? We believe it, and hope that the result
is not far distant when earth shall become a highway for God."

THE ROOM IN WHICH DAVID LIVINGSTONE WAS BORN

examination was sent with several other candidates to study for three months under the charge of the Rev. Richard Cecil at Ongar in Essex. This period of probation, short as it was, nearly proved fatal to the young man's prospects of final acceptance by the Society. It was expected, not unreasonably, that the probationers should be able to give evidence of some amount of aptitude for the work of preaching and teaching, and in this respect Livingstone did not acquit himself well. It is questionable if he ever would have done so under any system of homiletical training. One who heard his address in the Senate House at Cambridge on December 4th, 1857, after noting Livingstone's plea that he had been unaccustomed to the use of his own language for seventeen years, and consequently had lost facility in expressing himself therein, observes that his style was peculiar to himself; his sentences were short and jerky, and his delivery uneven; but the effect of the whole was somehow profoundly impressive, because of the force of the man's personality behind the utterance.

Naturally this had not begun to show itself in 1838. Livingstone was then a queer, awkward young fellow, provincial in appearance and manner, habitually rather silent, a mixture of shyness and stubborn self-confidence. A neighbour who remembered him in Blantyre in his teens, on being asked what sort of person he was in those days, replied: "Oh, just a sulky, quiet, feckless sort of boy." [19] The description is not inapt. The reserve of power in Livingstone's nature would not be readily apparent in early years, nor indeed at any time till his achievements spoke for him; neither with tongue nor pen was he notably gifted; he was far more a doer than a talker to the end of his days.

Mr. Cecil's method of fostering preaching talent in the young men under his charge in 1838 was not conducive to overcoming Livingstone's innate defects as a speaker. He was required to write his discourses in full, bring them to his tutor for criticism, then learn them off by heart and recite them to his congregations. These were real congregations, not merely audiences of classmates, for the students were sent out on Sundays to preach in various churches. Livingstone had a humiliating and all but disastrous experience in this way, for,

[19] W. A. Elliott, *Nyaka*, p. 5.

being appointed to preach at Stanford Rivers on one occasion, he gave out his text and found that a treacherous memory had played him false: the sermon was gone. Blurting out, "I have forgotten all I had to say," he abruptly quitted the pulpit and made haste home. It was a clear case of stage fright, but some of the blame must be attributed to the burdensome method of preparation. The discipline of writing was good, but the memorizing of what was written was bad, and would have detracted from the effectiveness of the sermon even had the preacher been word perfect. Add to this that Livingstone, when taking his turn at conducting family worship with his fellow-students, was equally poor in extempore prayer, given to making long and painful pauses, owing apparently to poverty of ideas, and sticking to repetitions of a commonplace and almost banal character, and it is not surprising that at the end of the three months Mr. Cecil should have felt himself unable to report favourably upon this particular candidate. The Board would in consequence have refused to accept him but for the action of one of the directors, who urged that the young man should be given a further trial. This was done; Livingstone's persevering efforts to improve himself, together with his manifest spiritual sincerity and retentive mind, won the respect of his superiors, and he was approved for specialized medical training before being sent abroad.[20]

A letter sent to the secretary of the London Missionary Society by Livingstone's father, and now printed for the first time, may have helped to influence the directors in his favour. It is of value as shedding light upon the young man's character as viewed by his intimates.

REVD. SIR,

It occurred to me some months ago that I ought to state some particulars to you relative to my son David Livingstone, whose application is under your consideration, in the hope that however un-

---

[20] It should be noted that part of Livingstone's disability as a speaker was physical. An over-long uvula caused a thickness and indistinctness of utterance unpleasant to his hearers. An operation in Cape Town afforded a measure of relief from this drawback from 1852 onwards, but he was never wholly freed from it, and neither in voice nor manner did he succeed in becoming at any time attractive to popular assemblies.

important the statements may be in themselves, they may assist you in coming to a decision regarding him.

When he was about 13 years of age, he asked me if I would allow him to learn Latin, our village schoolmaster being at that time commencing a class. Although we were in very humble circumstances I consented, not knowing what might be the design of the Most High respecting him; he had to work in the factory 12 hours every day, yet managed to keep at the top of his class while it existed; and, after the rest all got tired of it, studied by himself untill the master, I suppose, not wishing to be troubled teaching one person only, advised him to give it up unless he had the prospect of needing it, which he knew he had not.

As factory workers are very plenty in this part of the country it was long before he got that kind of employment which enabled him to save a little money, since then he has saved all he could for education except what he gave for the support of the gospel and other pious purposes.

When he first mentioned to me his design of attending the University in order to study medicine I was much opposed to it untill he informed me that it was not to gain a livelihood he thought of doing so, his anxious wish was to be enabled to spend his life in the service of the Redeemer among the heathen; I no longer felt inclined to oppose his design, but felt thankful that such a thought was in his heart. He has now finished his second session at the University, and such was his untiring perseverance and the good health with which he was favoured that I believe he was but one day absent during the whole session. We live rather more than eight miles from Glasgow, he came up to us every Saturday afternoon, and walked three miles farther to Hamilton every Sabbath morning to attend our place of worship. A kind gentleman, a member of our Church, Fergus Ferguson, Esq., of Rosebank, would have taken him down to Glasgow every Monday morning in his gig, but he chose rather to walk on foot in all kinds of weather during the last severe winter, rising every Monday at five in the morning that he might reach Glasgow between 8 and 9 o'clock, and if he had waited on Mr. F. he would have lost one lecture and part of another. His landlord—a Mr. Dove, with whom he lodged in Glasgow—said to him one day, "Well, Mr. L., I admire your perseverance, and if you will leave the dissenters and become a Churchman, I will undertake to get you a situation as a Teacher worth £150 a year"; he replied he could not do that for any money: Mr. Dove said one day afterwards: "Well, if you give me leave, I will recommend you, and I think you will be accepted even retaining your principles as a dissenter"; David said he was grateful for his kindness, but that was not the object on which his heart was set. As stated above he has now finished his second winter without any assistance from any person except his own brother. I wished him to walk about for a few days after his severe studies before commencing his work, but not wishing to lose any time, he began next morning after coming from Glasgow.

The manager of the factory, who is frequently under the influence of whisky, told him yesterday that if he went to Glasgow any more, following after education, he must lose his work as he would not keep it any longer for him. Still he is not greatly cast down.

I might say many more things similar to the above, but am afraid I have tired you already. David knows nothing of this communication, and I believe he would feel, were he to know of it. I have however followed my own sense of duty and am not sensible of colouring any statement in the least degree, and now may He Who has the hearts of all flesh in His hand guide you in either accepting or rejecting, as it shall most promote His own glory.

I am, Rev. Sir, Your Obedient Servant,
(<i>Signed</i>)   Neil Livingston.</div>

Blantyre Works,
April 26th, 1838.

With David Livingstone's formal acceptance by the London Missionary Society the break with the associations of his youth may be said to have been definitely made, though two years or more had yet to elapse before he entered upon the scene of his future labours. It was at his own earnest request that facilities were now granted him to complete in London the medical studies which he had begun in Glasgow. The first intention of the directors had been to send him out to the West Indies, but on his pointing out that in the British settlements there a sufficient number of qualified medical men already existed, and therefore that his own precious two years of medical study would be wasted, they yielded to his desire and decided to assist him to obtain his diploma and then send him to Africa. It was with this programme in view that under the auspices of the Society he now took up his residence in London.

The following letter from Livingstone to the secretary of the London Missionary Society, sent from Ongar, July 2nd, 1839, is the one wherein he gives expression to his views on the proposal to send him to the West Indies. It is of interest as illustrating his habitual attitude to the Society. Here in one of his earliest communications he shows the same respect without servility, the same boldness without discourtesy, and the same independent thinking which marked all his dealings with official bodies. The London Missionary Society's important influence in regard to the emancipation of the slaves in British West Indian possessions is well known, as is also the great work done by its agents subsequently in raising the status of the negro. Livingstone's judgment of the situation was correct. Little pioneer work remained to be done in this field.

Dear Sir,

Having been informed a few days ago by Mr. Cecil, that there had been some intimation of a wish on the part of the Directors, that I should be employed in the West Indies in preference to South Africa, and being desirous to enter upon that sphere of labour, and, I trust, that only, in which I may be able most efficiently to advance the great cause of our Blessed Redeemer; permit me to state the following particulars for their consideration, previous to coming to a final decision on my case.

When first I felt the expansive benevolence of the gospel in my heart, it became an interesting question to me. How can I spend the remainder of my days in bringing my fellowmen to the enjoyment of the same happiness and peace? After much prayer for the Divine direction, it appeared to be in accordance (with) the will of Providence that I should attempt to obtain a medical education in order to render service to the cause of missions by that means. After much exertion and overcoming considerable difficulties, in which I was sensibly assisted by the good hand of Providence, I spent two years in that study, all which time, in the event of my being sent to the West Indies, might be considered as lost. For I could not use the knowledge which I have obtained without in all probability incurring the displeasure of medical men who have gone thither for the sake of gain, and it is well known how easily medical men can destroy each other's influence and usefulness, when an unsuccessful case occurs, as many hundreds of young men have experienced in this and other countries. In this manner might not only that means which I had hoped to have exerted to subserve the cause of religion be rendered inoperative, but likewise my moral and religious influence be weakened.

Added to this I may be permitted to mention, that settling in the West Indies has always appeared so much like the ministry at home that my thoughts have not at all been attracted in that direction, but always to other parts of the world.

I beg leave to state likewise in reference to a proposal to send me out in the present year, my earnest desire for more education. This has always been my wish, and the more I contemplate the magnitude of the work, the greater does the necessity of good preparation for it appear to be; even when commencing study in prospect of being a missionary, so fully was I convinced of its importance, that it formed no part of my plan to offer myself to any society untill suitably educated lest I should be sent out unfurnished for the work, and I at length did apply in order to avoid the necessity of working during the summer to support myself through the winter so that being permitted to study through the whole year I might in a shorter time be properly furnished for going abroad.

I hope it will not be supposed from anything I have said that I at all mean to dictate to the Directors, but feeling anxious that in their deliberations, these as well as all the other circumstances of the case should be taken into consideration, and the decision may be in accordance with the will of the Head of the church and for his glory, I have taken the liberty of mentioning these circumstances.

I am, Dear Sir, yours truly,

(*Signed*) DAVID LIVINGSTON.

It is apparent from the date of this document that Livingstone's memory failed him when he stated seventeen years later in *Missionary Travels* and private correspondence that the abandonment of his hope of proceeding to China was a consequence of the outbreak of the opium war. The war had not actually begun, but no doubt the fact that it was looming governed the change of venue.

CHAPTER III

LONDON TO KURUMAN

It was through reading Gutzlaff's appeal, issued from Canton in May, 1833, that Livingstone's thoughts were first directed towards becoming a medical missionary. Gutzlaff had travelled north to Tientsin and Manchu Tartary, and had given medical assistance to Chinese in the course of the journey. This was in 1831, and the intrepid Christian pioneer's experience of the needs and opportunities thus presented to his observation and ministry led him to ask for volunteers to carry on the work. He pointed out the importance of combining medical skill with evangelization; he had found that the one opened up the way for another. In the appeal, avoiding rhetoric, he spoke of the glorious results which might follow from his own feeble beginnings—a prophecy overwhelmingly fulfilled in the present state of Christian missions in China. Gutzlaff's call to Britain and America had a great effect both upon men and methods in the work of spreading the gospel of Christ in the heathen world, and not least upon David Livingstone. Had events permitted he would have gone to China, and it was with the hope of giving himself to that country along the lines marked out by Gutzlaff that he determined to obtain a medical degree. It was with the utmost reluctance that by 1840, owing to the Opium War, he had to give up the expectation of proceeding to China and comply with the decision of the directors that he should go to Africa instead. His interest in and solicitude for China underwent no diminution, however, and when at a later date his brother Charles felt drawn to the foreign field, David strongly advised him to offer himself for China.[1]

[1] A letter of Livingstone to Edmund Gabriel, British Consul at Loanda, sent from Quilimane on June 27th, 1856, after the completion of his great transcontinental journey, states: "I think they (the L.M.S.) may propose to send me to China. The practice of medicine and surgery in China was my own idea of the best way of spending my life, but the Chinese Opium War prevented my being sent there. But I have now no desire to leave this land."

While attending medical lectures in London, David Livingstone lodged at a boarding-house for missionary students in Aldersgate Street, and here another event took place with far-reaching consequences for his career. The distinguished Robert Moffat, the Society's missionary at Kuruman, South Africa, happened to call there and had some conversation with the young man. This led to further intercourse; Livingstone became more and more interested in what Moffat had to tell and in the older man's strongly held views of the needs of Africa. At length Livingstone asked whether in Moffat's opinion he would do for Africa. Moffat made the memorable reply, which more than any other single influence shaped Livingstone's future. It was to the effect that a man in full health and vigour, with his best years before him, could undoubtedly advance the cause of Christ in Africa if he would be content not to settle down in an old station, but penetrate to the north, where no missionary had yet set foot, and where in the bright light of an ordinary morning there could often be seen the smoke of a thousand villages. The immediate outcome of this fateful talk was that with Moffat's backing Livingstone intimated to the directors that he was willing to go to Africa after passing his medical examinations if they were prepared to sanction the idea. This they eventually did, entry to China still remaining closed.

In the meantime he zealously resumed the medical and scientific study which had been interrupted by his probation at Chipping Ongar. Here he was more at home, and his native talent found freer expression than in the toil of composing and repeating memoriter edifying doctrinal addresses. He had both aptitude and liking for the subjects with which he was now required to familiarize himself, and was as orderly and exact in his methods of acquiring knowledge in the London hospitals as he ever afterwards showed himself to be in his reports on the fauna and flora of the territories he was the means of opening up to educational and commercial enterprise.

Among the new friendships he made at this time was that with Dr. (afterwards Sir Risdon) Bennett. Livingstone had begun to attend the church in Falcon Square of which Bennett's father, one of the most celebrated of London preachers, was then minister. It is not unlikely that the acquaintance with the younger Bennett may have arisen through Livingstone's connection with the elder, but their association soon deepened in other ways. Bennett was physician to the Aldersgate Street Dispensary and lecturer at Charing Cross Hospital. Livingstone attended his classes, and through his influence obtained the hospital practice of which he stood in need. The two men were greatly drawn to each other, and continued on intimate and affectionate terms to the end of Livingstone's life. The brilliant and cultured physician discerned in the plain unpolished student from the north a character of rare worth and a mental grasp much above the ordinary. That he was able to give Livingstone valuable guidance at this period of specialization is evident from the nature of the correspondence they maintained for many years. Writing to his friend from Kuruman at the end of 1841, after five months' acquaintance of work among people who knew nothing of medical science, Livingstone said: "I feel the benefit often of your instructions, and of those I got through your kindness. Here I have an immense practice." [2] It was Sir J. Risdon Bennett's opinion that Livingstone would have risen to eminence in the medical profession had he felt it consistent with his assurance of a divine call to devote himself to pathology rather than evangelization.

The celebrated Professor (afterwards Sir Richard) Owen also produced a deep impression upon Livingstone at this time. Owen was demonstrator in comparative anatomy at the Hunterian Museum, and Livingstone became his pupil and warm admirer. The goodwill was reciprocated, though the two were never on quite the same footing of private fellowship as Livingstone and Bennett; it was only with the lapse of years that the Professor came to realize how much he had meant to Livingstone while the latter was receiving instruction at his hands. They might have parted for ever without the discovery being made on the part of the older man, and Livingstone might have dropped out of his memory or remained in it merely as one of a long succession of students that had passed through his classroom and laboratory but for Livingstone's fidelity to his plighted word—conjoined, of course, to the splendid success that attended his determination to

2 Blaikie, *op. cit.*, p. 41.

make a way across Africa. Had Livingstone died in the attempt, as he very well might, Owen would have had little occasion to recall him to mind; as it was he had a great deal. On bidding him good-bye Livingstone had promised to forward to him any unusual organic specimen he might find. Similar promises had been made by other former pupils and failed to fructify; Owen probably gave little thought to this one. But to his surprise and gratification he found after sixteen years that in Livingstone's case a promise made was a promise kept. On the explorer's first visit to England in 1856 he called to see Professor Owen, bringing with him the tusk of an elephant with a spiral curve. It had been no slight task to transport this heavy piece of ivory from central Africa to London through trackless forest and fever-breeding marsh, the bearer himself often prostrated by sickness and borne down by weakness and physical pain. Little wonder that Owen should again and again have recurred to the feat in his references to Livingstone in public and private. Nor did he ever say too much; the bare fact is eloquent of the kind of man Livingstone was and of the work he did.[3]

In other respects Livingstone seems to have attracted no great amount of attention from those with whom he came in contact either in Ongar or London during his student days in both centres. He did not shine in general company, but the few intimate friends he made among his fellow-students held him in high esteem and remained devoted to him through life. This was in great measure owing to his tenacity in friendship. Once his regard was bestowed he maintained it indefatigably, and never allowed distance nor the development of new interests to diminish the care wherewith he followed up the fortunes of those whom he admitted to a share in his affections. He was an assiduous correspondent, and managed somehow to keep in touch with former associates in this way to an astonishing extent, considering his difficulties and the toilsome nature of his work from the time his travels began. Some of the most striking particulars of his discoveries were given in letters to friends made in Ongar and London who, with the exceptions named, never attained any great subsequent distinction. The Rev.

[3] He had previously collected and forwarded other objects to the Professor, which apparently were never received.

Joseph Moore, himself a missionary under the direction of the London Missionary Society for a time, and in later years minister of a Congregational church in Cheshire, was one of the earliest of these college friends. Mr. Moore was accepted by the Society on the same day as Livingstone, and lodged in the same house with him at Ongar while both were under the tuition of Mr. Cecil. Another was the Rev. Joseph van Someren Taylor, who went as a missionary to India, and whom Livingstone visited at Bombay on the notable occasion when he sailed thither to dispose of his boat the *Lady Nyassa* in 1864, an event which must receive further attention in its proper place. A third friend of this period, like himself of Scottish origin, was the Rev. D. G. Watt.[4] Mr. Watt went out as a missionary to India. He seems to have enjoyed Livingstone's confidence in a special degree, for the correspondence between the two continued regularly for a period of about fifteen years, and Livingstone was accustomed to pour forth his views and feelings unreservedly in lengthy epistles to this trusted friend. It is to the contents of some of these communications that we are indebted for our knowledge of the growth of Livingstone's mind in relation to the missionary problem in general as it gradually opened before him from the time of his first landing in Africa to the end of his first great missionary journey.

All of these companions of Livingstone's early manhood agree in their estimate of his character and the impression produced by his personality during his student days in England. Mr. Moore has recorded that he and Livingstone were through force of circumstances constantly together during their stay in Ongar, and that the more he saw of the young Scot the more he respected him, and along with the respect there gradually grew a love which he never lost. Livingstone's ways,

----

[4] To his friend Watt, Livingstone often wrote in a playful style, sometimes using the facts of physiology in illustration (as a doctor might be allowed to do), but more often simply relaxing himself, as in the following example:

"KURUMAN,
"*January* 10th, 1851.

"Dauede Watt, Maister of Airts, I commend me unto you, albeit I have not recyved the letters qhuilk manyfestlie yo dyde not wryte. I hereby advertyse and command ye sayde Maister Dauede Watt instantly to repayre to his wryting box and use his pen, or as the boards used to say, 'Beware of crow toes and spring guns and being prosecuted according to the utmost rigour of the law.' "

he says, were rather ungainly and his face by no means winning, but somehow, despite these drawbacks, people were attracted to him once they had broken through the barrier of his reserve. Mr. Watt, in giving his personal recollections of this formative period in Livingstone's career, mentions a roughness or bluntness of manner which may be said to have been a permanent characteristic of the man, sometimes misleading casual acquaintances as to his real nature. He was frank and straightforward to a fault, never suppressing nor disguising his opinions on any subject, and often adhering to them stubbornly notwithstanding the adverse verdict of the circle in which he happened to be. His strength of will was as marked as his firmness of mind. Once his resolve was taken nothing could turn him from it, though he was never in a hurry in carrying it out nor inclined to ignore or minimize obstacles in his path. His very walk, remarked one shrewd observer, the Rev. Dr. Isaac Taylor, was indicative of the combined qualities of simplicity and resolution. "Now, after nearly forty years," wrote Dr. Taylor, "I remember his step, the characteristic forward tread, firm, simple, resolute, neither fast nor slow, no hurry and no dawdle, but which evidently meant—getting there." [5]

His college course in London was interrupted by a severe illness, due probably to overwork. He was prostrated for a time by lung trouble and congestion of the liver, which proved so serious that recovery was thought to be unlikely, and as soon as he was strong enough to bear the voyage he was sent home to Scotland by sea. Fortunately the change and rest restored him to health, and he was able to come south again for a short time before finally returning to Glasgow to sit for his medical diploma. He graduated as Licentiate of the Faculty of Physicians and Surgeons in November, 1840. In the same month, before finally leaving London, he was ordained to the Christian ministry in Albion Chapel, London Wall, "by solemn prayer and imposition of hands." Among those who took part in this dedicatory act and afterwards signed the certificate of the young ordinand were Richard Cecil, Livingstone's preceptor at Ongar, and Arthur Tidman, Foreign Secretary of the London Missionary Society,

[5] Blaikie, *op. cit.*, p. 23.

with whom he was to have much to do in the immediate future, and
for years to come, in the shaping of policy and the discussion of
methods of service in South Africa.

It is worthy of mention, as illustrating the strain of obstinacy in
Livingstone's nature alluded to above, that he risked forfeiting his
medical degree owing to a dispute with the examiners on the subject
of the use of the stethoscope. As usual, he held firmly to his own view
and refused to accept theirs, an impolitic attitude to assume with
examiners at any time or place, but in this instance the competence
of the candidate was held to be sufficient on the whole, and he was
passed.

Another point of some significance should be noted here. Livingstone's connection with Glasgow, and especially with the ministry of
Dr. Ralph Wardlaw, had some influence in awakening his hatred of
slavery. In a city that thrived on tropical trade, the anti-slavery cause
could not have been popular, yet from 1829 onward the Glasgow
Emancipation Society took a leading part in the struggle, first for the
complete abolition of slavery in British overseas dominions, and later
against slavery in the United States. Wardlaw's stern denunciations of
the iniquity of the officially maintained slavery system in the West
Indian plantations—a system against which the Independent missionaries, notably William Knibb of Jamaica and Smith of Demerara
made heroic moral protest—could not fail to have a great effect on the
mind of a young man of Livingstone's stamp. He was still but a boy
when Smith died a martyr to the cause in a felon's prison in British
Guiana in 1824, but emancipations in British possessions did not come
till nine years later, and the so-called apprenticeship system which
succeeded it did not end till 1838. Throughout this whole period the
Glasgow Emancipation Society was in the forefront of the battle for
righteousness and justice. Livingstone was nurtured in a moral
environment which would naturally tend to make him the unrelenting
foe of oppression that he consistently showed himself to be in time
to come.

Three weeks after his ordination Livingstone sailed from London
for Cape Town on board the *George*. Another missionary, William

Ross, accompanied him. The voyage was a long one, eighty-two days in all, as the vessel was required to cross the Atlantic to the coast of South America and touch at Rio de Janeiro before making for the Cape and Algoa Bay. Long as it was, however, Livingtone did not find the voyage tedious, for with characteristic practicality and industry he made use of the time to acquire a knowledge of navigation which stood him in good stead in after years. The commander of the *George,* Captain Donaldson, rendered him kind and generous service in this way, for finding the young passenger eager and desirous to learn, he took a personal interest in him, and taught him how to take his bearings, steer a course, and acquaint himself with the equipment and management of a ship. Livingstone's brief glimpse of Brazil, too, from the harbour of Rio de Janeiro greatly delighted him, and helped to intensify and make permanent the interest he always felt in everything pertaining to the development of the American continent.

The *George* stayed a month in Table Bay to discharge cargo and refit, and the passengers spent the time ashore, but as Port Elizabeth, on Algoa Bay, and not Cape Town, was their ultimate port of disembarkation, Livingstone did not expect to take more than temporary duty during the period of waiting. This he did, using the time to make acquaintance with local conditions and learn what he could of the progress of missions in the colony. Here he met with his first disappointment, finding to his surprise and indignation that missionaries, speaking generally, were neither united nor energetic. Jealousy and bickering were rife, and in some cases laziness and lack of zeal bore evil fruit in an inconsistency of profession and practice which reacted unfavourably on the native mind. Livingstone never forgot the unpleasant impression he thus received at the very outset of his work in Africa; it set a deep mark upon his mind and coloured all his future activities. He saw clearly from the first that there was something radically wrong with the ordinary missionary outlook, and did not hesitate to say so, the result in his own case being to make him unpopular with a section of his brethren for a time. He found fault with the unenterprising spirit which showed itself in the grouping of mission stations amid comparatively small populations in the south, while away in the north there were enormous territories and denser populations totally neglected. His private correspondence from this time forward contains many allusions to what seemed to him a defective method of using the resources contributed by the churches at home, and as early as June, 1843, he took the bold course of stating his views on the subject to the directors themselves, an action on his part which evoked some resentment. There were those among his fellow-workers, both in South Africa and in London, who held that it was presumptuous for one with so little experience of the mission field to deliver himself on matters of policy not only directly affecting his own mode of service, but that of all the others. This not unnatural feeling occasioned him a good deal of trouble then and later.

Livingstone, as we have noted, was never one to conceal his cherished convictions, and on the point under review those convictions never changed from the first few weeks of his acquaintance with the needs of Africa to the very end of his strenuous and exacting endeavours to meet those needs. He soon came to the conclusion— how soon we cannot be sure, but his earliest letters home show that it was present to his mind in a degree that became intensified later— that the proper principle to govern missionary effort was that the missionary should found churches, after the manner of the apostles, and that native converts should be trained to take charge of them. The practice already existed; the London Missionary Society had adopted it to some extent from the first; but Livingstone was strongly of opinion that it ought to be the normal method of working. Before he had been many months in the country he was doing his best at the cost of some personal sacrifice to make it the accompaniment of his own pioneering efforts. He thought, too, that many of the settled churches ought to be left to support themselves.[6]

His judgment of the situation, as it forced itself upon his attention during the month of his stay in Cape Town in 1841, was a painful disillusionment to a new-comer with fervent expectations. Some of the earlier agents of the Society had so conducted themselves in their

[6] He was wrong in this. The experiment was tried on a larger scale twenty-five years later, and even then proved to be premature.

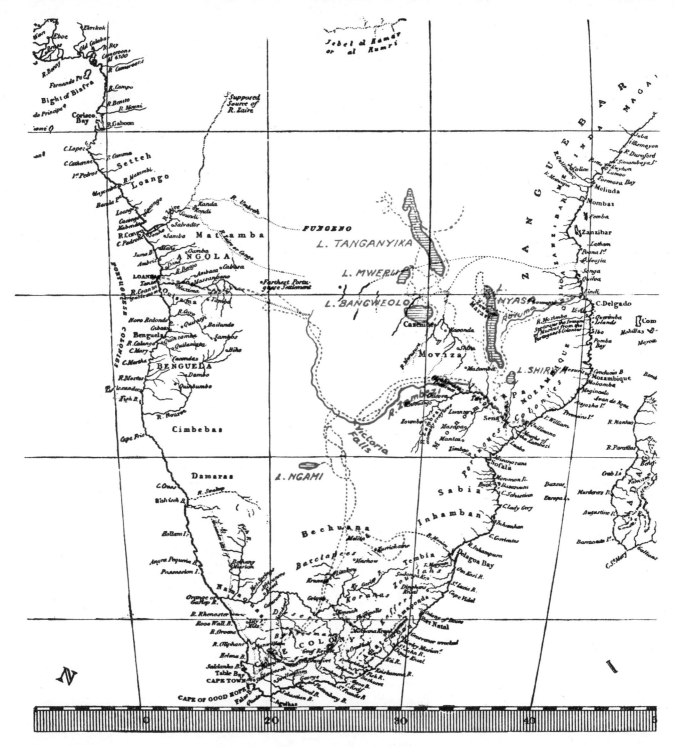

AREA EXPLORED BY LIVINGSTONE

relations with the natives as to bring discredit on the missionary cause; others against whom no such reproach could be levelled were living in a comfort and safety, far from the darkest zone of heathenism, which struck the young man as unheroic. They seemed to him to be more intent upon possessing good houses and gardens within easy reach of civilization than upon carrying the Gospel to those who had never heard it and who were outside the white man's sphere of influence. The great majority of the aborigines remained untouched; little was known of them, and where they came in contact with the whites the results were far from happy. There were two parties among the European population of the Cape, church-goers included—one that, like Smith of Demerara and others in the West Indies, befriended the black man and believed in his ability to rise in the intellectual and moral scale; and another which would fain have kept him in the status of a helot. The type of native who dwelt in the neighbourhood of Cape Town and was most immediately subject to white influence was not an admirable one, and it was this type more than any other, with the exception of the west coast negro, that was thought of in Europe as representing the entire African race The defects of the slave as known both in Africa and America, the product of generations of ignorance and the denial of civil rights, had given the world the impression that the negro was not educable, but by nature must remain in a more or less degraded condition. If Livingstone had done nothing else, his work in Africa would have been amply justified by the change he wrought in civilized men's views of the capacities of the African. The problem of the relations of the white and coloured peoples inhabiting the same territory is still far from being solved, but it is to Livingstone more than to any other man that the possibility of envisaging it in other terms than those of master and servant is chiefly due.

That he had predecessors in this field should not be ignored, and he was fortunate in coming directly under the influence of one of these during his month's stay at Cape Town as a neophyte in 1841. Dr. John Philip, a veteran L.M.S. missionary who hailed from Aberdeen, quickly established friendly relations with his newly arrived young brother Scot, to whom he acted as host, and gave him a perspective upon African conditions which proved of great importance to him and which he never lost. Philip had a fine record.[7] He was a man of great force of character and administrative gifts which had been unsparingly used for more than twenty years in championing the cause of the down-trodden and ruthlessly exploited native races. He had secured the complete emancipation of the Hottentots from their state of servitude in Cape territory, fought a ceaseless battle against the demoralization of the coloured inhabitants of Cape Colony by the sale of alcoholic drink to them, won the liberty of the press, and by his own consistent example and unselfish zeal converted a considerable body of public opinion to sympathy with missions and respect for their aims. It was well for young Livingstone that he gained his first impressions of what needed to be done in Africa from the lips of John Philip. That such a man should have been opposed and thwarted in his endeavours by some of his own brethren was a grievous thing and moved Livingstone's indignation. Henceforth the young missionary threw himself with ardour into the same cause that the older man had fought for through so long a period; he took the side of the negro in all the clashes of opinion, religious and political, that bore upon his labours from that time forward to the day of his death. First Philip, then Moffat, had the shaping of Livingstone's mind on the general question of the nature of the work he had come to Africa to do. These two noble men were the divinely used means of opening his eyes to the magnitude of the task before him and the stand he must take. They did not supply him with his programme; that was entirely his own; but from the standing ground of their ripe experience they enabled him to see just what the difficulties were and how they were to be faced. He had probably read Philip's great book, *South African Researches* (1828), before he went out. It was the book which finally secured the Hottentot emancipation, and if Livingstone had not read it earlier, he would be sure to do so while a guest in Philip's house for a whole month. The idea of raising the Africans by means of the Christian faith, and at the same time compelling the whites to see that

---

[7] *Cf.* W. M. Macmillan's *Bantu, Boer, and Briton*, which is based mainly on Philip's correspondence and literary remains.

the blacks were potential customers and consumers as well as producers, to say nothing of their being brethren in the sight of God, was one which entirely possessed Philip, and it is unthinkable that anyone could be a month in his house without hearing all about it.

Philip wrote to the L.M.S. on April 16th, 1844:

> The brethren, Ross and Livingstone, after having been here four weeks waiting for their ship, have left us for Algoa Bay.
> They will there find waggons and oxen waiting them. They seem to be worthy men.
> I have endeavoured to impress upon their minds that the first and perhaps the most important thing they will have to do in this country will be to make peace, and live in peace with their brethren.

Short as Livingstone's stay at Cape Town had been, it had some serious consequences. He caused offence to Philip's congregation by his manner of preaching, which seems strange considering that it was accustomed to strong meat from Philip himself. Perhaps it resented in the young man what it was prepared to accept from the older. Livingstone spoke straight out on the subject of the evils he had observed: the disunion among Christians, the lack of missionary spirit, the ill treatment of the natives. The strictures were resented, and created a prejudice against himself which operated to his disadvantage on subsequent occasions. Eleven years after, when trying to collect supplies in Cape Town for his expedition to the west coast, he could obtain no assistance, and very nearly found himself involved in a lawsuit with a local postmaster for libel, Livingstone having charged the petty official with extortion. The ill odour in which he found himself was directly traceable to the anger aroused by what he had said from Philip's pulpit in 1841. He was not unaware of the unpropitious beginning he had made at Cape Town, but does not seem to have felt any compunction on account of it, for writing home to his former preceptor, Mr. Cecil, he stated that the church was a house divided against itself and undeserving of the services of a man like Philip.

Disembarking at Port Elizabeth on May 19th, 1841, Livingstone set forth on his first long overland journey to Kuruman, a distance of five hundred and thirty miles. The novelty of the experience fascinated him, and in his letters to friends and kindred he gives glowing descriptions of it. Travelling was necessarily slow; roads were almost non-existent; great heights had to be surmounted; detours had to be taken to touch at two mission stations; the only available means of transport was the covered ox-waggon; hence it is not surprising that the party did not arrive at its destination until the thirty-first of July. The Moffats were still in England, but Messrs. Hamilton and Edwards were waiting to receive the new-comer and initiate him into the life of the most active missionary centre in Africa. Reporting to the directors of the L.M.S. on September 23rd, he enlarges upon the conviction which his stay in the south had already formed in his mind, that an effort should be made to penetrate from this frontier station into the very heart of heathendom, and asks leave to investigate possibilities in this direction; here was the true line of advance, not in maintaining disproportionately expensive establishments in sparsely populated localities within comparatively easy reach of coast towns.

How far did Livingstone foresee and intend at this time the special course his activities were to take? It is an error to suppose, as some do, that his purpose was fully formed from the first to make exploration and evangelization go hand in hand. This view does not accord with the evidence of his own words and needs. He began in the orthodox way by seeking individual conversions and deploring their paucity; it was only gradually that he came to see that individual conversions were, on the whole, of less value than the permeation of heathen society by purer and nobler ideals of living through the influence and example of Christian men and women. He came to believe more and more in the primary importance of endeavouring to raise the whole moral tone of African life by contact with what was most wholesome in European civilization. In this respect he was a typical child of the nineteenth century; his naïve belief in the ameliorating effects of civilization as such finds constant expression in his writings. We are not so sure now as the early Victorians were that civilization is to be trusted, but Livingstone never doubted it, though he had many misgivings about the character of some of its exponents in their impact upon the dark-skinned races. As far back as his first application to the L.M.S. he wrote in answer to a question as to what he considered the duties of a missionary to be: "To make known the Gospel by preaching, exhortation, conversation, instruction of the young—improving so far as in his power the temporal condition of those among whom he labours by introducing the arts and sciences of civilization." [8]

About a year after his arrival at Kuruman he sends to his father an enthusiastic report of the number of individual adherents made by appealing to the unconverted. "The work of God goes on here notwithstanding our infirmities. Souls are gathered in continually, and sometimes from among those you would never have expected to see turning to the Lord. Twenty-four were added to the church last month, and there are several inquirers." In 1846, when leaving the Bakhatlas to settle among the Bakwains, he confesses disappointment that, despite the apparent beneficial effects produced by his efforts in other ways, he had not succeeded in making converts.[9] But by September, 1853, he states in a letter to Blantyre, defending himself against critics who accused him of paying insufficient attention to this main object of a missionary's labours, that experience had taught him to distrust isolated gains of the character desired. "The conversion of a few, however valuable their souls may be, cannot be put into the scale against the knowledge of the truth spread over the whole country. In this I do and will exult. As in India, we are doomed to perpetual disappointment; but the knowledge of Christ spreads over the masses. . . . So very sure am I that I am in the path which God's Providence has pointed out, as that by which Christ's kingdom is to be promoted, that if the Society should object, I would consider it my duty to withdraw from it." [10] In December, 1850, pressing his kindred to emigrate, he says he believes the cause of Christ will be better advanced by emigration than by missionaries. This conviction deepened with him as time went on, and we meet it repeatedly in his utterances, public and private, written and oral. In the opening chapter of the *Missionary*

[8] L.M.S. archives.
[9] Blaikie, *op. cit.*, p. 63.
[10] *Ibid.*, p. 125.

Travels he gives emphatic expression to it in the challenging statement that the promotion of commerce would do more good than the missionary with the Bible under his arm; and so sure was he of his ground in so saying that out of the profits of this, his first and most widely circulated book, he offered two thousand pounds towards the cost of equipping and sending out selected British families to colonize the shores of Lake Nyassa if the Government would support the proposal. He was before his time in his belief in the psychological benefit of a good social example, and his foresight has been amply vindicated by the planting and growth of flourishing English and Scottish communities in this part of Africa; it is now one of the most prosperous coffee and cotton producing areas in the world, and nowhere have the natives made more gratifying response to the appeal of the Gospel. To Livingstone civilization never meant merely the provision of a better environment for human beings or the development of the world's material resources; he thought of it as a way of life, acceptance of lofty standards of conduct, the cultivation of habits of decency and refinement in social relations, and in the thoughts and feelings of the individual man, an ordered and secure mode of existence established on the foundation of Christian belief in righteousness and self-control. The longer he lived and wrought among the ignorant and rudely organized inhabitants of central Africa, the clearer became his vision of the end to be accomplished in bringing them under the influence of European culture as inspired and interpreted by the servants of Christ.

CHAPTER IV

IN SEARCH OF A PERMANENT STATION

It was not until June, 1843, nearly two years after his arrival at Kuruman, that Livingstone obtained the permission he had requested from the directors of the L.M.S. to proceed farther inland with the view of finding a suitable place for the establishment of a new missionary centre. The directors were cautious about giving this permission, rightly feeling that he must have time to acquaint himself with conditions on the spot before committing them to new ventures. He did not remain inactive, however. He had not forgotten Moffat's statement about perceiving the smoke of a thousand villages in a northerly direction, and was eager to make towards it without delay. While awaiting the solicited sanction he employed the interval in making experimental trips into the hitherto unknown region. In company with Roger Edwards he started in less than two months after reaching Kuruman to explore the country and make acquaintance with tribes lying to the north-east. In experimental conformity with his projected plan of making extensive use of native agency, two of the best of the Kuruman converts accompanied the party and proved of considerable service. One of these was later left to act by himself at a point where a beginning of Christian propaganda had been made; and though ere long he had to be withdrawn through illness, enough was done in this way to confirm Livingstone in the opinion he had formed, that native Christians could do more than white men in expounding the Gospel to their own race.

The expedition reached Lepelole in the territory of the Bakwains (or Ba-Kwena), about two hundred and fifty miles north by east of Kuruman, and here the colleagues decided to form their new centre, subject to the approval of higher authority. This done they returned to Kuruman, but in the February following Livingstone journeyed to

Lepelole again, without Edwards this time, his object being to live
with the natives for a few months in order to learn their language and
familiarize himself with their habits and institutions. Part of this
period he employed in making a beginning with the erection of buildings for the projected station.

The chief of the branch of the Bakwains established in and around
Lepelole was named Bubi, and merits attention mainly as the first
petty African potentate with whom Livingstone had independent
dealings. There had been a schism in the tribe, another portion of
it at a distance being ruled by Sechele, of whom more anon. Bubi gave
the missionary a warm welcome, apparently in the hope of obtaining
material advantages from the presence of a white settler; indeed, this
was the general attitude of the natives in this part of the continent.
They knew enough both for good and ill, but more ill than good, of
the prestige and power of the white race to be glad of such protection
and accruing benefits as the influence of a resident missionary might
afford. There was no corresponding readiness to respond to the Gospel
appeal, but Livingstone noted with warm approbation the scrupulous
honesty of Bubi's people; nothing was ever stolen from his belongings
during his stay in their midst, notwithstanding the fact that no guard
was ever set over his waggon. He was to come in contact with a very
different state of things later, when he penetrated into slave-raiding
districts, but, as he repeatedly records both in journals and letters, he
rarely found thieving practised among Africans except in the trail of
the slaver.

Livingstone did not confine himself entirely to Lepelole and the
Bakwains during this preliminary period of observing and learning
the ways of the heathen among whom he expected to labour. He
paid a short visit to Sekomi (or Sekhome), a chief of the Bamangwato.
Sekomi was the father of Khama, one of the most celebrated of
African chiefs in days to come, a noble-hearted Christian, and a wise
and capable administrator. Khama's visit to England in 1895 to meet
and interview Mr. Joseph Chamberlain, the then Colonial Secretary,
and petition among other things for the prohibition of the liquor

traffic in Bechuanaland, produced a great impression upon the public of Great Britain, as many still living will recall.

Sekomi gave Livingstone as warm a welcome as Bubi, and received a conditional promise that more should be attempted for the instruction of his people. His pathetic request for an elixir of regeneration is well known through Livingstone's report of it. "I wish you would change my heart. Give me medicine to change it, for it is proud, proud and angry, angry always." The messenger of Jesus Christ would fain have proceeded at once with the revelation of Him who has proved Himself able to remake sinful human nature and fill it with His own spirit of love, but the chief interrupted, saying, "Nay, I wish to have it changed by medicine, to drink and have it changed at once, for it is always very proud and very uneasy, and continually angry with someone." [1]

On this journey Livingstone penetrated to within ten days of Lake Ngami, which he was to discover later. He also visited the Bakaa, a tribe lying between the Bamangwato and the Bakwains, and here he met with his first experience of native hostility, due in this instance to a guilty conscience. The Bakaa had recently killed a trader with whom they had come into collision, and were apprehensive that they were now to be punished for it. Accordingly, they prepared to resist, and might have murdered the missionary and his little retinue had not Livingstone behaved with the coolness and forbearance which ever distinguished him in his treatment of uncivilized Africans. Exhibiting no sign of fear, he partook of food supplied to him in the Bakaa village and then calmly lay down to rest, knowing well that hundreds of suspicious eyes were watching him from hiding-places around. The method prevailed, and not only dissipated all danger of violence, but provided an opportunity for evangelization which was promptly put to good use, for it was here that Livingstone ventured for the first time to preach the Gospel in the Sichuana tongue, which he had been assiduously studying. He then passed on towards Kuruman, receiving *en route* a deputation from Sebehwe, a notable chief temporarily compelled with his following to settle at some distance to the west. The

[1] Blaikie, *op. cit.*, p. 39.

tribe had suffered greatly in conflict with the terrible Mosilikatse, paramount chief of the Matebele, who had long terrorized the vast tract of country to the north and west of the Dutch settlements. Sebehwe had borne himself well in the struggle with this dreaded warrior, but had had to give way before treachery and superior numbers, and was now in retreat. In response to his strongly expressed desire, Livingstone promised to pay him a visit at an early date, which promise was not fulfilled till the following year. For the present it was imperative to get to Kuruman in case instructions as to his future movements should have arrived during his absence. He finished the journey by June, 1842, having covered a distance of more than a thousand miles in less than six months and acquired much useful information.

The expected communication from the directors not yet having arrived, he would have gone north again after a brief rest in accordance with his promise to Sebehwe but in the interval disaster had overtaken this chief. In search of better quarters, he and the remnants of his harried tribe ventured forth from the corner of the Kalahari desert in which they had sought refuge, and were promptly assailed by another chief, Mahura, who had laid a trap for them. Somehow or other a part of the blame for this misfortune was laid at the door of the Christians, a group of Kuruman native converts happening to be with Sebehwe at the time. In consequence of this, no other native adherent of the mission station could be persuaded to accompany Livingstone, who was perforce compelled to wait for a more favourable opportunity; it was impossible for a European then, as now, to travel through trackless regions in Africa without a proper equipment of guides and carriers. The temporary check to his movements was not entirely without profit to his future labours, for it confined him to Kuruman and district for nearly eight months, and gave him a definite part in the ordinary everyday work of the establishment. It was not till February, 1843, that the territory to the north was sufficiently tranquillized to permit of his taking the road again, and even then not without hazard. Sebehwe gave him a chilly reception, partly on account of the supposed delinquency of the Christian converts, and partly because the missionary had been so long in fulfilling his undertaking to appear. The restraint soon wore off, and Livingstone was enabled to obtain for his message the most encouraging hearing it had yet received.

Meanwhile, finding that the Bakwains had been driven from Lepelole by marauders, he chose Mabotsa as the best available situation for the missionary centre he hoped to create. Mabotsa was a charming and healthy spot in the land of the Bakhatla, a tribe akin to the Bakwains, and it had the advantage of being sufficiently near to the Bakwains to render possible the carrying on of Christian work in both tribes simultaneously. With this end in view he decided to make acquaintance with Sechele, under whom the Bakwains were now united, Bubi having been accidentally killed by an explosion of gunpowder shortly after Livingstone's first visit to the tribe. Like Sebehwe, Sechele was at first inclined to resent the fact that his visitor had been so long in coming, and had paid prior attention to a rival, but with his usual wisdom and kindliness Livingstone overcame the prejudice. He cured the chief's child of an infantile disorder, and by this means attached the father to himself by a bond of affection that was never broken. Sechele became one of his firmest and most loyal friends, and the most satisfactory convert of the earlier part of his work in a purely heathen environment. No other man among the lesser native magnates with whom Livingstone came into intimate association at this period so won his respect, and deservedly so, for Sechele displayed an uprightness and strength of character remarkable in one of his savage antecedents. His profession of Christianity cost him dearly, as he could not carry his people with him, and they treated him with contempt and opposition because of it. At the beginning of Livingstone's ministry to the Bakwains the chief proposed to flog the whole tribe into acceptance of the Gospel by means of whips of rhinoceros hide, but as the missionary would not permit this, and succeeded in giving him a better conception of the meaning of Christianity, few cared to follow his example in becoming baptized. In a private letter to Thompson as late as September, 1852, Livingstone states with reference to this obtuseness of spirit: "The majority of the Bakwains have heard the Gospel repeatedly, but have not received it.

They treated me uniformly with respect, but when Sechele professed faith in Christ, they persecuted him bitterly." [2] An earlier note in his diary (September, 1848) says: "They cursed the chief with very bitter curses, and these come from the mouths of those whom Sechele would formerly have destroyed for a single disrespectful word."

Sechele was a man of remarkable mental capacity. He learned the alphabet in a single day, and speedily became a good reader with an appreciation of the literary beauties of the Bible. "He was a fine man that Isaiah; he knew how to speak," was his comment on one occasion after the reading of a magnificent passage from the book he loved best. He was accustomed after his conversion to conduct worship with his family, and Livingstone was greatly impressed by his simple and reverent manner of doing so. Christian missions in south central Africa owed not a little to Sechele in days to come.

The long-expected permission to extend having been received from the directors, Livingstone wrote to them in grateful elation, setting forth at some length the conclusions at which he had arrived through the excursions outlined above. It is now that he unburdens himself of the conviction he had formed before coming up country, that drastic changes should be made in the Society's mode of utilizing the services of missionaries and expending the funds contributed by the churches at home. If he could have had his own way, he would have closed a number of the stations he considered superfluous in the south, replacing the European by native teachers, and drafting the white missionaries to expanses hitherto outside their range. "The conviction to which I refer," he writes, "is that a much larger share of the benevolence of the Church and of missionary exertion is directed into this country than the amount of population, as compared with other countries, and the success attending those efforts, seem to call for. This conviction has been forced upon me, both by a personal inspection, more extensive than that which has fallen to the lot of any of them, either missionary or trader, and by the sentiments of other missionaries who have investigated the subject according to their opportunities." [3]

2 L.M.S. archives.
3 Ibid.

SECHELE AND HIS WIFE

The claim he here makes to special knowledge is already justified, as we have seen by tracing his movements during the previous two years; he knew at first hand the magnitude of the problem that awaited solution as no one else did at the moment, and he knew it because he had examined it for himself. But he could not prevail with the directors; it could hardly be expected that he should at this early date; his name did not carry the weight it came to carry thirteen or fourteen years later. But he never ceased to advocate a more courageous and aggressive policy in respect to missions. Writing to Tidman in 1852, he furnishes with careful accuracy statistics showing the cost of missions in part of Cape Colony as compared with the vast interior. "Who in England would believe," he remonstrates, "that the average expenses of Bethelsdorp would be £224, of Colesberg £211, of Uitenhage £251, while 'The Apostle of the Bechuanas' (Moffat) draws on an average not much over £100?" [4] His appeal in this instance is for more equitable treatment for Dr. Moffat, who had been doing outpost work since 1824, but the indictment of policy is based on broader grounds.

To this representation he received a reply promising that more should be done for Moffat, but objecting to the criticism of the policy hitherto followed, whereupon Livingstone somewhat sarcastically rejoins, quoting Tidman's own words: "I am sorry to find that my remarks on the relative expenditure in the Colony and countries beyond have appeared to imply a charge of maladministration on the part of the Directors. Those remarks were founded on data published in the Colony showing the average expenditure for a season of years, and though it is quite true that 'a missionary looking at an object from an isolated point of view is very liable to misinterpret the measures of the Directors when applied on a wide scale,' it is not quite so obvious that the relative or numerical value of these data can be affected by our mode of viewing them." [5]

It may truly be said that Livingstone gave his life for this nascent conviction of his career as the bringer of glad tidings to beknighted

4 *Ibid.*
5 *Ibid.*

Africa. It burnt itself into his soul, and reached its climax in the words he penned in his *Last Journals,* alone and ailing, amid scenes of horror and desolation in the deepest depths of African savagery—words vibrant with moral passion. He was near his end and knew it; hence this must be understood as his last message to the conscience of his fellow-Christians in the homeland he was never to see again. As such they were received, and effected immediately more than all his persuasions had been able to do when he braved the odds against him twenty years before. "I would say to missionaries, Come on brethren, to the real heathen. You have no idea how brave you are till you try. Leaving the coast tribes, and devoting yourselves heartily to the savages, as they are called, you will find, with some drawbacks and wickednesses, a very great deal to admire and love." "It would be a sort of Robinson Crusoe life," he remarks later in the same connection, and goes into details of his own habits of improvisation and going without many things that are ordinarily deemed necessaries. It was an austere mode of existence that he both commended and practised.

Without the systematic use of native agency, Livingstone's proposed plan of campaign would have been impossible of realization, and many years had still to elapse before it was fully operative. His private letters home on this subject had not been wholly without effect, for he found to his great gratification a helpful response awaiting him at Kuruman which had come by the same delivery as the directors' consent to the founding of a new station. Mrs. McRobert, the wife of a Congregational minister residing near Blantyre, had become so interested in his expressed view of the desirability of spreading the Gospel by means of native Christian converts, that she had raised and sent him twelve pounds in furtherance of this object. Livingstone took the gift as a direct mandate from heaven to proceed, and in his expression of thanks to this good lady and her helpers went far beyond his usual calm and matter-of-fact mode of utterance. The twelve pounds would provide maintenance for one native teacher, Mebalwe, who had already shown himself possessed of aptitude for the particular kind of work that was so urgently needed; henceforth he was to be con-

sidered the special representative of Mrs. McRobert and her friends.[6]
Encouraged by this evidence of sympathy with his aims, Livingstone in informing the directors of it in the communication aforesaid,
thanking them for permission to extend, begs hard for greater official
recognition of the worth of native agency and the results to be expected
therefrom. He offers to defray the cost of supporting a second agent
out of his own small salary, and states that he has had other promises
of a sufficient amount to justify the authorization of a third. This
letter of June, 1843, is only the first of a series wherein he persistently
champions the change of policy involved: the British missionaries to
lead the way into every abode of heathen darkness, and their converts
to maintain and extend under proper superintendence the work thus
begun in every fresh locality. It will be seen from this that Livingstone
was no mere visionary, but a man with a clear conception of what
should and could be done in destroying the strongholds of heathenism
and introducing the knowledge of Christian faith and life. For the
next ten years he continued to urge the creation of an efficient seminary
for the training of the native teachers required and sending them
forth as opportunity presented itself. At first he naturally thought of
Kuruman as the most suitable centre at which to establish such an

[6] Writing to Mrs. McRobert from Kuruman on June 24th, 1843, Livingstone says: "Your
representative is a Deacon in the church here, and one of the most sensible consistent converts
belonging to the Mission. The older Missionaries who are best able to judge say that he and
his sister have more principle than any others in the church, and they have been uniformly
consistent in their walk since their conversion. As to general information, he is at least equal
to the best informed of his nation. He always attends the school, though he is the father of
two children; but I should mislead you if I made you think his knowledge is extensive. No,
the Bechuanas have not yet had the means of acquiring much knowledge; he, however, knows
the way of life, and can preach to the point and with as much affection as any Scotsman I
ever heard. . . . His name is David Molehani, but he passes more frequently by his former
name, Mebalwe, the second sounding like 'a' in father. I shall give him some plain instructions in medicine in order to make a master for the rain-making Doctor of this country."
    Another letter, dated September 1st, gives still warmer praise to Mebalwe. "I wish to place
him with another tribe than that with which we have commenced in order that when he is
favoured to be the means of converting souls, his success may stand out distinct from ours,
and thus others may be stimulated to follow the excellent example of yourself and friends. I
earnestly desire this, but I fear it will be some time ere it can be put into execution. He is
at present with us, and *is invaluable*. He works as hard as either Mr. Edwards or myself,
and is not the least influenced by the example of a lazy Hottentot whom Mr. Edwards has
with him. The fellow feigns sickness in order to escape work. He (Mebalwe) endeavours
to instruct the natives, and from his great command of the language has a decided advantage
over us foreigners. Indeed, I cannot speak *too highly* of the spirit he has shewn. I magnify
the grace which has done so much for him, for he was once in the same state as those wicked
Bakhatla. I intend putting him through a course of instruction, and it may be by the time
that is finished an opening may present itself for carrying the Gospel to some other tribe."

institution, and ultimately it was placed there, the need for it having become recognized, not only through Livingstone's representations, but those of Moffat; but by the time the decision was finally taken both Livingstone and Moffat had come to see that it would have been wiser to choose another site, as the population around Kuruman was declining rather than increasing. The problem has since been solved in ways other than either of these pioneers could have anticipated.

Mention should be made at this point of the fact that Livingstone's early efforts on behalf of a policy so clear to his own mind occasioned some misunderstanding. He was accused of wanting to get the seminary established in order that he might become the head of it himself, and this so vexed him that for a time he refused to have anything more to do with the matter, a course he would not have taken in later years when he saw that an end needed to be accomplished and called for his support; no consideration of his own comfort or reputation was ever allowed to stand in the way in such a case. In the present instance he was made to realize that his tactics had been at fault. He was barely thirty and new to the work, and in the ardour of his perception of what he believed ought to be done he overlooked the desirability of winning older men to his side and letting them take the lead; and human nature being what it is he found himself thwarted. Later he resumed the agitation, but still without success. In 1849 the Society sent out the Rev. J. J. Freeman to visit the South African mission stations and report. To Livingstone's great disappointment this gentleman differed from him entirely in regard to the policy above outlined, and it is but just to say that on the whole the visitor's judgment was sound, taking into account all the difficulties of the position at the time. He and Livingstone do not appear to have been mutually attracted, nor did Freeman obtain a glimpse of the vision that dominated Livingstone's soul. Their meeting had momentous consequences, however, for had not Livingstone been defeated on the subject he had so much at heart it is probable that he would not have undertaken single-handed the seemingly impossible task of opening up the interior. He could never have remained long in one spot; his nature would not permit of it; but if the ideal that took

LIVINGSTONE'S
ROUTES. No. 1

⊙━━⊙ Livingstone's Apprenticeship Journey
" First Great Journey
■ Mission Stations founded before 1838
○ " " AFTER
○ Other towns
━━━ Railways

20 0 20 40 60 80 100
Scale of Miles

possession of his imagination within the first twelve months of his landing in South Africa had been approved by the Society contemporaneously he would have been content to share with his fellow-missionaries in the duty of carrying it out. As it was he had to act alone.

In August, 1843, he and Edwards started for Mabotsa to take up the new work agreed upon. Two English gentlemen, Captain (later Sir Thomas) Steele and Mr. Pringle, who were big game hunting in South Africa, accompanied the party and proved kind companions *en route.* They conceived a respect and liking for Livingstone which bore good fruit in after years. The first task of the missionaries on reaching their destination was to complete the buildings Livingstone had begun a year before for the housing of the new establishment. These were of the plainest character consistent with immediate needs. A hut fifty feet by eighteen had to suffice at first for living accommodation, schoolroom, and place of worship. Scarcely was the work finished when the accident befell Livingstone which of all his African adventures has become most widely known, his seizure by a lion and narrow escape from death. The facts are too familiar to need recital here, but it should be noticed that Mebalwe, who diverted the attention of the lion at the critical moment, was the native assistant of whom mention has been made as having been furnished by the contributions of Mrs. McRobert and a group of friends in the near neighbourhood of Livingstone's Scottish home. The lion's jaws so injured the upper part of Livingstone's arm that for the rest of his life he never could raise his gun to the level of his shoulder without steadying the barrel against some support. It was through the marks of this encounter that the body of the great explorer was identified after it was borne to the coast by his faithful attendants in 1874.[7]

A letter which has not hitherto publicly appeared, written by Livingstone from Mabotsa on May 28th, 1845, to his friend and former fellow-student, Robert Newton Hayward, of Edinburgh, some time surgeon in the Navy, gives his own account of the lion incident. The letter is

---

[7] At the Royal College of Surgeons there is a plaster cast of the broken humerus. The bad join makes an excrescence almost as big as the head of the humerus.

the property of Alexander Young, Esq., of Newton Stewart, and is lent for exhibition in the National Memorial to Livingstone at Blantyre.

I have had some trials since I last addressed you. Of one of these you may have heard, so I need not say much about it. I was without medical assistance, without house, and had very few attentions save *what the poor black fellows about me* could give. The lion left me with eleven ugly gashes and a shattered humerus, and these discharging excessively made me as weak as possible. They put up one of their own little huts to shelter me from the sun, and though that was so far good I often dreamed that I was in London and saw Dr. Bennett, etc., coming to put up my arm properly. But through the kindness of God I recovered beyond my expectations well. I had to begin my house before I was perfectly well, and a partial false joint in the upper third of the humerus is the result. But I don't complain. I never expected it to be so well, and while the other two who were bitten by the same lion feel pains at the changes of the weather, I feel none. One of them had an abscess among the wounds at the anniversary of the event. I can work very well with it, bad as you might call it. People in general condemn me for going near the lions, but they don't know that we live amongst them. Others say it was because the lion killed my sheep, but I had not one single sheep to kill. The reason I went was that the people with whom I dwell suffered so many losses by the attacks of lions they became discouraged by the belief that they had been given over to the power of lions by witchcraft. I went with them to encourage them to destroy one which had that morning killed nine sheep belonging to them, and in coming away went near to where one was wounded. A native teacher (Mebalwe) stood close by and tried to shoot him as he tore me, but his gun missed fire and he got torn for his faithfulness. Another native tried to assist him with his spear and he got wounded too. But a third finished the business by pitching his spear into the monster's heart. By the way, the second native was tossed up into the air by a buffalo the year previous to the above accident. I saw him immediately afterwards, and though he lighted on his head and was unconscious for some days afterwards, by a few bleedings he got quite well. The *vis medicatrix* is very potent in all these fellows. . . . They bear operations better than any other people can.

His sufferings were great, though we only learn this from Edwards; Livingstone himself says nothing of them, nor does he allude to the fact that he was indebted to his colleague for such nursing as he received. As soon as he was able to travel he went to Kuruman for more thorough treatment, and remained there until the following January when he had sufficiently recovered to be able to ride on horseback a hundred and fifty miles to the south to meet the Moffats, who were returning after their lengthy furlough in England.

This journey had the important consequence of leading him to fall in love with Dr. Moffat's daughter Mary, to whom he became engaged shortly afterwards and married in January, 1845. Up to this time Livingstone had not seriously contemplated matrimony nor seen much of female society; on the contrary, he had been inclined to believe that it might be a hindrance rather than a help in the breaking of new ground, which was what he had been attempting to do. In a letter to the directors, dated Mabotsa, December 2nd, 1844, announcing his approaching union with Miss Moffat, he says: "I do not regret having come out single. I rather think it would be advantageous if many of our young missionaries would spend at least as much time previous to marriage as would enable them to acquire the language and become acclimatized. In cases where young men would be kindly cared for by older brethren, a much longer delay would be advantageous for the mission. But where there is an almost total deprivation of European society and civilization long delay would be improper." [8]

The concluding sentence of this paragraph is probably an allusion to the well-known tendency to deterioration of habits only too apt to beset Europeans isolated in a savage environment; the most careful vigilance and rigid self-discipline are required to counteract it. Livingstone himself recalls at a much later stage that he was always scrupulous to observe home standards of cleanliness and decorum, not only

[8] L.M.S. archives.

for the sake of his own self-respect, but as a means of keeping his
relations with his uncivilized companions on a right footing; he
attributed not a little of his influence over them to his practice in this
regard.

His marriage is clear evidence that he did not as yet foresee the lines
on which he was to proceed in the not distant future, for had he done
so it is incredible that he should have been•willing to encumber himself
with the responsibilities of a family or to subject a wife and children
to the hardships he must himself undergo. That strange wanderer
in African wilds, Aloysius Horn, voices some of the disparagement
that fell upon Livingstone in the fifties on the point. Describing the
explorer as one of fortune's favourites lionized in London's drawing-
rooms for his exploits, Horn sneers at him for dragging "that poor
girl, Mary Moffat," up and down Africa in obedience to his own
craving to be always on the move. There is just enough truth in the
accusation to make it sting, and there were not a few among Livingstone's contemporaries who uttered and believed similar aspersions
on his motives and conduct. That he did unwillingly sacrifice his
wife's life and much of her happiness to what he came to feel to be his
duty must be admitted, as it must be conceded also that he was never
able, except in a minor degree, to act a father's part towards his
children. He was well aware of this, and felt it deeply, as his correspondence shows, and it is but reasonable to conclude in view of all
the facts that had the issue of his vocation been manifest to him in
1844 he would not have asked Mary Moffat to link her life with his.

Yet there never was a happier match. Livingstone and his wife
were devoted to each other to an extent that the world never knew in
the lifetime of either, and in remembering the heroic services of the
one the patient self-abnegation of the other should never be forgotten.
They shared one another's ideals and partook of one another's confidence as fully as any happily married couple could desire. The greatest
sorrow that ever befell Livingstone was his wife's death on the
Zambesi in 1862; his agony of mind, as both Dr. Stewart and Sir John
Kirk have told us, was more uncontrollably manifest on this occasion
than on any other of which his intimate friends had knowledge. He

himself testifies: "It is the first heavy stroke I have suffered, and quite takes away my strength. I wept over her who well deserved many tears. I loved her when I married her, and the longer I lived with her I loved her the more. God pity the poor children, who were all tenderly attached to her, and I am left alone in the world by one whom I felt to be a part of myself." "For the first time in my life I feel willing to die," he enters in his Journal a fortnight after the bereavement.

Mrs. Livingstone's character was one of simple goodness and benevolence conjoined to a reticence in regard to her own personal feelings and beliefs unusual in evangelical circles in the middle of the nineteenth century. She was to endure much suffering and some slander during the period of necessary separation from her husband, which had to be borne while he was fighting his way across unknown Africa between 1852 and 1856, and again from 1858 to 1862. Evil tongues whispered that they could not get on together, and there were even some malicious enough to suggest to her that her husband had succumbed to the same sensual temptations as many white travellers had been known to do in their intercourse with the aborigines. The calumny disturbed her not at all, but her loneliness did, and it is not to be wondered at that in some of her touching letters to her beloved one she confessed to having given way to spiritual depression. Her mother said of her that she was less openly pious than other members of the family, but not one whit less tenacious in her loyalty to the practical simplicities of Christian faith. "Accept me, Lord, as I am, and make me such as Thou wouldst have me to be," was the private petition found among her papers after her passing. Brave, humble, quiet, sensible, unpretentious, hard-working, ever more ready with service than speech, a worthy mate for David Livingstone was Robert Moffat's eldest daughter, and if their married life was no idyll of domestic felicity, the fault was not with either of them, but with the stern demands of a vocation unique in the annals of modern Christendom.

Their joint troubles soon began. Immediately after their marriage, Livingstone took his wife to Mabotsa in the expectation of remaining there and making it a centre of wide-spreading Christian influence on the model of Kuruman. This was not to be. Deplorable differences arose between him and Edwards, which within twelve months rendered it impossible for them to continue to work together. The facts of the dispute have not hitherto been fully stated or perhaps understood by Livingstone's biographers. Roger Edwards had been an artisan in Bury, Lancashire, previous to his acceptance by the London Missionary Society, and remained limited in outlook and sympathies by the lack of a good education. He was an honest, unimaginative, and rather peevish man, ready to take offence at trifles and to insist upon the deference due to his seniority in his relations with his colleague. He was eighteen years older than Livingstone, and, of course, possessed a much greater familiarity with missionary methods in Africa as hitherto understood. Livingstone, on the other hand, had but little regard for precedent, and was too forceful a personality to run easily in double harness with a man of Edwards' temperament. We are not without evidence from various quarters that Livingstone was apt to dominate any situation that he took in hand, and was not always successful in managing men who resented his assumption of leadership. This view of his character is well brought out in Coupland's account of the work of Sir John Kirk in the region of the Zambesi. Two volumes are required for the telling of the story instead of one, as the author confesses, because so long as Livingstone was on the scene Kirk moved within his orbit and was subject to his will. With other members of the expedition in which they co-operated this overmastering energy was not as readily submitted to, and ruptures ensued.

Something of this kind may be in part the explanation of the quarrel between Edwards and Livingstone in 1845. The former brought specific charges against the latter which betray a certain pettiness of mind on the side of the accuser, but point to an independent initiative on the other which at times may have been rather galling. Concerning the beginnings of their partnership at Mabotsa, Edwards hints at being left with a preponderating share of humdrum labour, and claims to be having to minister to Livingstone even to the extent of preparing his home for him, a claim which Livingstone's letters to his fiancée do not mention at all, nor, as we have seen, does he ever allude to having been nursed by Edwards after his dangerous accident. The spirit in which the service was rendered may have had something to do with this silence on the part of the beneficiary. "Livingstone getting into the hands of the lion," writes Edwards, "was soon laid aside. The watercourse and the hut, which we left a shell on poles with a roof on them when we returned to Kuruman, I finished with native assistance, but had to be in hourly attendance on Mr. Livingstone for three months. His sufferings were dreadful, and called for all our sympathies and all we could do for him, and when I had compleated (sic) his room it gave me great pleasure to see him take possession of it. When he returned from a visit to Kuruman I had got up the walls of a building 40 by 18 for a schoolroom, and collected the wood for roofing and that like. Three men he brought with him from Kuruman and two already here assisted me four and a half days to put on the roof. The house is a frail concern—have begun to build two houses of clay and stone." [9] Obviously Edwards does not intend the directors to gather that Livingstone's services so far are on a par with his own.

When a few months later he formulates his complaint against his colleague, he harks back to the initiation of the work itself; Livingstone had chosen Mabotsa as the station, he says, and begun operations there without consulting the directors or anyone else. Further offences alleged are that he had interfered with discipline in attempting to remove a ban which Edwards had placed upon Mebalwe's wife, and had flouted the senior's authority in various similar ways. The woman in the instance cited had stayed away from Communion because of something Edwards had said to her; Livingstone had tried to find out the reason and obtain her restoration. Another count against him was that he had usurped Edwards' rights over a man employed in digging a water-course. An illuminating outburst in Edwards' protest to the directors is the declaration that he refuses to be made any longer an

[9] L.M.S. archives.

"appendix" to this young man, which, indeed, was probably the root of
the whole trouble.

Livingstone and his wife decided that rather than continue in a position involving strained relations with an older fellow-worker it would
be wise to move away and begin afresh. The decision necessitated
giving up the home upon which they had expended much patient
labour and care, and addressing themselves to the strenuous task of
making another, but they could see no alternative. In a long communication of about four thousand words, written from Mabotsa on
October 17th, 1845, Livingstone informs the directors in detail of the
successive events which have led him to the conclusion that he ought
to leave Mabotsa. As he had already begun work among the Bakwains, he fixed upon Chonuane in Sechele's country, about forty miles
from Mabotsa, as the place for a new mission station. Hither he and
his household removed in 1846, though not for long. The district was
so disturbed by tribal warfare, complicated by drought, famine, and
hostility from the neighbouring Dutch settlers, that another migration
soon became imperative. In February, 1847, Livingstone induced
Sechele to remove with his whole tribe to the banks of the river Kolobeng, where it was thought that a constant supply of water could be
depended upon, and here the same heavy toil of building was recom-
menced amid the same physical difficulties and hardships that had had
to be battled with twice before. They were able to stay two years in
this spot ere irresistible forces uprooted them again.

Up to this time Livingstone's record in the mission field had not won
much favour with his superiors. His leaving Mabotsa and the unpleasant circumstances relating thereto not unreasonably exposed him
to the suspicion of being unstable and difficult to work with, and the
suspicion became irritation when one removal was followed by another, each involving some amount of financial expenditure. The
amount was but small; Livingstone only asked for a building grant
of thirty pounds for Chonuane; but small as it was it was opposed,
and it is owing to this opposition that we learn of the privations endured by Mrs. Livingstone and himself. "I can bear," he protests,
"what other Europeans would consider hunger and thirst without any

inconvenience, but when we arrived (at Kuruman), to hear the old women who had seen my wife depart about two years before, exclaiming before the door, 'Bless me! how lean she is! Has he starved her? Is there no food in the country to which she has been?' was more than I could well bear." [10] His description to his friend Watt of the daily routine at Kolobeng is a revelation of hard and continuous labour both for husband and wife, with slender resources and little or no relaxation. "We get up as soon as we can, generally with the sun in summer, then have family worship, breakfast, and school; and as soon as these are over we begin the manual operations needed, sowing, ploughing, smithy work, and every other sort of work by turns as required. My better half is employed all the morning in culinary or other work; and feeling pretty well tired by dinner-time, we take about two hours' rest then; but more frequently, without the respite I try to secure for myself, she goes off to hold infant school, and this, I am happy to say, is very popular with the youngsters. She sometimes has eighty, but the average may be sixty. My manual labours are continued till about five o'clock. I then go into the town to give lessons and talk to anyone who may be disposed for it. As soon as the cows are milked we have a meeting, and this is followed by a prayer-meeting in Sechele's house, which brings me home about half-past eight, and generally tired enough, too fatigued to think of any mental exertion." [11]

It will be seen from this enumeration of activities that the "better half" took a full part in the spiritual work of the station in addition to caring for husband and home. The mission house at Kolobeng was the only settled home Dr. and Mrs. Livingstone ever had, and they had it entirely to themselves, for after the dissolution of partnership with Edwards, Livingstone never again worked in association with a missionary colleague. Within the first four years of their married life three children were born to the couple—the first, Robert, during the Mabotsa period, the others, Agnes and Thomas, while dwelling among the Bakwains. One of Livingstone's profoundest regrets in later life, as we learn from a confession written by him in 1870, was that he had

[10] Blaikie, *op. cit.*, p. 64.
[11] *Ibid.*, p. 70.

not devoted more time to playing with his children when he had them
with him up to 1851; he never had the same opportunity again, though
his delight in their society while in England in 1857 was observed and
sympathetically commented upon by Sir J. Risdon Bennett and Mr.
Frederick Fitch, with both of whom the Livingstone family stayed for
a time. Says the former: "It was beautiful to observe how thoroughly
he enjoyed domestic life and the society of children, how strong was
his attachment to his own family after his long and frequent separations from them, and how entirely he had retained his simplicity of
character."[12] The latter remarks on the unity of spirit that characterized the parents. "Dr. and Mrs. Livingstone were much attached, and
thoroughly understood each other. The Doctor was sportive and fond
of a joke, and Mrs. Livingstone entered into his humour. . . . In society, both were reserved and quiet."[13]

It is not improbable that, despite all attendant difficulties and drawbacks, the life at Kolobeng was the happiest the Livingstones ever enjoyed together. They accepted the discomforts of their lot cheerfully,
and were so thoroughly absorbed in their duties that they had no in-
clination to repine. They kept in constant touch with Dr. and Mrs.
Moffat at Kuruman, and paid occasional visits there; indeed, it was
necessary to do so for the sake of supplies and mutual consultation, as
the new centre was officially regarded as an appanage of the old. The
moral problems which Moffat had to face furnished Livingstone with
valuable guidance when he came up against similar ones in his dealings
with native mentality, and we are not surprised to find that among
the most intractable of these were cases relating to sexual incontinence
and the native habit of concealing breaches of the Christian requirement of monogamy. Combating these evils had constituted Dr. Moffat's heaviest task, and Livingstone found it no less so. As he more
than once stated, his wife's presence and example were of greater usefulness in this connection than his own exhortations.

That he had much need for the exercise of both is evident from his
private reports to Thompson on the subject of the enforcement of spir-

[12] Blaikie, *op. cit.*, p. 177.
[13] *Ibid.*, p. 179.

itual discipline against the chief himself and the native teachers too. The lapses in each case were serious, and had to be firmly dealt with, all the more so because of the duplicity that accompanied them. As late as October 12th, 1852, Livingstone gives a discouraging account of the suspension, or rather excommunication, of his principal helpers. The story is a typical illustration of the severity of the struggle that has always to be maintained for the establishment of Christian standards of purity and truthfulness in a polygamous community. He writes:

The reasons which make me doubt whether I ought to draw anything for Mebalwe are the following. I mentioned to you that after three years' consistent conduct and profession of faith in Christ I baptized Sechele on the first Sabbath of October, 1848. In March or April, 1849, it was discovered that he had been cohabiting with one of his former wives whom, in consequence of having a young child and no parents, he had found impossible to send away with the others. He at once confessed his sin and added as an excuse that having been accustomed to her he had not at the time felt as if he were sinning by taking another man's wife. He professed much penitence, entreating me not to cast him off, "as he hoped to stand along with me before the throne of Jesus." I cut him off from fellowship, and as he entreated to be allowed to remain as a *spectator* only at the ordinance, and I felt I must not count him as an enemy, I acceded to his request. He sat back from the spot where the few believers communicated on two or three occasions which occurred subsequently to his fall, and his manner being no way changed from what it had been previously I indulged the hope that if he continued to walk uprightly for two or three years we might again receive him. Immediately after his fall I wrote to the Directors about it, knowing that they would sympathize with me in my sorrow, and I mentioned to them subsequently the fact of his walking consistently. I thought this was sufficient unless I had restored him again. . . . I was the more careful to give the facts of his case because they had in some speeches made reference to his conversion, and some who did not, of course, know what I had written thought that I must still be holding up Sechele to the Board as a convert. Well, eight or ten

months after Sechele was cut off, a worse affair came to light
amongst the young people belonging to the families of the native
teachers, very excessive impurity, and when I began to make enquiries I found out that the teachers must have known of it and kept
me in ignorance. This is a peculiarity among Bechuana believers.
They never will make known the sins of their fellow believers, and
when anything comes to light then they quietly remark, "Oh, we
knew all about it long ago." The wives of the teachers, too, had
been using enchantments. I felt very much vexed to think that I
had been administering the ordinance to them as consistent believers,
and the whole town knowing all the while what their conduct had
been. Their whole number being only seven, I cut the whole off
having had no ordinance at all since. None of them even asked
why they were kept so. They seemed determined to act as if they
had never been guilty or as if they believed that I knew nothing
about it. Paul's family being notoriously bad I requested him to
leave, but he did not go. Mebalwe, however, confessed to me before
I went to the Cape that they had done great harm to the cause. "In
fact," said he, "we have spoiled the teaching at Kolobeng."

This lengthy extract from a long and detailed report conveys a better
idea of the perplexities Livingstone had to strive with at this stage of
his life-work than a mere bald statement of them at second hand.
Here we see him and his brave young wife wrestling with the enormi-
ties of heathenism and realizing as they could not fail to do what obstinate forces were arrayed against them; not in one year nor two, nor
in an ordinary lifetime could they expect to break down and eliminate
the evil customs and practices of many generations of unchecked savagery. Yet disappointing as these facts are on the surface, Sechele's
change of habits was nothing less than a moral miracle. That a man
of such an upbringing and in mature life should turn his back upon
old beliefs and conduct and submit himself humbly to the inflexible
requirements of Christian faith is a marvellous evidence of the operation of divine grace and of the moral ascendancy Livingstone had
gained in this instance. Stern and uncompromising, too, is the missionary's handling of the problem. There is no palliation of the

offence, and the sentence imposed is no light one—an exclusion of two or three years from the Lord's table. The austerity of the discipline imposed recalls the similar sternness of the church's treatment of backsliders in the early Christian centuries, the reason for it being the same —namely, the life-and-death struggle of Christian ideals with pagan grossness in a social atmosphere where the latter was taken for granted as normal. The epistles of St. Paul furnished sufficiently instructive parallels to the grievous experience that now confronted Livingstone. Nor was the apostolic precedent confined to the moral lapse of the converts alone; misrepresentation by uncharitable brethren was added. In the same letter above quoted Livingstone expresses indignation at the calumny that he had lacked the moral courage to cut off Sechele, and so had fallen back on the device of holding no Communion services at all, and further that he had continued to claim Sechele as a convert in his communications to London, well knowing him to be an apostate. He warmly repudiates this construction upon the chief's conduct. A backslider he was; an apostate he was not. Strange, too, it is to read that the quarrel with Edwards, now nine years old, had not been forgotten. "The directors," observes Livingstone, "tell me that it still exists." [14]

So far, then, Livingstone's life as a missionary on the front line of aggressive Christian effort in South Africa had not been unattended by vicissitudes and disappointments. A greater hindrance to his aims than anything dealt with up to the present has now to be described, as it was the chief factor in determining him to give up service in a settled station and become a pathfinder on a scale hitherto unforeseen and by methods unpremeditated, one step leading to another till the whole world stood in amaze at what had been accomplished by one dauntless soul energized by simple faith in God.

[14] L.M.S. archives.

CHAPTER V

TO LAKE NGAMI AND BEYOND

DURING his brief residence at Chonuane Livingstone came into contact with the Boers. Not everyone knows even to-day how serious an obstacle these hardy settlers presented to the progress of Christian missions in South Africa throughout the greater part of the nineteenth century. The antipathy which sprang up between British and Dutch in Cape Colony and Natal, leading to the formation of the Transvaal Republic and Orange Free State, and culminating in the South African War with which the twentieth century opened, was due in large measure to a fundamental opposition on the subject of the treatment of the native. It is but just to remember in this connection that the British record is none too creditable; we are not entitled to pose as having been consistently the protector of the black man as against the Dutch farmers who consistently oppressed him; but from 1833 onward this did, on the whole, represent the facts of the case. British imperial policy stood for fair play for the native, and the Boer element, with the active or tacit support of some of the British colonists, resented the consequent restrictions upon their habit of using their coloured neighbours as they liked. Reduced to its simplest terms, this was the chief reason for the successive migrations whereby a portion of the Dutch-speaking population of the Cape tried to get away from British rule. Like the southern planter in the grimly humorous gibe, the Boer trekker sought for liberty "to whop his own nigger in peace." This fact of history seems to have been forgotten or overlooked by the pro-Boer party in Great Britain in 1900, when a fierce wordy warfare was waged against the supposed tyranny of annexing two free self-governing Dutch communities to the British commonwealth of nations. New issues had arisen to obscure the old, but, whatever the causes in dispute between Boer and Briton in 1900, there can be no doubt that the Boer conception of freedom half a century earlier did not include the recognition of the native's right to the same. Happily the cleavage of opinion has ceased to exist, and British and Dutch statesmen to-day in the vast South African Federation are at one in the endeavour to find a permanent solution of the complicated problem of white and coloured peoples dwelling side by side without placing the weaker in the position of a chattel to the stronger.

British administration in South Africa, as directed from the Colonial Office in London, was not invariably wise, equitable, or well informed. The carrying out of the policy of emancipation, for instance, was always a sore point with the Boer farmers, as it was in other parts of the Empire. The compensation given was insufficient, and there were large deductions which were nothing short of downright robbery. The money was not paid at the Cape, but in London, and this inconvenient arrangement mulcted the Dutch slave owner in the Colony of a commission of twenty per cent. to an agent in England. Altogether the transaction did not enhance the prestige of the British Government among the Dutch Afrikanders and left much bitterness behind it.

It should be remembered, too, that the remoteness of the Dutch farmers in the interior of Cape Colony from the great centres of European civilization had continued in them much of the same mentality as marked their seventeenth century progenitors. They were a fine type physically and in rude strength of character, as became the descendants of the tough-fibred Hollanders who resisted Philip II. of Spain and Louis XIV. of France; the French strain which mingled with the Dutch after the revocation of the Edict of Nantes was not inconsiderable. They were men of the Bible and the strong arm, these children of the Reformation over whom England hoisted her flag in South Africa in 1802, and they were a breed impossible to coerce and difficult to persuade. The view they took of the coloured inhabitants of the continent was derived from the Pentateuch. The heathen were accursed, in the position of the uncircumcised Philistine, outside the covenant, to be subdued and exploited rather than to be approached in friendship or even tolerated.

This repelled and disgusted Livingstone; he could not understand it, and it aroused in him a moral wrath he made no attempt to restrain. He did not see, as we see now, that the difference of attitude was due to a difference of moral background, itself comparatively recent. The plain truth is that the attitude of the Boer to the native was precisely that of the seventeenth century Englishman, Puritan, Cavalier, or Roman Catholic, and the earlier half of the eighteenth century was no better. "How is it," demanded bluff old Samuel Johnson with reference to the American colonists' plea for autonomy—"how is it that the loudest yelps about liberty come from the drivers of negroes?" And we have the strange anomaly of John Newton confessing that he never enjoyed sweeter communion with God than when on his way to and from the Gold Coast with cargoes of wretched beings torn from their homes and lying fettered and festering in the ship's hold beneath his feet.[1] This prosperous trafficker in human flesh could and did write with perfect sincerity one of the most familiar and beautiful hymns sung by Christian congregations to-day, the hymn beginning:

> How sweet the name of Jesus sounds
>   In a believer's ear!
> It soothes his sorrows, heals his wounds,
>   And drives away his fear.

There was more allowance to be made for the Boers than Livingstone perceived, and it is in no small degree owing to him that the Dutch Reformed Church of South Africa, to which most of the Boer farmers belong, has long ago reversed the attitude of which he complained, and is as active and zealous as any other Protestant communion in the prosecution of missionary endeavour in regions he was the first to open to Christian influence. It invaded Nyasaland in 1889, and the mission established there consists at present of twelve stations with over seven hundred out-schools and thirty-eight thousand pupils. This mission is entirely supported by the members of the Dutch Reformed Church of the Cape Province of South Africa, the children of the very people who tried to prevent Livingstone from carrying the Gospel to the native population at all. About 1898 the Dutch Reformed Church of

[1] Edwin W. Smith, *The Golden Stool*, p. 103.

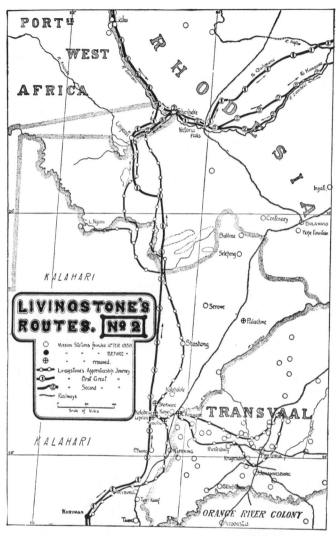

NOTE.—THE APPRENTICESHIP SERIES INCLUDES JOURNEYS FROM
THE COAST TO KURUMAN, KURUMAN TO LEPELOLE AND NGAMI,
AND TO THE CAPE AND BACK. FOR DETAILS SEE TABLE OF DIS-
TANCES TRAVELLED IN THE APPENDIX

the Orange Free State began a mission in Northern Rhodesia which has since grown into one of the largest and most successful on the whole African continent. In Southern Rhodesia a similar work began seven years earlier. This also may fairly be claimed as a direct outcome of Livingstone's brave and self-sacrificing labours in a cause which in the middle of the same century excited small sympathy in the Briton and sharp animosity in the Boer.

During his short period of residence at Chonuane Livingstone made two journeys to the Magaliesberg range on the borders of newly occupied Boer territory with the object of extending missionary operations in that direction and installing a native teacher there. One Dutch commandant was not unfavourably disposed at first towards the project, but it proved unworkable; the Dutch settlers in the neighbourhood refused to permit any attempt at evangelization among the natives, and some went so far as to intimate definitely that they would kill any native teacher operating anywhere near them. In face of this threat the idea had to be abandoned for the time.

Ere long the hostility thus evinced became more menacing. The Boers suspected or at least accused Livingstone of selling arms to the Bakwains, and denounced him to the Cape Government for this supposed offence, demanding his withdrawal and the disarming of Sechele's tribe. They also forbade the continuance of building operations for a permanent mission station at Chonuane. The facts of the case were that Sechele possessed no more than five muskets, which he had purchased from traders, and the only lethal weapon which Livingstone had parted with to him (on loan, not on sale) was an iron pot for cooking. Writing long subsequent to the event Livingstone makes merry over the terror excited in the Boer mind by this iron pot, which they persisted in believing to be a cannon.[2] The British officials at Cape Town were chary of offending the Boers and unsympathetic with the aims of the missionary; they seem, indeed, to have regarded Livingstone as a troublesome person likely to create difficulties for them. At this period, too, the official attitude was one of reluctance to intervene on the side of the native in any dispute with the Dutch settlers ouside

[2] Correspondence with Thompson. The fact is also referred to in *Missionary Travels*, p. 35.

the radius of direct British influence or even within it; the time had
not yet come for a more humane and enlightened policy. Any departure from the rule of official passivity was usually made by exerting
force on the side of the Boers instead of against them, the presumption
being that it were safer and wiser to back the white settler against the
native than to espouse the cause of the latter against the former. It
would take us too far from the main track of the present narrative to
attempt to give an account of the petty wars wherein British troops
came to the deliverance of the Dutch in their struggles against native
hordes, struggles mostly provoked by Dutch aggression; but it should
be recognized that these wars were neither few nor unimportant in
outcome.

In the circumstances, then, it was impossible for Livingstone to expect any countenance from the British administration at the Cape for
his protests against Boer persecution of his work at Chonuane. This
was one reason for the removal to Kolobeng. Here, too, the harassment went on and increased. Sechele was compelled to give hostages,
which really meant slaves, to the Boers for his own good behaviour.
One of his children was captured and carried off, to his great grief, and
neither he nor his missionary friend could obtain the restoration of the
child or any redress for other outrages. It is worthy of note that one
of the commandants whom Livingstone interviewed on poor Sechele's
behalf was the redoubtable Paul Kruger, who fifty years later was to
prove himself so formidable an enemy to the embattled might of the
entire British Empire. Little did the British Government understand
what it was doing when in 1852 it recognized the newly created Transvaal Republic, of which Kruger became President in the following
year. It was in 1848 that Kruger and Livingstone first came face to
face. The former was then on the point of leading a commando
against the Bakwains, and the missionary could only succeed in persuading him to postpone the intended subjugation of the tribe, not
to abandon it altogether. Less than five years later the arrested blow
fell with calamitous result, as we shall see.

As part of the price for holding his hand Kruger demanded that
Livingstone should furnish him with periodical reports of the be-

haviour of the Bakwains—in other words, to spy upon them secretly while ostensibly continuing their friend and preceptor. Compliance was firmly refused, but it was now clear that extension of missionary activity eastward was completely out of the question. A momentous conversation thereupon took place between the missionary and Sechele. The chief had quite reasonably refrained from putting himself in the power of the Boers by accompanying Livingstone to the conferences with Kruger. Livingstone now asked whether, as the road was blocked to the east, Sechele would join him in trying to find a more secure location towards the north. Sechele readily agreed, stating that on the north side of the great Kalahari desert dwelt a strong chief, Sebituane,[3] ruler of the Makololo, who might afford them protection and friendship. Thus was the idea born which was to have such a prodigious aftermath. From the day the decision was taken to leave Kolobeng Livingstone's work as a settled missionary was over and his work as an explorer began.

This he did not know, however, and the fact should be taken into account in reviewing his procedure. He expected to reach a point where he could do what had hitherto been frustrated on successive occasions: organize a missionary centre in a well-populated area unmolested by Boers and without the natural drawbacks of his two previous stations. This he never found. In one way or another he was determined to penetrate to the interior, and as the nearer route was closed, he chose the only feasible alternative. Once the great natural barrier of the Kalahari had been passed, he might expect to arrive at Lake Ngami, of which he had heard much, and to establish himself on its shores or in Sebituane's country.

The start was made on June 1st, 1849. Sechele did not feel free to leave his people at this time in their disturbed and anxious condition, but far more competent assistance was forthcoming. Two English sportsmen, Messrs. Oswell and Murray, were desirous of crossing the Kalahari, elephant hunting. Learning through Captain Steele, the helpful companion of one of Livingstone's former journeys, of the bold expedition in prospect, they asked leave to join it, a request which was

[3] He had saved Sechele's life in the childhood of the latter.

warmly acceded to. Livingstone had already made Oswell's acquaintance, and knew something of the man. Never was a more serviceable
partnership effected or a more lasting friendship established on a basis
of mutual respect and confidence. Oswell was intent upon exploration
even more than upon securing big game trophies, and he found in
the missionary a congenial spirit. Not enough has been made of his
part in the arduous task which the next two years were to see accomplished, for it is safe to say that it could not have been accomplished
without him. To his generosity the initial success of the expedition
was due. He furnished the guides at his own expense, and much of
the supplies also. At a subsequent stage of the adventure, taught by
experience, he did much more. Livingstone's gratitude to and affection for this noble-hearted associate of his first essay as an explorer
never underwent any diminution, and he took care to make adequate
public acknowledgment of his indebtedness to him.

The arid Kalahari was the great natural barrier which had hitherto
prevented access to the well-watered and fertile regions of which vague
rumours had reached the south, though little was thoroughly known
of them; the general belief of geographers was that the interior was
desert of the same character as the Kalahari. Few except Bushmen
had ever dared to attempt crossing the latter, involving as it did the
danger of perishing from thirst in a dismal wilderness of seemingly
illimitable extent. Livingstone and his party journeyed for two
months through this inhospitable expanse before they were rewarded
for their toils by a sight of Lake Ngami. The discovery of the lake
was made on August 1st, 1849, an event which the travellers rightly
regarded as of first-class importance, and sufficient in itself to justify
the exertions they had made. A fortnight earlier they had reached
the confluence of the fine rivers Zouga and Tamanak'le, which proved
to them that the central African basin was much more humid and
organically prolific than they had been led to believe. Throughout the
journey Livingstone made careful notes, as was his wont for the rest
of his life, of the principal topographical features and organic peculiarities met with day by day. Nothing new escaped his attention, and
everything of importance was recorded with scientific precision.

The expedition was not entirely without hindrances. Sekomi of the Bamangwato had been in the habit of deriving some profit from his virtual monopoly of the ivory trade with the interior, and being unwilling to see a possible competition set going, he first endeavoured to dissuade the party from setting out from Kolobeng, assuring them that they would perish in the desert or be murdered *en route,* and failing in this, he sent messengers in advance to warn the inhabitants of the Ngami country not to trade with them on any account, as their real object was to obtain plunder and slaves. The prejudice thus created had to be overcome by the exercise of Livingstone's usual methods of patience, fair dealing, and inoffensiveness of demeanour.

A further check appeared at the lake itself. While preparation was being made at Kolobeng for the contemplated journey, an invitation had come to Livingstone from a young chief named Lechulatebe, whose small tribe dwelt on the eastern shore of Ngami at the point where the Zouga debouched from it. Lechulatebe expressed a desire to have a resident missionary, and assured Livingstone of his readiness to welcome the white men to his country, should they see fit to come so far to pay him a visit. But on their arrival he changed his tone; he had no mind to allow them to proceed, and was especially opposed to their expressed intention of passing on to Sebituane, his mighty neighbour, two hundred miles farther to the north, to whom he stood in a sort of feudal subjection. With this intent he effectually blocked the way by refusing guides and stationing armed pickets to prevent the travellers from taking canoes to the opposite bank of the Zouga. There was nothing for it but to abandon the effort for the time being, and make their way home again with the purpose of returning later more fully equipped.

Livingstone's reports of the gains in geographical knowledge resulting from this expedition, made to the L.M.S. and to Captain Steele, were brought to the notice of the Royal Geographical Society by the latter, and gained him his first official recognition from that distinguished body in the shape of a gift of twenty-five guineas and public thanks for having made discoveries so valuable in concert with Messrs. Oswell and Murray. The compliment gave the recipient great pleasure, and he never omitted afterwards to despatch to the Royal Geographical Society full and accurate descriptions of new discoveries as soon as possible after making them This was the opening of a new chapter in his career, and he seems to have regarded it as such.

Reaching Kolobeng on October 10th, 1849, after retracing their course across the Kalahari, Messrs. Oswell and Murray took leave of their missionary companion, Oswell arranging to go on to Cape Town and get together all that might be necessary for a second attempt to penetrate to Sebituane's dominion. Without awaiting his friend's return, Livingstone proceeded with his design to leave Kolobeng and transplant his family and native associates to what he now knew, or thought he knew, to be a far better strategic centre for missionary work of the kind he most believed in and desired to do. Sechele accompanied him on this occasion, as did Mebalwe, Mrs. Livingstone, and her three children, and a few selected members of Sechele's tribe. Dr. and Mrs. Moffat did not view the upheaval with favour, preferring that Livingstone should consolidate his work among the Bakwains before abandoning it and moving his whole establishment to a point so far distant from it, so painful to reach, and of whose suitability for permanent residence so little was ascertained as yet. It must be admitted that Livingstone acted in this instance with an impetuosity and a lack of forethought which, in the circumstances, deserved to be found fault with. He should at least have deferred his departure until he could avail himself once more of Oswell's co-operation, which had been definitely promised; as it was, he exposed his family to much suffering. The want of water in the desert was the least of their trials—it was to be worse later; far more serious was the outbreak of fever in the company, the two younger children being the first to be attacked by the scourge which shortly afterwards laid all the bearers low. This untoward development took place at Lechulatebe's, which was now perceived to be a malarious district. So grievous were the effects of the sickness that the decision was taken, probably at the solicitation of the distressed mother, to get away from the disease-laden environment and return whence they had come.

This was a hard resolve for the ardent head of the party to be forced to acquiesce in, and a great disappointment to him, for they had not been many days in the Ngami country at this second visit, and he had been confidently expecting to pass on to the Makololo. Mrs. Livingstone, busy with her ailing children, had not even seen the lake whose discovery had meant so much to her husband, and it was only as they were leaving that he took her on a special trip of some six miles to enable her to have a view of it. He and Sechele had previously bargained with Lechulatebe for permission to cross the Zouga and a supply of guides to lead them to Sebituane. To secure the desired facilities, Livingstone parted with a much-prized gun to the chief, an unnecessary sacrifice, as matters turned out. Arrangements had been entered into for Mrs. Livingstone and the children to remain in Lechulatebe's care while Livingstone and Sechele made the journey to Sebituane and back, but all these plans were now hurriedly put aside, not only because of the dangerous severity of the fever, but because of the mortality among the cattle due to the attacks of the tsetse fly. It was imperative to pack up at once and be gone. This they did, the invalids soon recovering in the pure, dry air of the desert, where they met Oswell on his way north with the well-furnished travelling organization he had gone to the Cape to obtain some months before. With his usual courtesy and kindness, he at once turned round and escorted the Livingstone party to its destination at Kolobeng.

The strenuous experiment above narrated, of taking the missionary's whole household on a prospecting tour with insufficient resources, had not only proved unsuccessful in other ways, but was too much for poor Mrs. Livingstone's strength. Shortly after the enforced return to Kolobeng she was delivered of her fourth child, Elizabeth, who only survived for a few weeks. The mother herself became seriously ill, no doubt as the result of the hardships and anxieties she had endured. And as the malady was accompanied by paralysis of one side of the face, the whole family went for a few months to Kuruman for needful rest and care.

The temporary check to his hopes produced no change in Livingstone's resolve to make connection with Sebituane. He had by now come to believe in the possibility that readier access might be obtained to the interior from the west coast than from either the south or the east, and was desirous of putting this theory to the proof, his only way of doing so being to explore the routes westward from the Makololo country towards the sea. He was encouraged in this prospect by what he had now learned at first hand of the existence of great waterways in that direction which might be turned to good account both for missions and commerce. An ironical letter to his friend Thompson, written between three and four years later than the date of the return from the second attempt to reach Sebituane, shows how clearly Livingstone envisaged the object he had now set himself to achieve, and the reason for it. He pokes a little good-natured fun at his correspondent, not without some justification. "It is not likely I shall ever come your way again. Here one of your questions holds up its fiz at me—'Unless you discover a good way to the sea either to the East or West, how are we in future to send men to the region of the lake or to the parts beyond?' 'In *future!*' The dear man! How many has he sent in time past? 'Unless you discover a good way,' etc. An indifferent one will do for those who have any pluck in them. And for those who have none, the old overland route may be safely recommended, for they will discover some important and very large fields of labour, a long way south of the Orange River in which they will be associated with a Wesleyan, a Church of England Clergyman, a Dutch Predicant, and a Government schoolmaster, each of whom considers the ten shanties and eight shop-keepers' houses as his 'sphere of labour,' involving the most excrutiating (*sic*) (sacrifices)."[4] The irony is not without point in view of Livingstone's difficulties with his unenterprising brethren hitherto.

The first of a long series of attempts to deprive Livingstone of the credit due to him for his geographical discoveries deserves passing mention here, not because it was taken seriously by the public, but because it illustrates at once his methods of trying to introduce legitimate trade wherever he went, without directly engaging in it himself, and how those methods were continually baffled and diverted to unworthy ends by others. He was ever careful to avoid taking up com-

[4] L.M.S. archives.

mercial pursuits on his own account, lest he should lay himself open to the accusation of seeking personal gain, but, as we have seen, he thought it his duty to promote by every means in his power the growth of commercial relations between Europe and Africa in order to bring the latter under the influence of Christian culture. The time was to come, as we shall have to note in its order, when he found to his bitter sorrow that unscrupulous use was made of the facilities he thus provided to do the very opposite of what he expected and laboured for; advantage was taken of his discoveries by Europeans in many instances to render the state of the untaught African worse instead of better. This he did not foresee, but he found, to his annoyance, even at the very outset of his endeavours to introduce commerce along with the Gospel in the course of exploration of new territory, that his unselfish practice in this respect was liable to be abused. Personal profit never mattered to him; with ample opportunity for enriching himself, he lived and died a poor man; in every journey he undertook he was greatly hampered by lack of means; but he was ever sensitive, perhaps too sensitive, to depreciation of his work or denial of his title to being first in the field in any given instance. He was to endure plenty of this as time went on. In no single case did his claim to originality pass unchallenged, and his mortification was extreme when, in addition to the denial of his right to be accounted the discoverer of new ways into the interior, vile use was made of his maps and detailed scientific reports for the enslaving and fleecing of the inhabitants.

The relatively unimportant incident alluded to above is best explained in Livingstone's own words. Communication was so slow that apparently he did not hear till long after the discovery of Lake Ngami and the connected inland waterways that an impudent rival claim to the distinction of adding these great natural features to the world's knowledge of the African continent had been advanced at the Cape. Writing to Thompson from Kuruman on November 24th, 1852, Livingstone says:

We have a new claim out for the discovery of the lake—viz., Mr. Wilson, a trader who *asked and obtained* permission from me to accompany us as such. Oswell and Murray were not pleased with me for giving permission. His opinion was never on any occasion asked, he never spoke a word on any emergency, paid nothing to the guides, was fed and otherwise assisted, and got a fine load of ivory for next to nothing. Yet some of his friends, in order to detract as much as may be from my honours, set up his claim as the *true discoverer* of the lake. He, it seems, says we should all have turned back but for him. Now the question of turning was never mooted, except by Sekhomi's messenger—my answer was, "They must put me in my grave first." Mr. Oswell asked what I had said, and when I told him, he replied, "I am very glad to hear *you* say so." Murray may have spoken to Wilson about turning, but the idea never entered my head I know. On the single word "turn" hang all Mr. Wilson's claims. I perhaps ought to give him the medal on such serious grounds. But turn we didn't, so to us belongs the discovery.

After taking a few months at Kuruman for recuperation, the Livingstone family went back to Kolobeng, and from thence made a fresh start for the Makololo country. This was on April 8th, 1851. Again Oswell was the good genius of the party, the entire expedition being equipped at his expense. To Moffat's protest—a very reasonable one in the recollection of what had befallen the family on the previous journey—Livingstone replied that he had always been accustomed to think for himself and act in accordance with his convictions. "I have occasionally met with people who took it on themselves to act for me," he adds, "and they have offered their thoughts with an emphatic 'I think'; but I have generally excused them on the score of being a little soft-headed in believing they could think both for me and themselves." [5]

Truly Livingstone was not wanting in definiteness in his mode of expressing himself at any time when his resolution was questioned, if a little wanting in politeness. Dr. Moffat was assuredly right, and Livingstone was assuredly wrong in this further exposure of wife and children to the dangers and toils of a long journey through the African

[5] Blaikie, *op. cit.,* p. 98. Moffat expressed willingness to accompany his son-in-law at a later date when his translation of the New Testament into Sichuana should be completed (*cf.* Blaikie, p. 115).

wild, as events were shortly to prove. Moffat was thinking of his daughter, Livingstone of his goal. On the side of·the latter, be it said, that he wanted his family with him because it was his full intention to make his home with Sebituane's people. Mrs. Moffat had something to say on the subject, too, and she said it with a vigour equal to Livingstone's own. She objected vehemently to his taking his wife and children with him again on a journey which, as he very well knew, had already proved nearly fatal to every member of the family except himself, and had actually cost the life of his latest-born child. It is impossible to acquit Livingstone of want of consideration here. So firmly was his mind set on making a new home in the interior that it caused him to disregard all warnings and make light of the obstacles in his path; it was not till sheer disaster all but overtook his hopes in consequence of the agonies daily endured by his dear ones before his eyes that he was persuaded to face the facts as foretold by Mrs. Moffat, and come to the conclusion that his aims and the welfare of his family were incompatible.

This third journey to the north was more attended with pains and perils than either of the two previous ones. The party lost their way in the Kalahari owing to the errors and insouciance of their Bushman guide, Shobo, and nearly died of thirst in consequence. Writing to his friend Watt about this mischance, Livingstone mildly remarks on the merry-hearted ways of the Bushman folk as represented by friend Shobo, who, it appears, deserted them at one point, and might quite irresponsibly have left them to their fate. Being inconvenienced by the thorn bushes, which hurt his legs, the guide had taken to following elephant tracks, which went hither and thither, and so lost knowledge of his whereabouts. The drinking water gave out while they were wandering unguided—one of the containers had leaked through the carelessness of an attendant, and was found to be empty—and Dr. and Mrs. Livingstone were tortured through several successive days by hearing their little ones cry for the unobtainable means of cooling their parched throats. The father gratefully records that the mother never uttered a querulous or reproachful word during this dreadful period, terrible though her apprehensions must have been. On the fourth day after the failure of the water supply they came on the tracks of a rhinoceros, and allowed the oxen to follow them till they led to a muddy hole. The native carriers, who had gone a little in advance of the main body, promptly returned on the fifth afternoon with what few drops of water they could collect from this impure source, and never was draught more welcome; the discovery probably saved the lives of the travellers, young and old. Here, too, they found the errant Shobo, who coolly curled up and went to sleep in lieu of awkward explanations when the party arrived. Livingstone indulges in pleasantry at the recollection of the incident, but it is not improbable that Stanley would have taken sharp measures with Shobo.

This was the most serious danger they encountered *en route,* but there were many others. They had to be constantly on the alert for attacks by wild beasts and venomous creatures of all sorts, and by the time they reached the lake district the bodies of the children were covered with sores from the bites of ferocious insects. The Chobé river, within the territory of the Makololo tribe, was reached in July at a point five hundred miles from their starting point, and here the party was warmly welcomed by Sebituane.

This great African chief was a Basuto by birth, and, like so many other petty Bantu rulers, had headed several successful migrations before establishing himself on the banks of the Chobé, where Livingstone found him. He was a man of fine presence, of much magnanimity and charm of character, and by his genius and courage in leadership had built up a strong personal following composed of sections of various tribes which had coalesced under his command. Originally they had been mostly fugitives before the aggressive Zulu power under the formidable Chaka. Sebituane himself in his younger days had been driven from his home on the Vaal river by these assailants, and had settled for a time near Kuruman, whence in turn he was thrust by the Griquas. Moving to the north, he gained a reputation as a skilful and victorious warrior who could no longer be attacked with impunity; on the contrary, he overcame the Bechuana tribes that opposed him, and became the military master of the wide region of the upper Zambesi. The Makololo tribe or nation, if such it may be called, was thus composed of elements of differing origin held together by confidence in the all-round capacity of Sebituane. Of this amalgam the Barotse were perhaps the best constituents, as they undoubtedly were the most loyal and reliable in their relations with Livingstone. While Sebituane lived, his numerous subjects enjoyed a measure of security and peace unusual in the interior of Africa then or later. The only foes they feared were the Matebele, whose territory lay to the east and south, and even these were held firmly in check.

What the future might have been had Livingstone and Sebituane been able to co-operate for a few years, who can tell? The two men were mutually attracted, each recognizing in the other a kindred soul. The Christian European and the heathen savage possessed qualities of indomitableness and lofty purpose in common, and instinctively discerned the fact. Livingstone ever afterwards referred to Sebituane as by nature a true gentleman, and on the whole the best spcimen of indigenous chieftainship that he had ever made acquaintance with. To the great sorrow of all the British visitors and the dismay of the Makololo people, the acquaintance was short-lived. The chief was seized with pneumonia a few days after the party arrived, and died within a fortnight. On the Sunday previous to falling ill he had attended Livingstone's first service, and listened reverently to the preacher's words; this was the only occasion on which he ever heard the Gospel message. His death was a great blow to the expedition, and something of a danger as well, for it was possjble that the grief-stricken Makololo might charge the visitors with having brought this calamity upon them by witchcraft.

Happily, the apprehension proved to be groundless. Sebituane had designated his daughter, Mamochisane, to succeed him in the chieftainship. She was away in the north at the time of her father's decease, but on hearing from Livingstone, with the request that the party should be allowed to explore further with a view to settlement, she readily acceded, and promised to afford them whatever facilities might be necessary. Leaving his wife and children in the care of the head men of the Chobé district, Livingstone then went forward with Oswell to Linyanti, the principal town of the tribe, and a little later, at Sesheke, came on a great river which they subsequently discovered to be the upper reach of the Zambesi. Livingstone was in transports over this notable find, which he described in letters home as the first real river he had ever set eyes on, a noble volume of rolling water with an eastward current. But nowhere could the travellers find a district sufficiently free from fever and other drawbacks to warrant them in making a permanent home there for a missionary and his family. Warned by what the children had already suffered from malaria, the father yielded to the persuasions of Oswell not to expose them to further risk of sickness in a region so trying to European constitutions. For the third time, therefore, they turned back and made their way to Kolobeng.

They left Linyanti on August 13th, 1851, and on September 15th, while the party was still *en route,* Mrs. Livingstone was delivered of her fifth child, a son, who was named William Oswell, in compliment to the brave and generous friend who had done so much for them all. This latest accouchement throws a startling light upon the strain to which Mrs. Livingstone had been exposed in the two long journeys across the Kalahari desert, with a period of residence among savages, completely out of touch with the resources of civilization. No woman in such a condition ought ever to have been allowed to go through such an ordeal, and the reason for Mrs. Moffat's protest now becomes fully apparent.

The event did not lead Livingstone to contemplate for a moment the abandonment of his enterprise, but it compelled him to face the prospect of having to part from his family for a time. The facts were too much for him; the apprehensions of Mrs. Livingstone's parents were seen to be well grounded; it was clearly impossible to attempt again the distressing task of taking a delicate mother and her four surviving little ones through such perils and hardships as they had already borne, not to speak of the worse ones that might have to be encountered on any further journey into the interior. He must either fall in with Dr. and Mrs. Moffat's wish that he should be content to go on with his work at Kolobeng or somewhere else within reach of Kuruman, or he must take the drastic step of doing alone what he could not do while carrying his family with him.

Other considerations presented themselves also. A heathen environment was bad for children; they were only too apt to imbibe, consciously or unconsciously, ideas and habits they were better not to know. Their education had to be thought of, too, and nowhere in South Africa, let alone in a frontier station, could a missionary's children be as well educated or as cheaply as in certain institutions available for the purpose in the homeland. The decision was therefore taken to send Mrs. Livingstone and the children to England, while Livingstone himself completed the task that had been gradually shaping itself in his mind, and to which he was now convinced he was called of God—namely, to find a means of letting in the light of Christian civilization upon central Africa. "I will open a way to the interior or perish," he wrote to his brother-in-law.[6]

While sojourning with the Makololo he had been brought into closer contact than hitherto with the slave trade. The Boers had practised slavery without calling it such, but here was a new phenomenon, the systematic and organized harrying of one tribe by another in order to supply the slave markets of the Mohammedan, and even to some extent of the Christian world. The Makololo did not sell their own children—no African tribe did that—but they made raids upon their neighbours in order to obtain captives, which were afterwards sold to Arab traders and, though Livingstone did not then know it, to Portuguese. The object of engaging in this cruel traffic was to obtain firearms, and the suffering and waste of life that ensued were viewed with a callousness which struck the missionary with horror. Had there been no other reason for wishing to introduce the Gospel to the enormous region of the upper Zambesi, he would have deemed this sufficient. He believed that if he could only set a stream of legitimate commerce going and familiarize the natives with European, and especially British, habits of thought and ways of life, he would destroy the evil at its root.

[6] J. S. Moffat.

But how was it to be done? The Boers barred the way to the east—south of the Magaliesberg range, at any rate—the Zulus and Portuguese from Delagoa Bay northward, the Kalahari was a great natural barrier from Cape Colony to the Makololo and beyond. But there might be a hope of opening communications with Sebituane's country from the west coast, and this would have the advantage of being nearer for British ships and merchandise if the route were found to be practicable. Failing this method of trying to make contact between African heathendom and the Christian world, there would still be opportunity to approach the interior from the east. He lived to do both. His expectation was that he might devote two or at most three years to exploring the basin of the upper Zambesi and finding a way to the coast, and in the meantime, as he wrote to the directors, he hoped that his family might be cared for in England by the L.M.S. If the directors could not see their way to sanction this, he would commit his dependents to the charge of his parents in Scotland, with his own meagre stipend to eke out their subsistence.

It was a daring, indeed an audacious programme, for his stipend was but a hundred pounds per annum. No man but one who, like the apostle, was willing to be accounted mad for Christ's sake would have dreamed of such a sacrifice, or of so imperilling the future of those dependent upon him. He knew well what he was doing, and what it would involve. "To orphanize my children will be like tearing out my bowels," he wrote to his superiors; "but when I can find time to write you fully, you will perceive it is the only way, except giving up that region altogether." [7] Once more he met with opposition, some of his missionary brethren believing that he was actuated by selfish motives and was deserting his proper service for a venture outside the limits of his vocation. His answer to the criticism was: "So powerfully convinced am I that it is the will of our Lord I should, I will go, no matter who opposes." [8]

A lengthy letter to Tidman, dated March 17th, 1852, gives his views on the problem as he saw it at the time, and is helpful as illustrating

[7] L.M.S. archives.
[8] Blaikie, *op. cit.*, p. 102.

for present-day readers the difficulties that had to be faced by the Society as well as the missionary himself. It says much for the directors that they had vision enough to grasp what Livingstone proposed to do and why, and were willing to give it the seal of their approval despite the murmurs of their older representatives at the Cape.

After quoting Freeman's recommendation that he should apply to the Society for an increase of £20 or £30 per annum in salary in order to meet the extra expenses of his special work, he continues:

> It is scarcely worth while again to refer you to the peculiar obstacles which must be overcome before we can plant the Gospel in the densely populated country drained by the Zambesi.
>
> The swampy, boggy nature of a region more than two hundred miles in breadth, the tsetse, the death of Sebituane, the deep rivers, and the fever, prevented our proceeding at once to a part of the salubrity of which we could entertain a hope. The impropriety of removing the people from the only defences against the annual forays of the Matebele, and the fact that Sebituane's people, who were composed of Basutos, Bamangwato, Bakwain, and other tribes, have nearly all fallen victims to the fever, led me to the conclusion that separation from my family had become absolutely necessary— for though I may be justified in risking my own life in the service of our Master, I may not use the same freedom with the lives of my wife and children.
>
> As much less expense will be incurred in procuring education for the children in England than there would be in Cape Town, the propriety of deciding for the former will appear evident.
>
> Their mother was affected by total loss of motion in the whole of the right side of the head and face, and has frequently been threatened by symptoms of paralysis in the whole of the right side and extremities, and though now partially recovered, as the eldest of the children is only six years of age, it seems right on account of both parent and children that the expense of a voyage should be incurred.
>
> A residence in England of two or three years would prevent the frequent confinements which, notwithstanding the preaching of Dr. Malthus and Miss Martineau, periodically prevail and aggravate the complaint; and, besides the probable re-establishment of health,

the consolation of knowing that the children enjoyed a mother's care in passing from the extreme heat to which they have been exposed under many a bush in the wilderness to a cold and variable climate, time will also be given to me to form a mission in some healthy locality in the Barotse country or beyond.

I hope in that time, too, to solve some interesting problems in relation to the slave trade, my full conviction being that this nefarious traffic will be abolished by the influence of Christian missions, and that the London Missionary Society may hold as prominent a place as it did in the emancipation of the Hottentots.

We have been six months in travelling from Sebituane's country to the Cape, the whole of our stoppages not amounting to so many weeks. If I am spared for two years I may be permitted to establish a mission, and also to find a way to the Sea on either the East or the West coast. If so far favoured by Him on whose providence all depends, the long irksome land journey would be avoided, and much time saved. The act of orphanizing my children, which now becomes painfully near, will be like tearing out my bowels, for they will all forget me. But I feel it is a duty to Him who did much more for us than that. His command is, "Go ye into all the world and preach the Gospel to every creature."

Forbid it that we should ever consider the holding of a commission from the King of Kings a sacrifice, so long as men esteem the service of an earthly sovereign an honour. But for the disinterested kindness of Mr. Oswell we could not have come down to the Cape. He presented supplies for last year's journey worth £40; for that to Sebituane's upwards of £20, also a waggon worth £55.

I received also from a chief a present of three elephants' tusks worth £18. But one waggon was worn out and I was obliged to purchase another for £80, and for oxen to go to Sebituane's, I paid £47. New waggon sails £10: these are torn to tatters by each trip.

I have paid off nearly all our cows to extra drivers, leaders, etc. Most of our own oxen are dead, and but for Mr. O. presenting a number worth about £60, we could not have come down to the Cape. We have gnawed into the salary of 1853 a gap of £57.

I have now to crave your indulgence. I cannot possibly pay my people and go back with supplies of meat, tea, and coffee, unless I draw the salaries of '53 and '54. We have used no delicacies of any kind. I have been a teetotaller for twenty years. . . .

We were a queer looking lot when we came to Cape Town, clothes eleven years out of fashion.

Mrs. Livingstone and her four children sailed from Cape Town for London by the *Trafalgar,* Captain D. Robertson, on April 23rd, 1852. Livingstone was subject throughout life to fits of Gaelic gloom, and one of the worst of these possessed him at parting from his dear ones, and he gives sharper vent to his stress of mind in his correspondence at this time than was his wont. It is a cry of pain that comes from his heart as he commends his treasures to Tidman's care. He dares not keep them with him, he says; in his absence they would be no safer in Cape Colony than up country, and the moral dangers would be worse than the physical. "A slave population everywhere works the ruin and degradation of the class that employs it; the slave-holding farmers are themselves becoming as degraded as the natives whom they despise; tyranny and every other form of vice reproduce themselves, and the moral contagion spreads like leaven by means of the children owing to a contamination which they had no hand in producing. We expose them and ourselves for a time in order to elevate those sad captives of sin and Satan who are the victims of the degradation of ages. None of those who complain about missionaries sending their children home ever descend to this." [9]

There is a bitter note in the outburst, not unnatural in the circumstances, but perhaps, or let us hope, not quite justified by the facts. Missionaries were not popular in the Colony, and Livingstone, himself as we have seen was looked at askance by the British Administration and some of the non-official residents also; by the Boers farther north he was hated. Doubtless it was this knowledge which influenced him in writing as above, and evidently it is the pathetic questions of the children to whom he has just said good-bye that he feelingly quotes as follows:

[9] L.M.S. archives.

In regard to even the vestige of a home my children are absolutely vagabonds.

"When shall we return to Kolobeng?"

"When to Kuruman?"

"Never! the mark of Cain is on your foreheads. Your father is a missionary."

Our children ought to have both the sympathy and prayers of those at whose bidding we become strangers for life.[10]

Little did he imagine that in less than four years his name would be received with honour in this same city where now he stood poor, mournful, and alone. But it was not in his nature to give way to depression for long nor to allow his moods to modify his resolve.[11] He set to work at once, and spent the next two months at the Cape in making what preparation he could for the great effort to which he was committed. The Astronomer-Royal, Mr. (later Sir Thomas) Maclear, kindly gave him instruction in taking observations necessary for the accurate measurement of distances and altitudes, the fixing of positions, and the making of maps. Sir Thomas stated years afterwards, when the fame of Livingstone's exploits was electrifying the world, that he had never ceased to marvel at the amount his great pupil had accomplished with so small an equipment. It is much to be regretted that the instruments with which Livingstone obtained his wonderful results in redrafting the map of Africa should not have been preserved for the nation after being so faithfully protected and borne scathless for fifteen hundred miles by the heroic group of his native friends and followers who brought his remains to the coast in 1874.

As already intimated, he experienced great difficulty in obtaining the very minimum of absolutely necessary supplies for the great adventure he was resolved upon. Never surely before or since did a traveller prepare for a plunge into the unknown on a journey extending over several years with resources so small. The prejudice against him in

10 L.M.S. archives.

11 Almost at the same time as the above he writes to Thompson, "I enjoy a perpetual flow of good spirits."

Cape Town was still so strong and the authorities so suspicious of him that he could obtain very little help. To add to his embarrassments he had to part with what was to him a large sum abstracted from his small store of money in order to compose the frivolous lawsuit which would otherwise have detained him in the neighbourhood for a considerable time. The short-sighted Government officials with whom he had to deal were so much under the influence of the Boer calumny that he intended to sell arms and ammunition to the natives, that they would only permit him to take a very small quantity, far less than sufficient for his needs. In what he was enabled to accomplish on the astounding expedition which brought so much credit to British name and influence he owed little but hindrances to British Government servants.

He got away on June 8th, and reached Kuruman at the end of August after many vexatious delays due to the deficiency of his transport. As it happened, however, this drawback turned out to be the means of saving his life, though at the cost of the loss of all the property he had left at Kolobeng and expected to pick up *en route*. In his absence events had decided for him that there was to be no more return to this last scene of his labours as a missionary in a settled station. Henceforth there was to be no resting-place for him, no one spot that could claim him for its own. He belonged to Africa, the real Africa, not to any one corner of it, and least of all to the fringe that was under European control and was all that the outside world knew or cared about the mysterious continent.

CHAPTER VI

A CHECK AND A NEW ADVANCE

THE long-threatened blow had fallen. The Boers had attacked Sechele and his tribe and driven them from their habitations with great destruction of life and property, burning their kraals, seizing their cattle and carrying off to a number of the younger members of the tribe as slaves. The raiders sacked the mission station at Kolobeng, and left it an utter ruin, sparing nothing that they thought might be of value to Livingstone and his wife. What they did not take away they carefully destroyed—furniture, books and papers, doors and windows, tools, medicines, food stores and live stock. They openly expressed disappointment that the missionary himself was not there, as they had come intending to make an end of him.

Livingstone's anger at the news of this wanton outrage found strong expression both to the British Government and the L.M.S. To the former, through the official Resident, he sent in a claim for compensation, less in the hope of obtaining any than of exposing Boer disregard of treaty obligations. Writing to Tidman, he says:

> My property having been destroyed in express violation of the treaty, I scarcely expect any compensation, but I thought the more noise we made the less likely would they be to do the same thing over again. But the more I become acquainted with the present Governor, Sir George Cathcart's, feelings, the less hope I have of the least favour being shown to anything in the shape of either missionary or Hottentot. Indeed it would be unspeakably pleasing to Sir George to hang us all on one gibbet. He will never forgive the Hottentots for completely foiling him in war, nor us missionaries because our belief that the Hottentots have souls has turned out true.[1]

[1] L.M.S. archives.

To Thompson at Cape Town he is still more definite. Enclosing a statement of the destruction wrought by the Boers at Kolobeng, he asks Thompson to correct and forward it to the Lieutenant-Governor, and continues:

> They went the whole hog, attended church on Sunday, hearing Mebalwe preach, and then made the parson flee for his life on Monday. He ran the gauntlet—some of them calling out when they saw him with clothes on—"Here is the chief," and then the bullets whistled over, behind and before him. He seems to have become terrified, ran through the midst of the Boers, and so fast his feet were dreadfully bruised. He has lost all that he had, viz.: 27 head of cattle, all his furniture, etc. His house was burned by these *Christians.*
>
> He it was who stood by me when bitten by the lion, and got bit himself. Some fine young men whom I knew and loved have fallen. My heart is sore for them.
>
> Sechele had two bullets through his hat, and a third through his coat sleeve.
>
> The destruction of my property is a fortunate thing for me. There is not a native in the country but knows now for certain on whose side I am.[2]

The total of Livingstone's personal losses amounted to not less than three hundred pounds in value, partly the property of the Society. To be thus stripped bare of everything except what he carried with him in his ox-waggon was a grave misfortune for a traveller whose resources were so small to begin with, but not for an instant did he consider turning back; on the contrary, he looked upon himself as cut loose and with no alternative before him but that of pressing on at all risks. "The delays which have occurred have prevented me from falling into Boerish hands," he remarks, "so I am thankful, and indulge the hope that God has still some little work for me to do."[3] In the same context he declares:

[2] *Ibid.*
[3] *Ibid.*

Now that I can calmly look back to my sojourn among the natives who live in a hollow under Table Mountain, and who daily and nightly inhale effluvia known only to the initiated in the mysteries of Sanitary Reform, I do remember them with feelings of compassion. Poor creatures, living in a state of utter respectability, exchanging their "how d'ye do's"—their noddings, curtseys and ministerial breakfasts; and all the while the carnivori, the cannibals I may say, of the Law and State and Puseyite Church ready to spring upon them and devour them. They are obliged to live and walk as circumspectly as elephants among well-covered pitfalls. I do pity you from my heart. I could not breathe freely till I got over the Orange River.[4]

As has been observed, Livingstone was not destitute of humour, but he took his vocation in such deadly earnest that the humour seldom showed itself, and did so less and less as time went on. It was always of a rather grim sort with a vein of irony in it, a tendency illustrated by a piece of facetiousness displayed in the last letter written to Thompson at this time. The little fling at the "Puseyite Church" may explain it.

Fine fellows you Cape worthies are. Mr. Fairbairn tells his contemporaries that the connection of the Dutch Church with the State is very slender, and you believe it, of course. They get £200 per annum, and the State appoints the minister, or has all the patronage in its hands. Our connection with the Society is half as slight again, for we only get £100.

.   .   .   .

As I don't wish to be guilty of plagiarism I have to ask your permission to adopt the following flourish which, though similar, is not identical with yours.

(Signed) DAVID ZAMBEZI.[5]

His mark X.

Unto the Right Reverend and Venerable William Capetown with greeting (Scoticè).

---

[4] L.M.S. archives.

[5] The spelling is Livingstone's. The title he gives himself is strikingly prophetic in the light of after events. He was the first real explorer of the basin of the Zambesi.

Then follows a rough drawing intended to show Livingstone with the fingers of one hand extended in front of his nose. The drawing is marked, *"Not for everyone's eye, of course."* [6]

It is difficult to envisage Livingstone in this rôle, and there are few evidences extant of similar lapses into jocularity, though we have occasion to note his quiet appreciation of the ludicrous now and again.

But there was nothing to jest at in the ruin of his work with the Bakwains, and well he knew it. Poor Sechele, full of confidence in British justice, wanted to go to England and appeal to Queen Victoria for redress, and Livingstone had to discourage him. No redress was to be expected at that time, British Colonial policy being what it was. The chief got as far as Cape Town in the hope of making his way to London and stating his case to the Queen in person, but with Livingstone's full concurrence Thompson succeeded in dissuading him from making any further attempt, and sent him back to his people. Livingstone felt deeply his own inability to aid this sorely injured man and his bewildered tribe. All that he could do he did, as stated above, in his protest to the Lieutenant-Governor, a document worth quoting in full as at once the most exact and most detailed description now existing of what took place in the Boer raid on Kolobeng.

KURUMAN,

September 29th, 1852.

THE LIEUT.-GOVERNOR DARLING,

May It Please Your Honour—

In reference to the treaty entered into by Her Majesty's Commissioners with Emigrant Boers on the 16th of January last, I have the honour to inform the Government that the provisions therein made for the free access of British travellers to the Lake and countries beyond have lately been violated by a Commando of the above-named Boers. It was accompanied by some hundreds of natives, but the Commando was composed of six hundred mounted Boers, and as I know from repeated inspection of the entire district of Magaliesberg that the emigrant population is under four thousand souls, the violation of treaty, to which in the following particulars

[6] L.M.S. archives.

I respectfully call the attention of your Honour, is not the act of a small and unauthorized portion of the Community, but that of the body whose independence the treaty of the 16th January was meant to recognize.

The above-mentioned Commando made its appearance in the Bakwain country on the 27th ult. A party with four waggons was detached from the main body in order to plunder my house which is situated eight miles north from the town of Secheli.[7] They destroyed books, medicines and surgical instruments worth upwards of £150, and carried off or destroyed furniture and other property of more than £185 value, making my personal losses amount to £335. They also took away or destroyed the stores and cattle of some respectable English travellers, viz.: Messrs. Webb, Codrington, Green, etc., etc., who are now exploring the country of Sebitoane.[8] The distance from the Colony to that country renders relays of cattle absolutely necessary. It has therefore become customary for travellers to leave a portion of their stores at my house and half of their cattle in charge of Secheli, the Chief of the Bakwains. Both goods and cattle have always been held sacred by the inhabitants of the country; and when the town was removed eight miles from the house they of their own accord placed a guard on the spot, and every article remained in as much security during my absence for the last two years as when present in the house.

Guides have always been frankly furnished by Secheli to English travellers, and except in the case of Mr. Moyle, who did not return the people given by the Chief to take him to the Colony, no unpleasantness has ever occurred.

With the plundering of my house was associated the destruction of the town of Secheli, and considerable property deposited there by Mr. Macabe. The Boers were allowed to form their camp unmolested before the town. Some of them even attended Divine Service held in the middle of it on Sunday, 29th; and they informed Secheli that they had come to fight because the Queen had given over the country and people to them, and they would abolish Chieftainship. Considerable stress was also laid on the refusal of Secheli to obey their orders to prevent Englishmen from going to the Lake Country.

[7] The spelling is Livingstone's, but on other occasions he writes the name with a final "e."
[8] The spelling is Livingstone's. Usually he spells the name with "u" instead of "o."

(That these orders have been given I can testify, having seen the documents sent by the Boers containing them.) On Monday, the 30th, the Boers commenced their attack by means of swivels, which soon set the town on fire. The smoke and heat caused much confusion; many of the women running away were captured and shot. The men held their position on a small conical hill in the centre of the town during the whole day, and there being no water near, both Boers and natives retired when it became dark.

The number of natives killed is upward of sixty; of the Boers thirty-five; several of both parties have since died of their wounds, but these are not reckoned in the above numbers. The shooting of women was probably accidental, but not so the capture of children; they reduce them to a state of slavery. I have seen numerous instances of this in cases of children taken from other tribes; and have ascertained the facts from the children themselves in their own language. Among those captured from the Bakwains are a former wife and two children of Secheli. In the division of spoil the mother and children were given to different Boers. The possession of horses enabled the Commando to carry off the cattle belonging to the English travellers before the Bakwains could secure them by flight. Those of two Native Teachers and my own, on which I trusted for assistance in my northern journey, shared the same fate. Three cattle stations belonging to Secheli were also robbed, and the Bakhatla and Bangwaketse lost all their cattle. The corn in the country is entirely consumed, and the people have only stealing or starvation in prospect. There is a probability of a struggle altogether different from any which has yet taken place in the interior. I have made careful enquiries among eight different tribes who have been attacked by the Boers during the last ten years, and also among the Boers themselves; but never could discover the loss of a single man on the side of the latter. In only one instance was a wound inflicted. The above-mentioned engagement is therefore peculiar, and the known determination of Secheli's character evinced in the late skirmish, even after two bullets had pierced his hat and a third his coat sleeve, makes me fear that the work of retaliation for a most wanton and unprovoked attack will be carried on with vigour.

The loss of thirty-five men will be peculiarly galling to the Boers, inasmuch as while professing to wish to prevent the trade in guns and gunpowder by Englishmen, they are fully aware that much of this slaughter has been inflicted by weapons which members of their own community have sold.[9] It is highly probable that those parties of Boers who have gone to the Lake in order to trade in arms and ammunition will be cut off on their return. Secheli has warned the English travellers to keep apart from them, and I believe they are quite safe, as the difference between Boers and Englishmen is recognized throughout the interior.

The above facts showing that the first blow has been struck by the Boers, and that too on a tribe which has never given them the smallest provocation, nor for the last eight years at least the slightest trouble to any of its neighbours, are, I conceive, worthy of the observation of the Government, for if the policy of the Boers takes its usual course, the natives become exasperated and reckless; gradually learn to fight well, and then, when the Boers perceive their real danger, they back out on such contemptible pleas as that of not being paid by the English Government.

I have the honour to be

Your Honour's

Obedient Servant,

(Signed) DAVID LIVINGSTONE.

Livingstone was no pacifist, though patient to the extreme in his dealings with armed and hostile parties or individuals. He believed in the moral use of physical force to restrain the predatory and homicidal proclivities of the unruly and malevolent among whom his lot was cast. We shall have to take cognizance of instances wherein he found himself compelled to act on this belief. There is no doubt that he would have coerced the Boers by British military force if he could, as the tone of the foregoing communication indicates, and it is not too much to say that had his advice been followed at this period much subsequent trouble and bloodshed would have been saved in South Africa. Writing to his wife in England with the news of the raid

---

[9] A fact of moment in view of the charge of arming the natives formulated against Livingstone.

fresh in his mind, he pours out his indignation and forebodings in pungent staccato sentences.

The Bakwains will plunder and murder the Boers without mercy, and by and by the Boers will ask the English Government to assist them to put down rebellion, and of this rebellion I shall have, of course, to bear the blame. They often expressed a wish to get hold of me. I wait here a little in order to get information when the path is clear. Kind Providence detained me from falling into the very thick of it. God will preserve me still. He has work for me, or He would have allowed me to go in just when the Boers were there. We shall move more easily now that we are lightened of our furniture. They have taken away our sofa. I never had a good rest on it. We had only got it ready when we left. . . . I wonder what the Peace Society would do with these worthies.[10]

The belief that Livingstone had been engaged in gun-running in the endeavour to furnish the natives with the means of assisting Boer aggression was deeply rooted, and has been revived from time to time. J. A. Agar-Hamilton, Senior Lecturer in Modern History, Transvaal University, has written a book, *The Native Policy of the Voortrekkers,* in which he renews the suggestion that Livingstone supplied firearms to the natives. Both Moffat and Livingstone expressed themselves freely against the one-sided enactment which enabled Boer farmers to obtain guns and ammunition, but forbade the same facility to the natives. That on military grounds the prohibition was defensible may be admitted, but its incidence was demonstrably unfair. As soon as the effectiveness of guns in the procuring of food became apparent, the chiefs and their people quite naturally wished to have them. Missionaries and hunters, too, had guns; their daily food depended upon them. Livingstone no doubt mended guns, but to magnify his little workshop at Kolobeng into an "arsenal" and his few small gifts of guns into the supply of arms in any military sense, was absurd. He himself makes fun of the charge in *Missionary Travels,* but he saw the advantage of leaving the Boers to suppose that the Africans were better armed

[10] Blaikie, *op. cit.,* p. 111 *f.*

than they actually were.[11] Agar-Hamilton (who warmly thanks the L.M.S. for courtesy in allowing the examination of records) does not press the charge of gun-running against Livingstone, leaving it to be thought that he was imprudent.

Correspondence on the subject appeared in the *Cape Argus* in 1928. Sir Clarkson Tredgold took up Livingstone's case, and pointed out the paucity of the evidence—the absence of any sign that Livingstone ever made any money out of the hypothetical sale of firearms, the fact that such ammunition as he took with him was no more than was needed for the hunt or for Messrs. Oswell and Murray, and the difficulty they all had in securing even the indispensable minimum in Cape Town.

The old rumour crops up in other ways. Aloysius Horn writes about Livingstone's fondness for a "stand of arms" with a knowing wink, as though there were damning facts behind the words. Recently a receipt from Gordon Cumming, the big game hunter, was found which showed that Livingstone had purchased ammunition from him; but obviously anything purchased from such a man would be for shooting game.

Nowhere is there a shred of evidence that Livingstone provided, or caused to be provided, arms or ammunition of such character and quantity as would be of service against a Boer Commando.

The treaty above referred to, arranged between Sir George Cathcart and the Transvaal Boers in 1852, recognized the independence of the latter, but expressly stipulated for the free passage of British subjects to the country beyond, and also that no slavery was to be allowed. The Boers infringed these provisions without scruple; as Livingstone stated in his reports and correspondence, they never had any intention of abiding by them. His experience of their intransigence was much the same as that of his stout-hearted preceptor, John Philip, a generation earlier. Dr. Philip was as bitterly detested by Dutch and British oppressors of the natives as Livingstone came to be, and, like Livingstone, was more than once in danger of death at their hands. W. M.

[11] P. 32.

Macmillan relates [12] that in 1832, when emancipation of slaves through-out the British Empire was on the eve of being accomplished, Philip made a tour through the northern part of Cape Colony at the imminent risk of his life. He was not unjustly credited with having been the chief factor in a measure of enfranchisement to which the Boers never consented except under duress. He resisted manfully the Boer practice of seizing the lands of the natives at their pleasure and forcing the original owners to cultivate them for their new masters' profit. In 1838 he wrote to Dr. Thomas Hodgkin, of the Anti-Slavery Society: "Compensation money has turned their heads, and they turn it into powder and shot to expel the Canaanites from the Land of Promise." [13] Macmillan comments:

> It is true that all but irresponsible adventurers among the Trekkers accepted the prohibition of slavery. The slave-owning mentality remained and could hardly conceive of an educated "Kafir" or of an order of society in which the "Kafir" should have legally enforcible rights. The argument weighed heavily in 1910 that only a single-united South African Government could hope to deal effectively with the twentieth-century "Native Problem"; but the need for unity of control was still more clamant in 1840. The powers, the coherence, the machinery and resources of the mushroom republics being then, and for a long time to come, utterly contemptible, the British Government at the Cape was the only possible one to attempt to control the relations of black and white throughout South Africa. As the forties progressed there was some hope that the British Government would shoulder its responsibilities and attempt to cope with the situation as a whole. Early in the 'fifties Her Majesty's Government, having put its hand to the plough, looked back. The tangled problem of the twentieth century is the direct result. [14]

It was in the looking-back period that Livingstone and the Bakwains were victimized by Boer aggression and disregard of treaty obligations. It was useless to protest; the British authorities would not

[12] *Bantu, Boer, and Briton*, p. 47.
[13] *Ibid.*, p. 180.
[14] Macmillan, *op. cit.*, p. 181.

listen. It had been mainly owing to Philip's agitation that in 1843 the
Trekkers had been brought under control in Natal and the condition
laid down that "there shall not be in the eye of the law any distinction
or disqualification whatever founded upon mere distinction of colour,
origin, language or creed, but the protection of the law, in letter and
in substance, shall be extended impartially to all alike." [15] Sooner than
submit to the consequences of the enforcement of this principle, a large
number of the Boers trekked again. Philip would have had them followed up, but could not carry the Governor or Colonial public opinion
with him. His name was, as Macmillan remarks, "a hissing to the
Colonists" because of his exertions on behalf of the Hottentots, and
his prescience in regard to the stronger Bantu tribes in the north was
slighted. In more ways than one, notwithstanding his long and expert
acquaintance with Colonial problems and the respect felt for his
personal character, his experience anticipated that of Livingstone.
"My own countrymen," he sadly reflects in 1842, "who were born in a
land of liberty, I have invariably found to be most virulent in their
prejudices against me for my exertions in favour of the rights of the
coloured population in this country." [16] It was the British Government's refusal to listen to the representations of Philip and the few
who supported him on the subject of Boer interference with the
Bechuanas that led ultimately to the tragedy of Kolobeng.[17]

But, as we have seen, the catastrophe had one great result fraught
with a benefit to Africa that neither Boer nor Briton could at the
moment have conceived. It left Livingstone no alternative but to
seek another means of bringing the basin of the upper Zambesi into
active relations with Christian Europe. As he declares in *Missionary
Travels:* "The plundering only set me entirely free for my expedition
to the north, and I have never since had a moment's concern for
anything I left behind. The Boers resolved to shut up the interior,

---

[15] Macmillan, *op. cit.,* p. 185.

[16] *Ibid.,* p. 200.

[17] How complete the change of sentiment has been on the part of the Dutch community,
not to speak of the anti-missionary prejudices of many of the British colonists eighty years
ago, is illustrated by the fact that the successors of the men who destroyed the mission station
at Kolobeng have lately gone to the trouble and expense of enclosing and preserving what
remains on its site. The gesture is a fine one, and symbolical of the new spirit that is passing
over the civilized world with reference to the treatment of less advanced races.

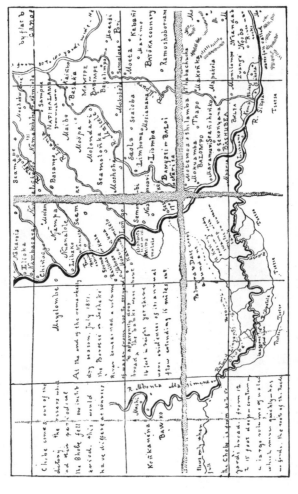

PART OF LIVINGSTONE'S MAP OF HIS EXPERIMENTAL JOURNEY IN BAROTSELAND

In possession of the London Missionary Society

and I determined to open the country; and we shall see who have been most successful in resolution—they or I." [18]

After a delay of several months due to the unsettlement caused by the troubles recorded, he left Kuruman in December, and taking a westward detour in order to avoid Boer raiders, reached Linyanti on May 23rd, 1853. His companion on this journey was a coloured trader named George Fleming, whom he brought along in the hope of instituting legitimate commercial intercourse with the Makololo and thus discouraging the slave trade. Fleming was to act as the authorized representative of Mr. Rutherfoord, of Cape Town, who heartily approved of Livingstone's policy in this respect. Unfortunately the attempt was not successful at this preliminary stage. Too many obstacles were put in the way, and though Livingstone was able to see Fleming safely established, as he thought, on Makololo soil and making a promising start in the exchange of European products for ivory and pelts, the experiment soon had to be abandoned and the trader sent back to Kuruman. The dishonesty and incompetence of the native assistants whom Fleming had introduced were chiefly to blame for the failure. [19]

But the reception accorded to Livingstone himself lacked nothing in fervour and friendliness. Mamochisane had abdicated in favour of her brother Sekeletu, a youth of eighteen, giving the truly feminine reason that she did not want to be a chief, but preferred to have her own home and her own children to look after like other women. Sekeletu had neither as fine a presence as, nor the ability of, his father Sebituane, but was equally glad to welcome a resident missionary. In the hope

[18] P. 39.

[19] The third page of the Journal, begun in November, 1853, reads: "I now became aware of a theft inflicted on me by the people I brought from Kuruman. We were compelled to take the very dregs of the people of that place. It was with difficulty I could get them to do half their duties; perpetually threatening to turn, I had to submit to almost everything which lazy, dirty, greedy servants can invent to annoy or destroy.

"The slightest sickness was an excuse for doing nothing; they lay by and eat (*sic*) heartily all the while.

"When I was absent seeking a ford at the Chobé, they allowed the oxen to wander by day and by night, and wander they did into the tsetse, by which I lost ten, which cost between £25 and £30.

"I wished to get rid of these, the first which I have been unable by kind treatment to manage; but some of them had been weakened by fever, and I allowed them to remain till their strength was renewed. The first use the worthies made of their strength was whoredom."

that Livingstone would be content to fix his abode among the Makololo, he at once offered to provide everything needful in the way of land, labour, and provisions. The entire population of the capital, which consisted of about six or seven thousand persons, issued to meet and escort the visitor and his retinue on their progress from their last camping ground to the quarters provided for them in Linyanti itself. Great was the curiosity exhibited at seeing the waggon-wheels turning, for never before had these unsophisticated folk witnessed such a phenomenon. This is not wonderful, considering that it took the ancient Egyptians fourteen hundred years to discover that a grindstone might be set on edge and made to carry burdens. In the *Missionary Travels*[20] Livingstone describes the extravagant rejoicing wherewith his noisy hosts celebrated his arrival and the expectations they had formed of the advantages likely to accrue to themselves therefrom. The greatest of these advantages was protection. "We want sleep"— that is, rest—was their pathetic greeting; and they hoped that the presence of a white man would give them the needed security from the dangerous Matebele beyond their borders and the Arab slave raiders whose occasional incursions had begun to be dreaded.

Within a week Livingstone was down with fever, the first of the many attacks he was to suffer from henceforth. He did not as yet know what the enemy was, but imagined it to be a chill caused by exposure to a sudden change of temperature. His Makololo friends knew better, and he allowed them to doctor him, but speedily came to the conclusion that his own remedies were more effective as well as less disagreeable than theirs. As soon as he recovered, which he did in the course of a few days, he made preparation for a further trip with the object, which he had not yet abandoned, of finding a healthy location for a new mission centre. Leaving Linyanti in the last week of June, he and Sekeletu with one hundred and sixty attendants went to explore the Barotse country, whose chief town, Naliele (or Nariele) lay about three hundred miles to the north of Linyanti. Taking Sesheke on the way, the party reached Naliele in a little over three

<hr />

20 P. 178.

weeks' time, but without finding or hearing of any district in which settlers of European race could be reasonably sure of immunity from disease together with accessibility to the tribes among whom they would have to work. The country was fertile enough, rich in food-producing plants and animals, but subject to heavy rains and floods, with the attendant drawbacks which had already proved so serious a handicap to the Livingstone family. This was Sekeletu's first visit to the principal Barotse centres since his succession to the chieftainship, and everywhere he and his guest were received with acclamation, though for the latter the expedition was marred by some barbarities which shocked, and with exhibitions of grossness which nauseated him.

This preliminary exploration decided Livingstone to pursue forthwith his intention of seeking a means of communication with the west coast, if possible. They returned to Linyanti in September, and on November 11th he set forth on the long fifteen-hundred-mile journey to Loanda, which first opened the eyes of the civilized world to the true facts concerning the interior of Africa and the resources awaiting development there. Livingstone's notes and correspondence, much of them hitherto unpublished, give a better idea of the impressions made on his mind by what he had learned up to the point we have now reached, while these impressions were still fresh, than the pages of the *Missionary Travels*. The book does not give the reader an adequate conception of the difficulties that had to be surmounted and the perils, sufferings, and bad usage that had to be endured in breaking new ground amid a population hitherto untouched by ameliorating influences. The Journal tells the story better, though necessarily in an irregular and disjointed manner.[21] Livingstone made a practice of repeating himself in his various communications to the Society and private correspondents, lifting whole sections of description word for

---

21 The Journal he carried with him on this expedition is a big quarto MS. book with a lever lock. There are 849 pages of carefully written notes in it, including an index. It covers the period from November 11th, 1853, to May 26th, 1856, and is introduced with the words: "This Journal is intended to be a private record of the incidents which may occur in my intercourse with the people of the interior in order that I may in future years, by reading it, reproduce the feelings which animated me in endeavouring to open up Africa to the sympathies and succour of Christian and more favoured lands. I mean to note down even trivial incidents such as will interest none but myself."

word out of his daily record and despatching them as best he could
to the Cape and England. Many of these communications never came
to hand, but on the whole it is probable that the practice here specified
has preserved the greater part of what he thought worthy of attention.
Because of this method of duplication his letters are usually long and
detailed, and both corroborate and supplement what he later saw fit
to publish. This is particularly so with regard to the period leading
up to the journey to Loanda; what he tells of it in *Missionary Travels*
is slight compared with what found its way into other channels.

The men he had brought with him from Kuruman not having
proved satisfactory, he sent them all back with Fleming, and with
Sekeletu's authority engaged a company of twenty-seven bearers in
Linyanti. These were not all Makololo, as usually stated, and as
Livingstone himself describes them for convenience; only two of them
were of that tribe; the rest were Barotse, Batoka, and Ambonda. As
some apprehensions were felt by the Makololo people that in the event
of the explorer's death they would be blamed for allowing him to
pass on with so small a force to wild and possibly hostile tribes, he
replied that he would leave a book with Sekeletu to be sent to Moffat
explaining everything up to the time of his leaving Linyanti. This was
a volume of his Journal, which, faithful to their trust, the Makololo
subsequently gave into the hands of a trader to be delivered as directed.
Through some mischance the volume was believed to be lost, as Livingstone states in *Missionary Travels;* but it came to light long afterwards, and its contents confirm in a remarkable degree what had been
previously written and published of his recollections of the period
covered. But had it never been found at all, most of his observations
could have been verified from his letters. In a report to the L.M.S.
dated September 24th, 1853, he gives details of his relations with
Sekeletu and his people, from which the following extracts are taken: [22]

> The idea seemed universal that with a missionary some great
> definite good had arrived. Many expected to be elevated at once
> to a condition equal to that of the Bakwains and inhabitants of
> Kuruman, of which they had received very exaggerated accounts;

[22] L.M.S. archives.

others imagined that they would very soon be transformed into civilized men, possessing the clothing, horses, arms, waggons, etc., of Europeans.

. . . .

"Jesus had not loved their forefathers," hence their present degradation. "He had loved the white men, and had given them all the wonderful things they now possess."

And as I had come to teach them to pray to Jesus, and to pray for them, "their wants would soon be all supplied."

. . . . . .

A very great deal was expected also from medicines and my liberality in giving things I have not in my possession. Patient industry and perseverance in learning were never thought of. The chief, not yet nineteen years of age, frequently pressed me to name something I wished, so that he might by presenting it show his affection, and, I expected, induce me forthwith to commence the work of metamorphosis by means of enchantments.

But when I steadily refused to mention any object I desired more than to secure their temporal and spiritual welfare by means of the Gospel, he seemed to test my sincerity by presenting 4 small and 8 large elephant tusks. I had not the opportunity of refusing them, as they were brought and laid down by the waggon during my absence. And then the chief came and begged me so earnestly to accept them, I felt at a loss how to act.

In other circumstances I should have felt no hesitation in appropriating them to defray expenses incurred entirely on account of his people. But as it was, though I had no direct evidence that the chief's object was such as I have described, the mere suspicion led me, when departing for the Barotse country, to request him to leave orders, that if any traders came, my ivory must be used as well as his own. By this means no offence was given, as might have been the case, had I at once sent them back.

I never had a touch of fever until my employment became sedentary here.

I have had eight attacks since. The last when going north to Nariele was very severe—loss of blood—fits of vertigo.

Everything seemed to rush to the left and I had to lay hold on something to prevent a fall.

He is still thin from these fevers, but is only waiting for the rains before starting for the west.

In a further letter to Tidman, November 8th, he writes:

I leave in company with Barotse people alone. The people we have brought from Kuruman have been rendered useless by fever, so I send them back.

I am again through God's mercy and kindness quite recovered from the effects of that disease. I think I am getting rid of intermittent too, and if spared will impart some knowledge of Christ to many who have never before heard His blessed name.

There are many and very large tribes in the direction in which we go. All are sitting in darkness and in the shadow of death. I hope God will in mercy permit me to establish the Gospel somewhere in this region; and that I may live to see the double influence of commerce *and Christianity employed to stay the bitter fountain of African misery.*

"In case of my being cut off," he points out how the region can be reached from the east by means of the Zambesi and Maninche rivers.

A letter to Thompson dated September 17th, 1853, after his return from the excursion through Barotse land, contains the striking passage afterwards printed in substance in *Missionary Travels,* and evidently copied from a diary:

I had been, during a nine weeks' tour, in closer contact with heathenism than I had ever been before, and though all, including the chief, were as kind and attentive to me as possible, and there was no want of food (oxen being slaughtered daily, sometimes ten at a time, more than sufficient for the wants of all), yet to endure the dancing, roaring, and singing, the jesting, anecdotes, grumbling, quarreling, and murdering of these children of nature, seemed more like a severe penance than anything I had before met with in the course of my missionary duties. I took thence a more intense disgust at heathenism than I had before, and formed a greatly elevated opinion of the latent effects of missions in the south, among tribes which are reported to have been as savage as the Makololo. The indirect benefits, which to a casual observer lie beneath the surface and are inappreciable, in reference to the probable wide diffusion of Christianity at some future time, are worth all the money and labour that have been expended to produce them.[23]

Another, dated October 11th, also has its parallel in the Journal. "If I allowed my mind to dwell on the miserable degradation, wickedness, and the prospects of the people here, I might become melancholy, and soon die."[24] The Journal of October 28th has the significant entry: "The conduct of the people whom we have brought from Kuruman shows that no amount of preaching or instruction will insure real piety. . . . The old superstitions cannot be driven out of their minds by faith implanted by preaching. They have not vanished in either England or Scotland yet, after the lapse of centuries of preaching." Yet over against these items we have once more the explicit statement that "a merry heart doeth good like a medicine . . . I am never low-spirited. It might be different if I had a crusty companion. I have experience in the matter, and my thoughts never turn with any longing except for my family."[25]

We must not expect too much consistency from his temperament; he has his moods. An undated letter in the same connection states that he has been trying to get on with the work he undertook but never completed—the compilation of a dictionary of the Sichuana language. We hear no more of it after his arrival at Linyanti, though he had kept assiduously at it in his lumbering conveyance on the way north. "The waggon is most inconvenient for writing. I can only write on my side, and must doff and trek on my 'inexpressibles' only when lying flat on my back. I must be getting old and ill-natured now, for the constrained positions of my waggon life rather make me crusty than gentle."[26]

He would have been spared much sickness, finally resulting in pre-

[23] L.M.S. archives. *Cf. Missionary Travels*, p. 226.
[24] *Ibid.*
[25] L.M.S. archives.
[26] *Ibid.*

mature death, had the discoveries of Sir Ronald Ross and others in relation to tropical hygiene been made two generations earlier. "I would like," he writes in his Journal, "to devote a portion of my life to the discovery of a remedy for that terrible disease, the African fever. I would go into the parts where it prevails most, and try to discover if the natives have a remedy for it." He saw clearly that it was the most fatal obstacle to the penetration of central Africa by European trade, and he came very near at one time to guessing how the disease was transmitted, for in chapter xix. of *Missionary Travels* he notes that it sometimes ensues from the bite of an insect, and in chapter xxii. observes a connection between the symptoms and the drinking of contaminated water. At a much later date, 1865, in *A Narrative of the Expedition to the Zambesi* (chap. viii.), dwelling on the symptoms of a severe attack of malaria, he says (the passage is almost certainly of his inditing): "When our posterity shall have discovered what it is which, distinct from foul smells, causes fever . . . they will pity our dulness of perception." The remark is suggestive. He notes further (chap. x.) that Dr. Kirk, who suffered greatly from malaria in the steamy lowlands, recovered quickly on the dry heights. Livingstone was on the track of a cure for the scourge, though he never found it. How near he came to it is shown by a passage in the *Narrative of an Expedition to the Zambesi* (chap. xix.), written in connection with the launching of a four-oared gig on the upper Shiré at the entrance to Lake Nyassa in 1861: "Myriads of mosquitoes showed, as probably they always do, the presence of malaria."

During the period of Livingstone's daily intimacy with Sekeletu he offered to teach the young chief to read, but the wary savage declined the privilege, or rather postponed experimenting with it, fearing, as he said, that it might change his heart—in other words, might lead to his having to give up his troop of wives and modify his habits in other respects also. As a compromise, after the return from Barotseland, he suggested that the instruction might be tried on his father-in-law and step-father. This was done, and the two deputies and several others learned with such good effect that they mastered the alphabet in a single day.

Not so pleasant was the missionary's knowledge of the fate of another relative of Sekeletu. Mpepe, half-brother of the chief on the mother's side, engaged in a plot to assassinate the latter and replace him in the chieftainship. To this end he caused the report to be circulated that Sekeletu was not really the son of Sebituane; but, as Mamochisane had publicly and definitely stated the contrary and recognized Sekeletu as her father's lawful heir, Mpepe proceeded to more desperate measures. He entered into communication with the Mambari, half-caste Portuguese slave traders, who promised him their support on the understanding that he would furnish facilities for the traffic in the regions to which the Makololo had easy access or held in subjection. The arrival of Livingstone at Linyanti was felt to be a blow to these designs, and the Mambari envoys withdrew in company with Mpepe to the north. Sekeletu and the missionary followed; a conference was summoned at a certain village to which Mpepe came with armed followers. Had it not been for Livingstone's accidental intervention, by rising up in the council hut at the same moment as the chief and thus screening him with his own body, Sekeletu would have been murdered there and then. The fact becoming known through the confession of a few of Mpepe's attendants, the would-be usurper was quietly arrested in the night, led aside, and executed. Livingstone did not know of this nocturnal tragedy until the next day, but it had a bloody sequel against which he protested in vain. Mpepe's father and another headman had been privy to the conspiracy to put Sekeletu to death. They were seized in their own village not long afterwards, briefly interrogated by the chief in presence of his principal councillors, as promptly condemned, led forth, cut to pieces, and their bodies tossed into the river to feed the crocodiles. The missionary was a horrified spectator of the trial and its swift and terrible ending, but the only answer he received to his remonstrance against such brutal butchery was: "You see, we are still Boers; we are not yet taught." [27]

These and such-like repellent scenes were demonstration enough, had he needed it, that what awaited him in his journey up-country would be a greater trial of his physical and moral endurance than any-

[27] *Missionary Travels*, p. 215.

thing he had yet encountered. As he says in *Missionary Travels:* [28]
"It was now quite evident that no healthy location could be obtained
in which the Makololo would be allowed to live in peace. I had thus a
fair excuse, if I had chosen to avail myself of it, of coming home and
saying that the 'door was shut,' because the Lord's time had not yet
come. But believing that it was my duty to devote some portion of my
life to these (to me at least) very confiding and affectionate Makololo,
I resolved to follow out the second part of my plan, though I had
failed in accomplishing the first." He would go forward whatever
befell.

[28] P. 222.

CHAPTER VII

ON TO LOANDA

A GLANCE at the map of Africa will show that the nearest port on the west coast from the Makololo country would have been St. Philip de Benguela, but after consideration Livingstone decided to avoid this because it was a customary slave-trading route,[1] and, as he had grievous occasion to know in later years, a route marked by the trail of the slave trade was an undesirable one to follow for many reasons. He therefore came to the conclusion that it would be preferable to strike farther north and make for the town of St. Paul de Loanda, where, as he knew, because it was the most important Portuguese port on the west coast and the outlet of the extensive province of Angola, British merchants had established commercial relations, and a British Government agent resided to do what was possible towards the suppression of the slave trade. After making all the inquiries he could—he soon found that native reports on topography were nearly always hazy—and carefully studying the lie of the country, he resolved to go by canoe down the Chobé river to its junction with the Zambesi, then on the Zambesi upstream till he reached Libonta; thence, still keeping almost directly northward, to Shinte's Town. Half-way between this point and Katema's Town, after leaving the canoes and going on foot, the course taken turned westward and kept on the whole in a westerly direction to the sea.

Properly speaking, no road existed. All that the explorer could do was to feel his way from village to village, relying upon his compass and astronomical observations, and hire guides wherever obtainable. In this manner he eventually succeeded in covering a range of territory which no man, white or black, had yet been known to make a way

---

[1] And infested with the tsetse fly.

through.[2] From Katema's Town he went by the banks of the Kasai river through Katende's country into the country of the dangerous Chiboque, where the path diverged to the north. Skirting this wide area and turning towards the setting sun again, he crossed the Quango river and came on the first Portuguese outpost at Cassange. Thence he was able to proceed more surely by Ambaca and Golungo Alto to Loanda.

When he and his company of twenty-seven bearers left Linyanti on this perilous and protracted venture they took with them a few tusks of ivory, the property of Sekeletu, to trade with; a few pounds of tea and sugar; a large supply of coffee; forty shillings' worth of beads; a small stock of medicines, the most valuable part of which was soon stolen; a magic lantern, the gift of Mr. Murray to Livingstone after the first expedition to Lake Ngami; the missionary's kit of scientific instruments; a small tin trunk containing a change of clothing and several books, including the precious Journal; a tent, five guns, and a meagre supply of ammunition which had to be carefully husbanded, as their subsistence as well as defence depended mainly upon it. Ere long, in fact, Livingstone found that he had to stop doling out the ammunition to his followers as they were bad shots and wasted it. Upon him fell the chief responsibility thereafter for shooting what game was needed for the food of the whole party, a task which he found a heavy one owing to the difficulty of taking aim with his damaged arm.

All Livingston's explorations, except during the comparatively short period of his partnership with Oswell, were prosecuted with similarly inadequate resources. Contrast with the above the equipment that Stanley had at command when he set out from Bagamoyo to find the missing missionary on February 18th, 1871. Gordon Bennett, of the *New York Herald,* had given him *carte blanche* to draw whatever money might be necessary to finance the expedition at any stage. He was accompanied by two white men, twenty-three native soldiers, one hundred and sixty porters, twenty-seven donkeys, one cart bearing six

---

[2] Two coloured Portuguese traders had previously covered within a thousand miles of the distance, but were incapable of taking observations or making reports of value.

tons of cloth, beads, wire, provisions, utensils, boats, instruments, medicines, and "every conceivable article." The party was armed with thirty-nine guns and revolvers. Livingstone travelled over approximately three thousand miles of hitherto unknown ground; Stanley covered sixteen hundred miles of partly explored country. Had Livingstone possessed on his first great journey even a third of the resources furnished to Stanley by American generosity—furnished, too, because of the world-wide interest felt in Livingstone and his work—his achievement in forcing his way from Linyanti to Loanda would still have been a wonderful one; but when the fact is realized that it was accomplished with resources so small and by living almost entirely on the country as he went through it, sharing the food of the natives and availing himself of such rude hospitality as they could provide, we can but marvel at the intense concentration of purpose which sustained him and brought the arduous effort to success. Sir H. H. Johnston rightly says:

He suffered incessantly from attacks of fever, but really one cannot wonder at his ill-health when it is considered what very little care he took of himself. . . . He had to cross streams or rivers daily, and on these occasions was always wetted up to his thighs, if not up to his neck. It never seems to have occurred to him to change and dry his clothes; he either attempted to dry himself by walking on through the blazing sun, or he did not even make that attempt, but sat down or remained stationary in his wet clothes whenever he had occasion to wait for his men or to stop for any purpose on the line of march. Is it surprising under these conditions that he was attacked with fever? Is it not rather surprising that he lived through such experiences at all? [3]

The same eminent authority, writing in 1891, also says that if Livingstone had travelled from first to last with a reasonable amount of comfort such as is considered necessary by European explorers, "he would have completed his great scheme of geographical discovery and have been alive now in the enjoyment of honours and competence, as are several of his old companions." [4]

[3] *Livingstone and the Exploration of Central Africa*, p. 160 f.
[4] *Ibid.*, p. 149.

With the exception of what his gun procured him, his staple food during this exhausting journey of nearly seven months was the same as the natives lived on; often he was reduced to a diet of birdseed, manioc roots, and meal, and now and then had to go hungry. Little wonder that for the greater part of the time he was a very sick man. Nothing but his indomitable will enabled him to keep going and overcome the multitudinous difficulties that daily beset him and his companions. These companions, though essential to his safety and ultimate success, were themselves a constant source of anxiety to him. Their liability to gusts of passion, unreasoning changes of mood, silly superstitions, dread of the unknown, and readiness to give way in face of every obstacle were an ever present trial to the lonely leader. Fellowship he had none, for, as he records, it was impossible to share thoughts and feelings with minds so differently constituted from his own. He was forced back on himself for consolation and refreshment of soul, a habit that grew on him and characterized him markedly for the rest of his life; he was ever a solitary man, sufficient for himself, and neither needing nor desiring much in the way of human society. He relates in *Missionary Travels* that in order to withdraw his thoughts from the marring influences of the heathenism around him, he made a regular practice of endeavouring to learn all he could of the botanical and biological phenomena that came successively under his keen and trained observation. In this respect, indeed, he is almost without a peer in the field of African exploration, as his beautifully written Journals bear witness.

By this means he succeeded in detaching himself in some degree from the harassments and revolting features of daily life among savages, wherein he was wise and psychologically sound, more so, probably, than he could have been fully aware of at that time. He says of this salutary method:

> I shall not often advert to their depravity. My practice has always been to apply the remedy with all possible earnestness, but never allow my own mind to dwell on the dark shades of men's characters. I have never been able to draw pictures of guilt, as if that could

awaken Christian sympathy. The evil is there. But all around in this fair creation are scenes of beauty, and to turn from these to ponder on deeds of sin, cannot promote a healthy state of the faculties. I attribute much of the bodily health I enjoy to following the plan, adopted by most physicians, who, while engaged in active, laborious efforts to assist the needy, at the same time follow the delightful studies of some department of natural history. The human misery and sin we endeavour to alleviate and cure may be likened to the sickness and impurity of some of the back slums of great cities. One contents himself by ministering to the sick and trying to remove the causes, without remaining longer in the filth than is necessary for his work: another, equally anxious for the public good, stirs up every cesspool, that he may describe its reeking vapours, and, by long contact with impurities, becomes himself infected, sickens, and dies.[5]

Sir Thomas Maclear and Sir H. H. Johnston have both given high praise to Livingstone's qualities of exactitude and patient care in registering his facts. Commenting upon the acquisitions made on the journey to Loanda, the former states in a letter to Livingstone himself on March 27th, 1854: "Upon the whole I do not hesitate to assert that no explorer on record has determined his path with the precision you have accomplished." At the Cape Town meeting on November 12th, 1856, the same high authority said: "You could go to any point across the entire continent, along Livingstone's track, and feel certain of your position." Johnston's testimony is no less emphatic: "Livingstone was perhaps the most exact computer of astronomical observations who has yet appeared among African explorers." [6]

The missionary was never sunk in the scientific observer, however. At every point on his route where a pause was made Livingstone held divine service and preached to assembled crowds unless prevented by illness. Curiosity probably gained him a hearing in most cases, for the number of listeners was nearly always large, sometimes as many as a thousand persons being present, though there were few signs of permanent interest in the teaching given. Of this, on the other hand, Liv-

[5] P. 259.
[6] Op. cit., p. 63.

ingstone says (*Missionary Travels*, chap. xvii.): "In beginning to speak on religious subjects with those who have never heard of Christianity, the great fact of the Son of God having come down from heaven to die for us is the prominent theme. No fact more striking can be mentioned. 'He actually came to men. He Himself told us about His Father, and the dwelling-place whither He has gone. We have His words in this book, and He really endured punishment in our stead from pure love,' etc. If this fails to interest them, nothing else will succeed." Notwithstanding which, the teaching is plainly heretical! [7] Livingstone was a better geographer than expounder of Christian doctrine, though no man ever had a firmer grasp of the essentials of Christian life. He repeatedly insists that real influence with the natives is only to be gained by setting a good example. Savages, he declares, have a clear idea of the difference between right and wrong, however vile their own conduct may be, and they are not deceived by a profession of superiority which is not supported by corresponding behaviour. This was one reason why he was ever careful to maintain habits of personal cleanliness and modesty, however difficult it might be to do so while travelling. The natives respected a European who showed that he respected himself in this particular, and were quick to discount the worth of one who allowed himself to fall into slovenly ways or adopted those of the natives themselves.

An entry in the Journal under date August 5th, 1855, referring to a religious service with the Barotse at Naliele, stresses the point:

A large audience listened most attentively to my morning address. Surely some will remember the ideas conveyed, and pray to our merciful Father, who would never have thought of Him but for this visit. The invariably kind and respectful treatment I have received from these, and many other heathen tribes in this central country, together with the attentive observations of many years, have led me to the belief that, if one exerts himself for their good, he will never be ill-treated. There may be opposition to his doctrine, but none to the man himself.

[7] Neither the New Testament nor historic Christian doctrine inculcates that Christ was "punished" for human sin, though He suffered for it.

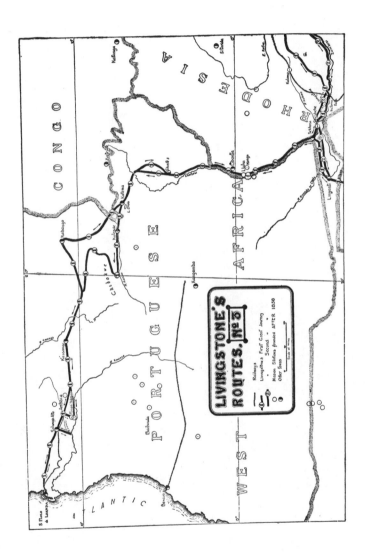

And in *Missionary Travels* (chap. xxv.):

Although the Makololo were so confiding, the reader must not imagine that they would be so to every individual who might visit them. Much of my influence depended upon the good name given me by the Bakwains, and that I secured only through a long course of tolerably good conduct. No one ever gains much influence in this country without purity and uprightness. The acts of a stranger are keenly scrutinized by both young and old, and seldom is the judgment pronounced, even by the heathen, unfair or uncharitable. I have heard women speaking in admiration of a white man, because he was pure, and never was guilty of any secret immorality. Had he been, they would have known it, and untutored heathen though they be, would have despised him in consequence. Secret vice becomes known throughout the tribe; and while one unacquainted with the language may imagine a peccadillo to be hidden, it is as patent to all as it would be in London, had he a placard on his back.

This conviction of his received strong confirmation in days to come and was a theme to which he often recurred.

Murray's magic lantern he found to be a most useful gift. He could always obtain a hearing by means of it, though sometimes its effect upon the audience was as disturbing as that of the cinema upon the Scottish islanders of St. Kilda in recent years. When the picture of Abraham preparing to offer up Isaac was shown in Shinte's country, for instance, the audience became panic-stricken at the movement of the knife, believing that there was devil magic in it of which they would speedily be the victims, and fled the scene in headlong disorder. Yet once apprehensions were allayed no method of instruction was so popular; people came long distances in order to witness the entertainment, which was the only kind of Christian propaganda Livingstone was ever asked to repeat.

It was on the journey to Loanda that for the first time he beheld captured slaves chained together in gangs, a spectacle which also shocked his followers. On the whole, however, he encountered no atrocities in connection with the evil system at all comparable to what he was to find in the Nyassa region a few years later. Writing to his wife after his arrival at Loanda, he confesses to having received much kindness from some of the very men, Portuguese, who were engaged in the traffic, and acquits them of deliberate cruelty. In comparing Portuguese slavery, as it now came under his notice, with what he had already known of Boer treatment of the natives he believes the former to be milder and the more humane of the two. There is no colour bar, and slaves and masters live much the same kind of life, greatly to the moral hurt of the latter without raising in any way the status of the former. In a letter to Thompson from Linyanti on September 13th, 1855, he reports: [8]

> The Portuguese men marry black women, there being very few white ladies in the country, and (unlike our immaculate Transvaal Congregation) never disown their children.
> I made enquiry and found one person only whose children might answer like Topsy, "Never had any father or mother."
> Persons of colour of respectability sit at the tables of the richest without, as far as I can observe, any distinction on account of race, and I met a Canon of the Church who was as black as a Kaffre with short woolly hair, thick lips, etc. He is greatly respected.

But apart from evidences of the demoralizing effect of the slave trade the vicissitudes experienced *en route* were sufficiently troublesome to call for all his reserves of wisdom and courage. The ferocity, treachery, and rapacity of the various tribes with whom he came in contact were wearying and baffling in the extreme, and not seldom all but disastrous to the expedition. Beyond the border of Sekeletu's domains the tribes met with were suspicious of the party's intentions because of the raids in which the Makololo had been in the habit of indulging. Beyond Libonta Sekeletu could give no protection to the travellers, and the Balonda people through whose land it was necessary to pass were smarting from the recollection of an attack which had recently been made upon their villages by a Makololo party under the leadership of a warrior named Lerimo, and the carrying off of a number of prisoners

[8] L.M.S. archives.

as slaves. This act of aggression was contrary to the wishes of Sekeletu, and a considerable embarrassment to Livingstone as likely to expose him and his slender retinue to the danger of reprisals, perhaps to massacre. The raid had been accompanied by the burning of a number of kraals and the destruction of Balonda property. Livingstone sought out Mpololo, the head man of the Barotse district, whence the marauders had come with his knowledge and approval, and rebuked him sternly, threatening him with condign punishment from Sekeletu if evil befell the expedition in consequence of this flagrant infringement of his commands; for, so far from wishing to do harm to the Balonda, the missionary was bringing with him a quantity of gifts for the very chiefs upon whom the injury had been inflicted. He demanded that the captives be restored, and, to make sure that the order would be complied with, stayed to see it executed, taking some of them in his train and handing them over himself. Nineteen enslaved persons were thus released on Livingstone's intervention, the first case of the kind wherein he took an active part, but not the last, as we shall see when we come to the record of his relations with Bishop Mackenzie in 1861.

Masiko, an independent Barotse chief from whose subjects some of the captives had been taken, was not blameless; he had given provocation by trying to seduce the Barotse from their allegiance to the Makololo power, and was also guilty in his turn of selling slaves to the Mambari. It was his vicious custom to seize orphan children or isolated adults who could not protect themselves, and treat them as merchandise to be exchanged for cloth and other products of European manufacture. In returning to Masiko two little boys, a little girl, a young man, and two middle-aged women who had been torn from his tribe by the Makololo, Livingstone took the opportunity of sending him a message animadverting upon the cruelty and meanness of enslaving the weak and friendless members of his own tribe. The message had the effect of stimulating Masiko to send an embassy to Livingstone untruthfully defending himself from the imputation, and saying that he only sold prisoners of war. The chief's representatives brought gifts of food and an elephant's tusk for the white man, and in thanking the donor and welcoming these evidences of a friendly spirit Livingstone successfully entered upon negotiations for bringing about a peaceful understanding between this border princeling and the lord paramount of the Makololo State.

This piece of good work was effected on Balonda ground, for by this time the Livingstone party had arrived at a village belonging to a chieftainess named Manenko, to whom a captive boy and girl were to be restored in Sekeletu's name. Nyamoana, mother of Manenko, and sister of a great Balonda chief named Shinte or Kabompo, who ruled farther to the north, was also visited at her village in the same locality. Nyamoana pressed Livingstone not to ascend the river Leeba any farther at this point, but leave his canoes and go on ox-back to her brother's headquarters. While the proposition was being debated Manenko arrived and promptly took charge of the whole proceedings. This redoubtable lady was something of a termagant, and seems to have amused the missionary highly. He had left her village in disregard of her orders that he should await her coming there, and her purpose in following him to her mother's village was to make sure that he should not proceed without paying due deference to her authority.

She began by falling foul of the Masiko embassy, which was still in conference with Livingstone, and poured upon its members a tirade of merciless abuse for having dared to call at her village and sleep in one of her huts without receiving her august permission to do so. The petty chiefs against whom her invective was principally directed listened to it in stolid silence, as men in more enlightened communities are wont to do when under the lash of a woman's tongue. The spectacle entertained the white onlooker vastly, because, as he remarks, in attitude, gesture, and screaming eloquence Manenko's performance displayed a certain similarity to what might be observed in England in corresponding circumstances when feelings find unrestrained expression.

Manenko's femininity showed in other ways. She was an important person and meant the missionary to know it. A strapping, healthy young woman of about twenty years of age, she could outdo most

men of her entourage in physical prowess and was well able to keep
her conceited husband in his place. Her costume approximated more
closely to that of English ladies of the present day than of Victorian
times, and perhaps would not scandalize Livingstone now as much as
it did then. Seconding her mother's desire that her visitor should go
overland to her uncle Shinte, she announced at the same time her
intention of going with him. Livingstone demurred, but his objec-
tions were useless; Manenko was more than a match for him. The
story runs in his record:

> Manenko gave us some manioc-roots in the morning, and had
> determined to carry our baggage to her uncle's, Kabompo, or Shinti.
> We had heard a sample of what she could do with her tongue; and
> as neither my men nor myself had much inclination to encounter a
> scolding from this black Mrs. Caudle, we made ready the packages;
> but she came and said the men whom she had ordered for the service
> had not yet come; they would arrive to-morrow. Being on low and
> disagreeable diet, I felt annoyed at this further delay, and ordered
> the packages to be put into the canoes to proceed up the river with-
> out her servants; but Manenko was not to be circumvented in this
> way; she came forward with her people, and said her uncle would
> be angry if she did not carry forward the tusks and goods of Seke-
> letu, seized the luggage, and declared that she would carry it in spite
> of me. My men succumbed sooner to the petticoat government than
> I felt inclined to do, and left me no power; and, being unwilling to
> encounter her tongue, I was moving off to the canoes when she gave
> me a kind of explanation, and, with her hand on my shoulder, put
> on a motherly look, saying, "Now, my little man, just do as the rest
> have done." My feelings of annoyance of course vanished, and I
> went out to try and get some meat.[9]

Manenko wheedling the austere Livingstone must have been a funny
sight. She got her way and proved of service to the party *en route,*
though her arbitrary whims and fancies were more than a little trying.
But she displayed a kindliness and capability for which the missionary
had cause to be grateful. The bad cooking of the manioc porridge,

[9] *Missionary Travels,* p. 279.

which was often the only article of diet obtainable, had given him in-digestion habitually, and she saved him from this in addition to caring for his comfort when he was prostrated by fever. Again his own testimony should be cited:

> Whilst delayed, by Manenko's management, among the Balonda villages, a little to the south of the town of Shinti, we were well supplied by the villagers with sweet potatoes and green maize; Sambanza (Manenko's husband) went to his mother's village for supplies of other food. I was labouring under fever, and did not find it very difficult to exercise patience with her whims; but it being Saturday, I thought we might as well go to the town for Sunday (January 15th, 1854). "No; her messenger must return from her uncle first." Being sure that the answer of the uncle would be fa-vourable, I thought we might go on at once, and not lose two days in the same spot. "No, it is our custom"; and everything else I could urge was answered in the genuine pertinacious lady style. She ground some meal for me with her own hands, and, when she brought it, told me she had actually gone to a village and begged corn for the purpose. She said this with an air as if the inference must be drawn by even a stupid white man: "I know how to manage, don't I?" It was refreshing to eat food which could be eaten without producing the unpleasantness described by the Rev. John Newton, of St. Mary's, Woolnoth, London, when obliged to eat the same roots while a slave in the West Indies.[10]

The path to Shinte's Town lay almost entirely through tropical forest, the first time that Livingstone had made acquaintance with this type of scenery on a large scale. The luxuriant tropical growth inter-ested and charmed him, notwithstanding the personal discomfort to which he was exposed from ceaseless rain. At Shinte's Town the party had a ceremonious reception in a great public square in the pres-ence of about thirteen hundred people of both sexes. The chief, a man of about fifty-five years old and of good appearance, sat on a throne under a shady tree. He wore a checked jacket, a scarlet kilt edged with green, and heavy necklaces of beads; his arms and lower limbs

[10] *Missionary Travels*, p. 287.

were covered with metal rings; his headpiece consisted of beads arranged in a pattern and tufted with feathers. Behind him squatted his harem of about a hundred women, and in the rear and on either side a force of some three hundred armed warriors stood in rank. As no one was allowed to approach within less than forty yards of the potentate, and as the visitor seemed likely to be left standing in the sun while long-drawn-out formalities of introduction were gone through, Livingstone retreated to another tree and seated himself where he could have an uninterrupted view of what went on. He noticed that Shinte seldom took his eyes off him, and he returned the scrutiny with careful attention. Furious drum-beating and other conventional noise-making continued without cessation for a long and wearying time, no less than nine orators making elaborate speeches.

The tedious ceremony was at length brought to an end by the chief rising and moving off surrounded by his court, but, to the missionary's surprise, was not followed by an invitation to a private audience, nor was any further communication made to him that day. Another day passed, and then, in the middle of the night, came a request from Shinte that the white man should pay him a visit immediately. This Livingstone refused to do, as he was in the sweating stage of an intermittent fever and the way to the chief lay through a swamp. He went next morning and was graciously received, Shinte beginning the interview by expressing his disappointment that a visitor so illustrious should not have approached and talked with him on first arriving. Livingstone replied that the delay had been of the chief's own making, and not his, that he had come two days before fully expecting to be able to see the chief personally at once, explain his mission, convey Sekeletu's greetings, and obtain facilities for going farther, whereas the interval had simply been so much wasted time. Shinte took this frank statement in good part, expressed the liveliest approval of Livingstone's intentions, and promised to help as far as he could.

We have here a typical instance of Livingstone's ways of establishing relations with uncivilized Africans. He always considered it bad policy to allow them to think they were condescending to the stranger or conferring a favour in admitting him to their presence, and he found from experience that a candid and self-respecting manner, albeit inoffensive and undemonstrative, was the best mode of dealing with them. Acting on a broad hint that the chief would like to taste some ox-flesh, he presented him with one of the riding beasts furnished for the expedition by Sekeletu, at the same time advising Shinte to obtain more for himself by legitimate trading with the Makololo. The recommendation was acted upon, as Livingstone found on the return journey fifteen months later.

Shinte's delight in the gift was exuberant but short-lived, Manenko irrupting again. Learning of her uncle's good fortune, she rushed to the scene at high speed, and declaring indignantly that the white man belonged to her, that she had brought him there, and therefore that the ox was hers, not Shinte's, she ordered her men to take it away at once. The peremptory command was promptly obeyed, the ox slaughtered, and a leg only sent to Shinte, who made no protest and exhibited no displeasure. Admittedly Manenko had a way with her.

Ten days passed before the missionary and his party were able to take the road again, much time having been consumed in negotiations ere the necessary guides and provisions for the next stage of the journey were forthcoming. One great hindrance to the preparations was the prevailing drunkenness of the people. They brewed a fermented liquor resembling mead, which had the effect of stupefying them, and it was no uncommon thing to see them sprawling in great numbers in stertorous slumber at all hours of the day under the influence of this potent drink. Evidently the European trader has not been entirely to blame for introducing the native African to intoxicating beverages.

The incessant rains were another cause of delay, but as it was hopeless to expect any lessening of the universal humidity, Livingstone decided to push on in spite of it. It accompanied him all the rest of the way, and caused him chronic discomfort, rusting everything metallic, covering his clothes with mildew, and rotting the canvas of his tent. Day after day without intermission he rode, walked, rested, ate, and slept in steaming or chilling dampness from which there was no escape in any direction. "Never did I endure such drenchings," he writes to Thompson. . . . "I don't care much for fatigue. If we could

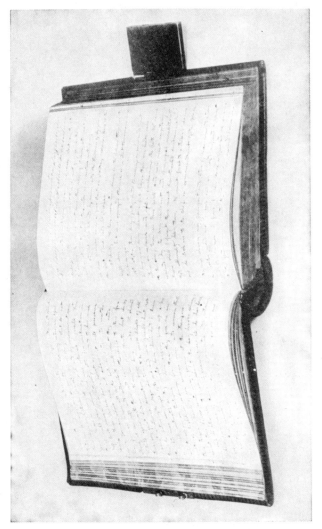

march I got on very well, but when compelled to stand still by pouring rains, then fever laid hold with his strong hands on my inner man, and lying in a little gipsy tent with everything damp or wet was sore against the grain." [11] He followed the course of the Leeba till clear of Shinte's country, and then made his way through the flat Lobale region to the village of a chief named Katema, near the shores of the little Lake Dilolo. This wide plain or spongy tableland, with a mean elevation of about five thousand feet, he correctly conjectured to be the watershed between the great river systems of the Zambesi and the Congo which flow from it in opposite directions. It is an enormous saturated area, almost water-logged, as the traveller found to his serious inconvenience, for it incommoded him at every step, especially on the Congo side, water spurting out of the sodden soil everywhere, or lying but a few inches below the surface.

Shinte supplied him with eight guides and bearers to conduct him to Katema, and had the climatic conditions been less trying, the journey would have been very enjoyable, as the valley traversed was of exceeding beauty and fertility. The party had been provided with plenty of food by Shinte's orders, though, as before, Livingstone's stomach did not accommodate itself very kindly to the rough-and-ready mode of preparing the manioc porridge which formed the basis of the daily regimen. He writes:

> When intended to be used as food, this meal is stirred into boiling water: they put as much in as can be moistened, one man holding the vessel and the other stirring the porridge with all his might. This is the common mess of the country. Though hungry, we could just manage to swallow it with the aid of a little honey, which I shared with my men as long as it lasted. It is very unsavoury (*Scoticè* wersh); and no matter how much one may eat, two hours afterwards he is as hungry as ever. When less meal is employed, the mess is exactly like a basin of starch in the hands of a laundress, and if the starch were made from diseased potatoes, some idea might be formed of the Balonda porridge, which hunger alone forced us to eat. [12]

[11] L.M.S. archives.
[12] *Missionary Travels,* p. 303.

There was no Manenko on this trip to mitigate by more careful cooking the worst effects of this bad dietary on the missionary's fever-enfeebled frame.

He pays grateful tribute in many entries of his Journal to the loyalty and generous care of his simple Makololo followers. He was much touched by their faithful attention to his wants at night; never did they resort to their own rough resting-places without first seeing that their white master was made as comfortable as was possible in the circumstances. "As I glance over their deeds of generosity recorded in my Journal," he states, "my heart glows with gratitude." On one occasion they jeopardized their own lives to rescue him, as they thought, from drowning. The incident is related in Livingstone's public account of this part of the expedition, but his shorter and earlier version of it in the correspondence with Thompson is as well worth quoting: [13]

> My Barotse did not know I could swim, and the first broad stream we came to excited their fears on my account.
> "Now hold fast by the tail. Don't let go."
> I intended to follow the injunctions, but tail and all went so deep I thought it better to strike out alone for the bank, and just as I reached it, I was greatly gratified to see a universal rush had been made for my rescue.
> Their clothes were all floating down the stream, and two of them reached me, breathless with the exertion they had made.

Katema gave the missionary as friendly a welcome as Shinte, without the long preliminary formalities. With considerate hospitality, as soon as the introductions were over he placed sixteen large baskets of meal before the party, a few fowls, and a plentiful quantity of eggs, saying that no visitor must go hungry in his town. "Go home," he added, "and cook and eat, and you will then be in a fit state to speak to me at an audience I will give you to-morrow." This genial conduct was in marked contrast to what Livingstone was to experience during the remainder of the journey. He was particularly struck with Katema's laugh, which was spontaneous and hearty. "This is a good sign," he shrewdly comments, "for a man who shakes his sides with mirth is seldom difficult to deal with." [14] The only conspicuous drawback to their intercourse was the chief's unwillingness to listen to any religious teaching; he was more than indifferent, he was frankly bored. But there was no fault to be found with his willingness to further the more utilitarian objects of the expedition, giving and receiving presents and promising to do what he could in establishing commercial relations with the coast if Livingstone could succeed in making a way for him to do so. Altogether he made a good impression on the missionary, and they parted well satisfied with each other.

Less agreeable was the party's reception at the town of Kangenke, on the banks of the Kasai river. This shifty chief was as mean in supplying food, even at a price, as Katema had been generous. Like all the chiefs on the route hitherto followed, he consented to furnish guides to conduct the travellers to the borders of the next considerable tribe located on the line of march; nothing, indeed, displays Livingstone's resourcefulness in a clearer light than his success in obtaining such facilities as he proceeded, for without guides he and his companions would have been helpless on strange ground remote from every European settlement. But Kangenke's guides were untrustworthy. Shinte had cautioned Livingstone to keep a sharp eye upon their movements, as they would be likely to play him some trick if they caught him at a disadvantage. The warning was well grounded, as was soon apparent, for at the fording of the Kasai Kangenke's people waited till half the party had crossed, and then suddenly sprang the charge that one of the Makololo had stolen a knife, and that the theft must be paid for by a heavy fine. Knowing that his men were honest, Livingstone readily agreed to have the baggage searched, when to his discomfiture the missing knife was discovered in the kit of one of the bearers. On being questioned, the man admitted that he had picked it up at their last encampment, where, as the missionary presently perceived when the wrangling and threatening had accomplished their purpose, the knife had been placed with the very object of luring one of the strangers to appropriate it. Later on he learned that this was a

[14] *Missionary Travels,* p. 319.

common device employed by the emissaries of slave traders, and he made it a rule in consequence never to allow any of his followers to touch, much less carry away, articles, however small, which had not been paid for or received in lawful exchange in the presence of witnesses. In the case narrated there was nothing for it but to pay the exorbitant demands, and pay they did, or Livingstone himself would have been seized as a hostage, as, following his usual custom, he was the last to cross, and was left by himself on Kangenke's side of the river and in the power of the latter's armed men.

This was only the beginning of a series of equally vexatious occurrences. Katende, who ruled on the western bank of the Kasai, would not see the white man at all, but sent representatives to demand presents and payment for permission to pass through his land. Livingstone had to part with some of his own undergarments to satisfy the requirements of this haughty invisible personage, and in return received only a single fowl and a little meal. They had to pass on without meeting Katende, but not without one more attempt at exacting tribute for an imaginary offence. Noticing a certain facial resemblance between one of Katende's villagers and a member of the Barotse community at home, one of Livingstone's bearers jocularly addressed the former by the name of the latter. This was promptly dubbed an insult only to be atoned for by handing over some more property; but this time Livingstone stood firm and refused to submit to the imposition. At a bridge a little farther on they had to pay toll fees to an able-bodied gatekeeper, and the climax was reached when Kangenke's guides who had come thus far with them sat down on the ground and coolly announced that there were three paths in front and that if they were not given a present of cloth immediately they would not show the travellers which of the three to take. Again Livingstone was mulcted ere advance could be made.

Worse awaited him. They were now entering the wide-spreading country of the Chiboque, as the Portuguese call the tribe, the fiercest and least placable people yet encountered, probably because more directly under the influence of slave traders than the tribes farther south. It was Livingstone's invariable experience that wherever the slave trade prevailed the worst characteristics of savagery became accentuated. He had avoided the route to the coast at St. Philip de Benguela because he knew this, but here he found himself in a similar environment and with constant evidence of its demoralizing effects before his eyes. The first chief at whose village he paused in this region was a truculent individual named Njambi, whose attitude was the reverse of friendly. As this was a country where cattle were scarce—owing to the former prevalence of the tsetse fly, so Livingstone inferred—he killed one of his small stock of oxen and sent Njambi a present of the meat with a complimentary message. The reply was a demand for a gift more in accordance with the dignity and importance of so high a personage; he must have either a man, an ox, a gun, powder, cloth, or something equally valuable; if the requirement were not complied with instantly the expedition would not be allowed to proceed farther. Some of the insolent Chiboque who brought the ultimatum were overheard saying: "They have only five guns." This reconnoitring of the defensive armament of the visitors was quickly followed up by a hostile demonstration, Njambi surrounding the encampment with a large force equipped with firearms. This was the most perilous moment the party had yet known, and but for Livingstone's coolness and intrepidity would have seen its complete destruction. Although the assailants had covered him with their guns, he seated himself without exhibiting any sign of perturbation and invited Njambi to do the same. As Africans never can resist an invitation to a palaver the suggestion was acceded to, and the missionary with his gun across his knees began in quiet tones to reason with the chief and appeal to his better feelings. It did not appear that Njambi's better feelings were easy to reach, for in argument he simply proceeded from one pretext to another for stripping the travellers of all they possessed. The first misdemeanour which he insisted could only be compensated for by the gift of a slave, an ox, or a gun was the fact that one of Livingstone's men in spitting had accidentally caused a little saliva to fall upon one of the Chiboque. The involuntary offender had actually been handing the said Chiboque native a present of meat at the time, had apologized for the spitting mischance, and wiped off the very small evidence of it, but Njambi refused to accept this as sufficient, and loudly demanded that the unfortunate perpetrator of the supposed wrong should be surrendered as a slave in punishment. Livingstone firmly declining to listen to this, tribute for passing through their territory was next demanded—another sure sign of contact with slave raiders. This he also refused as inequitable, and offered various gifts instead in token of good will; but the more he offered the higher their terms became until at length he stated that he would do no more, that he was not afraid of them, and if they wanted to fight he was quite ready, but that they must strike the first blow.

While the conversation had been going on his trained Makololo warriors had been gradually surrounding the chief and his councillors, and these at last perceiving themselves to be entrapped yielded to the missionary's representations and went away without committing any overt act of violence. The incident is worth relating for the illustration it affords of Livingstone's methods in dealing with recalcitrant natives. Patience, forbearance, and reasonable persuasion were always put into operation, and were usually successful; but he knew the virtue of armed force, and would not have shrunk from using it as a last resort.

Half-starved and shaking with fever, he moved on, keeping carefully on his guard against ambush, and continually harassed by Chiboque attempts at robbery. Being too feeble to walk, he rode on ox-back most of the way, but his special mount, "Sinbad," was a difficult beast to manage. With malignant ingenuity he would often sweep his rider off by darting under a low-hanging branch, in which event he never failed to aim a kick at his prostrate victim. It was an unhappy mode of progressing for a man as ill as Livingstone now was without intermission.

Trouble also began to show itself among his followers, partly on account of the continuous harassments to which they were subjected by the unfriendly Chiboque and partly because of mutual jealousy occasioned by Livingstone's discriminations in distributing gifts and assigning duties. Grumbling culminated at length in disobedience and open mutiny. Thinking their white chief too ill to exercise effective control, some of them jeered at him when he issued a specific order. Knowing he dared not allow them to gain the upper hand, as their very lives depended upon discipline being maintained, the dauntless leader sprang to his feet, pistol in hand, and rushed upon them with a determination so unmistakable as to reduce them to instant submission. This was the only occasion when he had any difficulty of the kind on this his first long journey; the crisis never recurred. It had been necessary to show that he was master, and there was no pretence about the action he took; he would have taken sterner measures had they been necessary. As it was, the very sight of his anger terrified the malcontents and quenched all tendency to insubordination.

But rebellion was succeeded by loss of heart. The ceaseless exactions and attempts at spoliation by the natives of one district after another through which the expedition had now to pass made the poor Makololo feel that it was hopeless to expect to reach their destination in safety. Again and again their way was barred by armed parties bent on brigandage, and the need for vigilance night and day to preserve themselves from sudden attack wore down their resolution, and they united in begging their leader to give up his quest and turn back. Livingstone replying that if they forsook him he would go on alone, they held a consultation together and then came in a body with the announcement that they would not desert him. "We will never leave you," they said, and the promise was more than mere words. The subsequent behaviour of everyone concerned, and not least of the one or two who had earlier attempted disobedience to Livingstone's authority, was proof enough of the sincerity of their profession.

When the party reached the river Quango, which marked the eastern boundary of the Portuguese sphere of influence, Livingstone had become so weak that he could neither ride nor walk, and had to be led by his men in order to be prevented from falling down. The scenery here was magnificent, the dark and swampy forest belt having been left behind and replaced by undulating fertile savannahs rolling west and north as far as the eye could see. But here, too, the party was greeted with hostility. The Bashinje people who inhabited the beautiful region along the right bank of the river refused to allow them to pass unless given a slave in payment, and matters assumed so menacing an appearance that even the dogged Livingstone almost began to despair of getting any farther. They had parted with almost everything negotiable; he himself was so wasted by fever and suffering such severe pain that the chaffering and noise about him were almost intolerable to his nerves; privacy was impossible, for his tent was now in shreds and his every movement exposed to the view of swarms of peering, gabbling natives of both sexes.

Just when matters were at their worst a young half-caste Portuguese sergeant of militia, Cypriano di Abreu, appeared and saved the situation. Acting on his advice, Livingstone and his men moved down to the ferry in spite of a scattered fire from their assailants, and under the same skilful pilotage succeeded in getting punted across. Once on the other side they were safe, and their new friend who had descended upon them in their extremity like an angel from heaven entertained them hospitably and furnished them with full rations for the four or five days' travel which lay between them and the Portuguese military and trading station of Cassange. Here Livingstone arrived in a pitiable state of destitution, his clothing in rags, his body a bag of bones. The commandant, Captain Neves, and his fellow-officials were amazed to behold him, and did not at first know what to make of him, but after hearing his story treated him with lavish kindness. He was entertained in the commandant's own house and re-arrayed from head to foot in decent habiliments contributed by his brotherly host. "I feel deeply grateful to him for his disinterested kindness," writes Livingstone; "he not only attended to my wants, but also furnished food for my famishing party free of charge." [15]

The same welcome and ungrudging assistance were given all the rest of the way to the coast. A black Portuguese corporal was detailed to guide them and requisition whatever might be needed *en route*. From first to last, indeed, the same unvarying courtesy was extended to the expedition by the Portuguese authorities, as Livingstone ever willingly and gladly acknowledged, and it was only with extreme reluctance that in after years, and on the opposite side of the continent, he had set himself in opposition to them on account of their slave-dealing policy.

[15] *Missionary Travels*, p. 369.

Passing through Ambaca and Golungo Alto, in the latter of which stations he was entertained by Lieutenant Canto e Castro—"a young gentleman whose whole subsequent conduct will ever make me regard him with great affection," Livingstone records—the party came at length to St. Paul de Loanda, their earnestly desired goal. The date was May 31st, 1854. His brave and faithful but simple-minded Makololo companions were sorely troubled during the last stage of the journey by the suspicion which had been implanted in their minds by some of the inhabitants of the Portuguese territory of Angola, through which their road now lay, that they were being taken to the coast to be sold as slaves. Their leader reassured them by telling them that nothing would happen to them which did not first happen to him.

He had his own feelings of misgiving, and it is not surprising to learn that he approached the town in a state of mental depression, wondering what his reception would be on making contact with civilization again. He does not seem to have anticipated in the slightest degree the sensation that the news of his exploit would cause in England. He was so ill that he could not sit on his riding ox for more than ten minutes at a time, and it was a poor broken wreck of a man that stumbled down the hill into the streets of the Portuguese settlement and anxiously inquired for the British Consul, Mr. Edmund Gabriel. Much depended on the character of this compatriot, and the worn and weary traveller was as apprehensive of a rebuff as his Makololo followers had been of being sold into slavery. He was not long in realizing that his doubts were as groundless as theirs. Mr. Gabriel, having already been informed of his coming by Portuguese traders, had sent messengers to meet him on the way, and although these had unfortunately missed him, nothing was wanting that could be done in preparing for his comfort who had so long known little of it. One characteristic touch deserves mention. As Livingstone approached the Consul's residence he noticed a quantity of carefully cultivated flowers growing in front of it, and took the fact as evidence that the man within must be of an estimable nature. He was right. A warm British welcome awaited him, and Mr. Gabriel, seeing that he was half-dead with fatigue and disease, wisely postponed all attempts at an account of the expedition and put him promptly to bed. "Never shall I forget," runs Livingstone's heart-felt chronicle of the event, "the luxuriant pleasure I enjoyed in feeling myself again on a good English couch, after six months' sleeping on the ground. I was soon asleep; and Mr. Gabriel, coming in almost immediately, rejoiced at the soundness of my repose." [16]

[16] *Missionary Travels*, p. 389.

CHAPTER VIII

ACROSS AFRICA

Not for some weeks was the exhausted traveller able to leave the couch on which he had been so compassionately thrust. Fever and dysentery combined had reduced him to a mere skeleton, and the first effect of rest and proper attention was actually to aggravate instead of remove the symptoms of the complaint, and he suffered greatly. Mr. Gabriel nursed him personally, administered with his own hands such remedies as were obtainable; but ere long, by a fortunate coincidence, a squadron of British warships entered the harbour, and a doctor was sent ashore who quickly brought the patient to convalescence. A passage to England on board one of the vessels was offered, and Livingstone might have availed himself of it, but felt bound by his promise to see his twenty-seven followers safely home again. It was, however, imperative to rest and recuperate for a time before renewing the ordeal of the past seven months; he was therefore content to remain as Mr. Gabriel's guest while writing up his Journals and preparing his reports for the London Missionary Society, the Royal Geographical Society, and his family and friends at home. A severe recurrence of his malady laid him aside in August, and it was not until September 20th that he felt himself able to take the road again.

In the meantime, great interest had been taken in him and his plans by the Portuguese administration of the town and province. The acting Governor-General, the Bishop of Loanda, received him and his whole party formally, and gave warm approbation to the design of bringing Sekeletu and his people into commercial touch with Europe. Mr. Gabriel, at his own expense, attired Livingstone's Makololo in robes of striped cotton cloth with red caps for this auspicious occasion, to their great delight. During their master's illness in Mr. Gabriel's home the Consul had kept a wise and friendly eye on the men and helped them to obtain work at loading and unloading cargoes in the port, so that Livingstone should be under no anxiety as to their means of livelihood. They became favourites with the British seamen on board the men-of-war, who showed them over the ships, explained to them that these had been sent to put down the slave trade, and with the permission of one commander allowed them to fire off a cannon. This fraternization had a good effect on their morale. Livingstone remarks that though they had been normally respectful to him heretofore, and shown confidence in his leadership, he was now much elevated in their estimation. They saw that he had spoken the truth about his country-men; henceforth they always distinguished between the British on the one hand, and the Boers and Portuguese on the other, and their reports to the interior tribes in this sense had a permanently beneficial influ-ence. They were lost in wonder at the size and grandeur of the Euro-pean houses and the warships, which surpassed everything they had previously been able to imagine; and when they saw the respect with which Livingstone was greeted everywhere, both on shore and afloat, they began to treat him with a new deference, which was never relaxed during the whole period of their subsequent association with him.

The return journey was begun very happily, and with far better prospects than the outward journey had been. On the initiative of the Bishop, Livingstone was entrusted with a cordial message for Sekeletu, inviting him to set commercial activities on foot, and promising encour-agement to the same; as a present, a Colonel's uniform and a horse were sent specially for the chief. All Livingstone's men were provided with suits of clothing, and the merchants of Loanda by public sub-scription furnished the party with specimens of all the articles suitable for trade. Two donkeys were also taken along in the hope of intro-ducing the breed in the interior, as these animals are immune from the poisonous effects of the bite of the tsetse insect. Abundance of sup-plies, including arms and ammunition, was carried; instead of five guns in all, every one of the twenty-seven Makololo now had a musket. Twenty new carriers were commissioned to carry the baggage; a good new tent made by the capable hands of the British sailors on board the *Philomel* contributed greatly to Livingstone's comfort; and he was

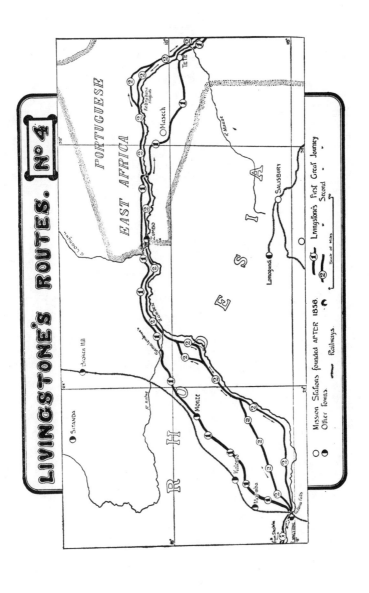

LIVINGSTONE'S ROUTES. Nº 4

given letters to all the commandants of the districts through which he was likely to pass directing them to afford him every assistance in their power. It was a cheerful and confident company that set out from Loanda under his command on September 20th, 1854, *en route* for Linyanti.

At Golungo Alto he had the satisfaction of being able to return in some measure the kindness earlier shown to him by Lieutenant Canto, for the latter, being in the grip of a particularly malignant form of fever, was both prescribed for and nursed by the missionary, without whose ministrations he would probably have died. The horse intended for Sekeletu did die, whether of neglect or of some local infection was not discoverable, while the expedition was thus detained. This loss was the more disappointing, as the utmost care had been taken while passing through tsetse-infested neighbourhoods to preserve the animal from being bitten by the pest.

During the stay at Golungo Alto, Livingstone took the opportunity of viewing the ruins of the former Jesuit establishments in the neighbourhood. He was greatly impressed by what he was able to learn of the heroic and useful Christian work that had been done in Angola by the members of the order. He found that the tradition concerning them was all in their favour. Though generations had passed since their mission ended, the natives still spoke of them with warmth and reverence. They had been expelled in 1760 by the order of the then Governor for doing exactly what Livingstone was doing now, resisting the oppression of the aborigines by white men. The secular priests who succeeded them were not, in the missionary's judgment, of the same moral worth, and there were many evidences of deterioration in manners. The Portuguese settlers had done little or nothing to raise the tone of the natives they ruled, whereas they themselves were undoubtedly the worse for being in daily contact with an uncivilized race. Livingstone's conclusions on this subject were greatly strengthened in after years by what he saw of Portuguese administration on the east coast, the mingled lassitude and callousness, the inefficiency and disregard of the welfare of the native population—the absence, indeed, of any conception of duty towards the undeveloped heathen Africans.

That there had been a sharp decline from the vigour and enterprise of the earlier days of Portuguese colonization was evident on every hand, and he put this down to the combined influence of slavery and concubinage. Portuguese officials did not come out with the intention of making a real home in Africa or of benefiting the country in any way; their object was to acquire a competence as soon as possible and return to their own land. Hence they did not bring their women-folk with them, but set up mixed domestic establishments, which had the result of bringing into existence large half-caste communities which were, as they still are, a perplexing problem in African life. Livingstone became increasingly of opinion that all-round demoralization must inevitably proceed from the habitual intercourse of white and black races which recognized no moral obligation on the part of the former to raise the status of the latter, and had for its main object the making of an economic profit out of flesh and blood. That the profit was illusory, and the methods of obtaining it prodigally wasteful, he suspected from the first, and was to realize with certainty and deepening indignation as time went on. He was repelled by the type of Christianity which was quiescent in the presence of so much that was plainly debasing and corrupt.

But it was only gradually that his detestation of the system as a whole found vent in unrestrained language. Up to the present, and for some time to come, his lively gratitude for the spontaneous kindness and helpfulness of Portuguese military and civilian authorities is given repeated expression in the strongest terms both in his Journals and correspondence. The acknowledgment was deserved, for it is difficult to see how the stupendous task he was now attempting could have been accomplished had the Portuguese chosen to adopt the policy of the Boers and block the way. Everywhere they did the opposite, and it was not until his denunciations of the Portuguese connivance at the barbarities of the slave trade with Zanzibar reached Europe in 1860 that their friendly attitude changed to one of resentment and opposition.

At Pungo Andongo, remarkable for its gigantic and picturesque rocks, he was the guest of Colonel Pires, and here he had the mortification of learning that all his despatches to England had been lost in the wreck of the mail steamer *Forerunner*. The news reached him in October, and on the invitation of his host he set to work to rewrite the whole voluminous set of reports and letters that had gone to the bottom of the sea, and to redraft the maps wherewith to illustrate them. The task occupied him for several months, he and his whole company living at the expense of Colonel Pires the while. This gentleman, though a slave owner like the rest of his countrymen in Angola and other Portuguese possessions in the African continent, was highly esteemed by Livingstone, both on account of his personal character and the beneficial effects of his work. He had risen from lowly beginnings until he had become the richest merchant in the province, and had others been content to follow his example would have made it the most prosperous on the coast. His slaves, Livingstone remarks, were more like freely hired servants than any who had hitherto come under his observation. "Everything is neat and clean, while generally, where slaves are the only domestics, there is an aspect of slovenliness as if they went on the principle of always doing as little for their masters as possible." He notes that Colonel Pires' success was proof of what might have been achieved both in trade and agriculture in Angola, had intelligence and industry been brought to bear upon the cultivation of the products of its naturally rich and prolific soil. But little had been done in this way, and the general impression made on the observer was that little interest was taken in any subject except the traffic in ivory and human beings.

On the rest of the return journey to the Makololo country Livingstone's comments are comparatively brief. He and his followers were longer on the way than on the outward journey, mainly because of the continuous rains and floods and the repeated attacks of sickness. He states that after crossing the Kasai river he was prostrated by his twenty-seventh attack of fever. His men were no more fortunate, for almost all of them succumbed to fever at one time or another, and had to be doctored by him. The same applied to his further association with Captain Neves, who had shown him so much courtesy and given him such valuable assistance at Cassange when he reached that station in dire extremity on the way to Loanda. Here, as in the case of Lieutenant Canto, he found himself able to repay his kindness. Captain Neves was seriously ill, and Livingstone was able to minister to him with speedy and gratifying success, but became convinced, from what he was able to see of this and other cases, that the district was as unhealthy as it was productive. The description was true, indeed, of the whole vast sodden area traversed from the coast back to the Zambesi. These were the days before the great advance in tropical hygiene to which reference has already been made. Writing to Thompson after arriving at Linyanti again, Livingstone draws special attention to the obstacle which the prevailing disease presents to Christian enterprise. "Concerning missionary prospects in this region," he says, "I feel perplexed on one point—the insalubrity of the climate. It is no obstacle to myself personally [the twenty-seven attacks of fever notwithstanding, apparently]. I think no London Society's 'Zendeling' would bolt at that. My better half would go as readily as anyone, but I am not clear on exposing my little ones without their intelligent self-dedication. As far as opportunity goes, there is no lack. Tribes and villages without number would be proud of the presence of a white man.

"Every day we hear of commerce extending its ramifications. Only think of the way this letter goes—by an Arab from Zanzibar who takes charge of a party of Makololo with ivory from Loanda. Before my trip the Makololo never visited another tribe except to plunder." [1]

There was a marked diminution of the tormenting demands and attempted robberies by hostile natives on this return journey, and Livingstone makes no secret of his belief that the chief reason for the improvement was that he was better armed. In a letter to his wife, written from the very district where, as we have seen, he had had to endure some of the most unpleasant and dangerous aggressions of the whole route, he sardonically adverts to the different reception he was now having:

> We have passed two chiefs who plagued us much when going down, but now were quite friendly. At that time one of them ordered his people not to sell us anything, and we had at last to force

[1] L.M.S. archives.

our way past him. Now he came running to meet us, saluting us, etc., with great urbanity. He informed us that he would come in the evening to receive a present, but I said unless he brought one he should receive nothing. He came in the usual way. The Balonda show the exalted position they occupy among men, viz., riding on the shoulders of a spokesman in the way little boys do in England. The chief brought two cocks and some eggs. I then gave a little present, too. The alteration in the gentleman's conduct—the Peace Society would not credit it—is attributable solely to my people possessing guns. When we passed before, we were defenceless. [2]

A collision with a Chiboque chief nearly led to bloodshed, an eventuality which Livingstone would have regarded as nothing short of calamitous had it been forced upon him, though he would not have shrunk from fighting in order to save the lives of his men. Probably the trouble would not have arisen had he been in fair health at the time and able to attend personally to the intercourse of his followers with the turbulent tribesmen around, but this happened to be wanting. For no less than twenty-two days he was detained at one village by a crippling attack of rheumatic fever brought on by constant exposure to damp. Night after night he had lain down to sleep in a tract of country covered with water through which he had waded all day. The only bed he could obtain was made by dragging a quantity of earth up above the surface of the flood and laying grass on the top. This comfortless couch was rendered all the worse by the fact that the rain beat pitilessly down without intermission, soaking the traveller through and through; a change to dry garments was an impossibility. That agonizing illness should supervene was the least that might have been expected from hardship so constant in its inroads upon vitality. The natives thinking that the white man was too far gone to be able to interest himself in the affairs of the camp, altercations began. The headman of the village, haggling arrogantly over the price of a piece of meat, was struck on the mouth by one of Livingstone's men. Uproar ensued amid vociferous demands for instant and heavy compensation for the insult. Pitsane, the missionary's lieutenant, offered five pieces

[2] Blaikie, *op. cit.*, p. 144.

of cloth and a gun in satisfaction of the claim and to spare his master annoyance, but, as usual, the more was offered the higher the demands arose, until at length the matter had to be referred to the sick and exhausted leader, who refused to yield to any further imposition and gave orders to his party to move on. Before they had gone far a formidable number of armed natives, drawn from all the neighbouring villages, began firing upon them through the trees, knocked down the baggage of the rearmost of the bearers, and showed clearly their intention of encircling and overwhelming the whole company. The rest of the dramatic story cannot be better told than in Livingstone's own version:

I fortunately had a six-barreled revolver, which my friend Captain Henry Need, of her Majesty's brig *Linnet,* had considerately sent to Golungo Alto after my departure from Loanda. Taking this in my hand, and forgetting fever, I staggered quickly along the path with two or three of my men, and fortunately encountered the chief. The sight of the six barrels gaping into his stomach, with my own ghastly visage looking daggers at his face, seemed to produce an instant revolution in his martial feelings, for he cried out, "Oh! I have only come to speak to you, and wish peace only." Mashauana [Livingstone's body-servant] had hold of him by the hand, and found him shaking. We examined his gun, and found that it had been discharged. Both parties crowded up to their chiefs. One of the opposite party coming too near, one of mine drove him back with a battle-axe. The enemy protested their amicable intentions, and my men asserted the fact of having the goods knocked down as evidence of the contrary. Without waiting long, I requested all to sit down, and Pitsane, placing his hand upon the revolver, somewhat allayed their fears. I then said to the chief, "If you have come with peaceable intentions, we have no other; go away home to your village." He replied, "I am afraid lest you shoot me in the back." I rejoined, "If I wanted to kill you, I could shoot you in the face as well." Mosantu called out to me, "That's only a Makalaka trick; don't give him your back." But I said, "Tell him to observe that I am not afraid of him"; and, turning, mounted my ox. There was not much danger in the fire that was opened at first, there being so many trees. The enemy probably expected that the sudden attack would make us forsake our goods, and allow them to plunder with ease. The villagers were no doubt pleased with being allowed to retire unscathed, and we were also glad to get away without having shed a drop of blood or having compromised ourselves for any future visit. My men were delighted with their own bravery, and made the woods ring with telling each other how "brilliant their conduct before the enemy" would have been had hostilities not been brought to a sudden close.

I do not mention this little skirmish as a very frightful affair. The negro character in these parts and in Angola is essentially cowardly, except when influenced by success. A partial triumph over any body of men would induce the whole country to rise in arms, and this is the chief danger to be feared. These petty chiefs have individually but little power, and with my men, now armed with guns, I could have easily beaten them off singly; but, being of the same family, they would readily unite in vast numbers, if incited by prospects of successful plunder. They are by no means equal to Cape Kaffres in any respect whatever.[3]

The fearlessness exhibited by Livingstone on this occasion was one of his most distinguishing characteristics, as Sir John Kirk and other comrades of his later travels have pointed out. Few even of the bravest men can pass through similar perilous scenes without sign of trepidation or at least of taut nerves, but the testimony of all who ever saw Livingstone in danger of his life is that he was more than cool and collected; so far as a spectator could judge, he was quite indifferent; his pulse beat no faster; he knew no tremors. That this quality of his nature helped him in dealing with savages, as it would with animals, is certain. On the other hand, his equally extraordinary forbearance and abstention from giving provocation to the inhabitants of the territories through which he passed gained him a good name which permeated everywhere. Over many hundreds of miles of Africa which he never visited his reputation went and smoothed the way for others, a fact which at one time slave-traders were not slow to take advantage of, as we shall have to note when we come to the record of his

[3] *Missionary Travels*, p. 445 f.

explorations in the Nyassa region. To this day connection with Livingstone is an open passport through the heart of Africa.

On only one other occasion on the homeward journey to Linyanti was there any serious unpleasantness with a native chief, and this preceded the passage of the Kasai river some distance from the ford where the party had crossed on the outward journey. A detour had been made for the purpose of obtaining a better supply of provisions than on the route formerly followed, and this led to the village of a chief named Kawawa, who presumably had not heard of Livingstone previously or only vaguely. This personage was friendly enough at first, but later became truculent in his demands for payment for according permission to pass through his land. Hearing that the traveller had been forced to give an ox to the Chiboque, he insisted on a still higher price; he must have not only an ox but a gun, ammunition, and a black robe (the missionary's rug) which he had seen hung out to dry; in default of an ox he must have a man.

Kawawa had been infected with the slave-dealer's cupidity, owing to the influence of half-caste Portuguese traders of whom he was a regular customer. An unpleasant example of his tyrannical methods in this connection was exhibited in Livingstone's presence. A poor man and his wife were accused of witchcraft and brought before the chief, the charge probably originating with the chief himself. Kawawa condemned them unheard, telling them that as they had deprived him of a tribesman by their enchantments, they must bring all their children to him and let him choose one or more as substitutes. He showed himself unable to believe that the white visitor had any real objection to striking a bargain involving the sale of a human being into bondage in this manner, and acted throughout on the assumption that Livingstone's purpose in coming there was the same as that of the half-castes —namely, to buy slaves and pay the usual commission for facilities in so doing.

This invincible scepticism led to conflict. With cool effrontery the chief sent to say that he had inspected all the goods in the white man's camp and meant to exact his full price or prevent the party from leaving; this he could do easily, he added, because he had control of the banks of the Kasai, and would neither furnish canoes for crossing nor allow others to do so.

Livingstone's reply was a calm defiance; he would neither submit to the exactions nor remain where he was; he would cross the Kasai in spite of the embargo. Kawawa thereupon ordered his people to arm, and, on their rushing hastily to obey, Livingstone's company became excited and bellicose. Prompt action was necessary if an encounter were to be avoided, so Livingstone gave the word to march, and forbade his men to fire unless Kawawa's warriors struck the first blow. Apprehensive of an attack in their rear, and resentful of Kawawa's manœuvres, some of the missionary's party did not respond to his command with their usual celerity, and matters reached a crisis. Here again Livingstone's own narrative gives a vivid and succinct description of the scene:

I took the lead, and expected them all to follow, as they usually had done, but many of my men remained behind. When I knew this, I jumped off the ox, and made a rush to them with the revolver in my hand. Kawawa ran away amongst his people, and they turned their backs too. I shouted to my men to take up their luggage and march; some did so with alacrity, feeling that they had disobeyed orders by remaining, but one of them refused, and was preparing to fire at Kawawa, until I gave him a punch on the head with the pistol and made him go too. I felt here, as elsewhere, that subordination must be maintained at all risks. We all moved into the forest, the people of Kawawa standing about a hundred yards off, gazing, but not firing a shot or an arrow. It is extremely unpleasant to part with these chieftains thus, after spending a day or two in the most amicable intercourse, and in a part where the people are generally civil. This Kawawa, however, is not a good specimen of the Balonda chiefs, and is rather notorious in the neighbourhood for his folly. We were told that he has good reason to believe that Matiamvo (his suzerain) will some day cut off his head for his disregard of the rights of strangers.

Kawawa was not to be balked of his supposed rights by the unceremonious way in which we had left him, for, when we had reached the ford of the Kasai, about ten miles distant, we found that he had sent four of his men with orders to the ferrymen to refuse us passage. We were here duly informed that we must deliver up all the articles mentioned and one of our men besides. This demand for one of our number always nettled every heart. The canoes were taken away before our eyes, and we were supposed to be quite helpless without them at a river a good hundred yards broad and very deep. Pitsane stood on the bank, gazing with apparent indifference on the stream, and made an accurate observation of where the canoes were hidden among the reeds. The ferrymen casually asked one of my Batoka if they had rivers in his country, and he answered with truth, "No, we have none." Kawawa's people then felt sure we could not cross. I thought of swimming when they were gone; but after it was dark, by the unasked loan of one of the hidden canoes, we soon were snug in our bivouac on the southern bank of the Kasai. I left some beads as payment for some meal which had been presented by the ferry-men; and the canoe having been left on their own side of the river, Pitsane and his companions laughed uproariously at the disgust our enemies would feel, and their perplexity as to who had been our paddler across. They were quite sure that Kawawa would imagine that we had been ferried over by his own people, and would be divin-ing who had done the deed. When (we were) ready to depart in the morning, Kawawa's people appeared on the opposite heights, and could scarcely believe their eyes when they saw us prepared to start away to the south. At last one of them called out, "Ah! ye are bad." To which Pitsane and his companions retorted, "Ah! ye are good; and we thank you for the loan of your canoe." We were careful to explain the whole of the circumstances to Katema and the other chiefs, and they all agreed that we were perfectly justifiable under the circumstances, and that Matiamvo would approve our conduct. When anything that might bear an unfavourable construction hap-pens among themselves they send explanations to each other. The mere fact of doing so prevents them from losing their character, for there is public opinion even amongst them.[4]

With these exceptions, no grave hindrances from native chiefs were experienced at any stage of the journey to Linyanti, though, as we shall

[4] *Missionary Travels*, p. 469 f.

have occasion to note in its place, more than one of a similar kind had to be reckoned with afterwards on the way to the east coast. Dangers and painful visitations of another sort are chronicled from time to time, such as a fierce onslaught by carnivorous red ants, which seemed determined to devour the missionary alive. Obnoxious creatures of various kinds, insects, reptiles, and beasts of prey, had to be guarded against constantly, especially at night. Alligators and leeches abounded in the swampy stretches through which the marchers had to swim or wade. At one point Livingstone had a narrow escape from a charging buffalo, the most vicious and implacable of herbivorous animals; at another, in the Makololo country itself, a female hippopotamus upset the canoe in which he was passing down the Zambesi (here called the Leeambye), and tossed him and his paddlers into the water, whence they only escaped by diving and keeping away from the infuriated beast, which, as is well known, is not quick-sighted. An earlier mishap detained the party for some days. In the forest near Cabango a branch of a tree, released with some force, struck Livingstone a severe blow on one of his eyes, virtually blinding him for a time, and causing troublesome inflammation and swelling from the concussion. The consequent delay he employed, in his usual Spartan manner, in preparing a sketch of the country to be sent back to Mr. Gabriel for transmission from Loanda to England.

Libonta was reached on July 27th, 1854, and thenceforward the company moved in triumphal procession. Everywhere they were received with the liveliest expressions of delight and admiration. The people streamed forth to meet them, dancing, shouting, singing, and manifesting in many extravagant ways their surprise and gratification at seeing them again alive, for they had long been given up as dead. Livingstone's original twenty-seven bearers were saluted as heroes and persons of renown, and evidently felt themselves to be such. Most of their own personal possessions were gone; the goods with which they had started from Loanda had gradually been bartered *en route* for food and transport facilities; but they had somehow managed to keep their European finery supplied by Mr. Gabriel, and this they now donned to impress their compatriots, which it certainly did. They

strutted and posed like the big children they were, doing their best
to imitate the walk of the soldiers they had seen in Loanda, carrying
their guns over their shoulders with a great air of dignity and self-
importance which made their leader smile. At the public reception
in Libonta, Livingstone asked that the following day might be set
apart as a day of thanksgiving and praise to God for the safe return
of all the men he had taken with him on the long and perilous tramp
to the ocean and back, and for their deliverance from so many ills.
The request was agreed to, and the missionary held service and
preached. Other similar services followed almost daily, and it is not
too much to say that Livingstone's own hope and belief, as expressed
in his Journal, that the hold he had now gained on the mind of the
Barotse and Makololo tribes would win a hearing for further and
permanent missionary effort in the same districts have been fully
justified by subsequent events. After a mournful set-back, to be
described in a later chapter, and the break-up of the Makololo power,
the tide of the Christian evangel began to flow from several different
directions into the valley of the upper Zambesi, never to recede again.
The Paris Missionary Society, the Primitive Methodists, the Brethren's
Mission, and the representatives of the Methodist Episcopal Church of
America have all established themselves in these vast districts and
changed the entire character of the life of the communities inhabiting
them.

Great was the rejoicing at Linyanti when the party, augmented by
numerous camp followers and voluntary helpers, reached the town.
Every Barotse village on the route furnished them lavishly with provisions and entertained them without stint, so that they arrived in
better fettle than they had been in for many a day. They had been
almost twelve months on the road from Loanda, though even this
slow rate of travelling was much quicker than that attempted by
ordinary traders in the same roadless regions. The whole tribe was
now assembled by proclamation to hear the report of their adventures
and receive the presents and messages sent by the Governor and merchants of Loanda. Livingstone gave his men full opportunity of
relating their exploits in public, and pawky remarks like these lost

nothing in the telling! Sekeletu was particularly pleased with his Colonel's uniform, and appeared in it at Christian worship on the following Sunday, to the exclusion of all interest in the sermon.

Livingstone was surprised and gratified to find that the two horses he had left behind when starting for Loanda had not suffered from the tsetse fly, and measures were afterwards taken with success to introduce the breed in the entire valley of the upper Zambesi. He was still more pleased to find his waggon and stores intact. A consignment of goods sent by Moffat some months previously had also been carefully preserved on an island in the middle of the river and sheltered from the elements. These goods had been entrusted by Moffat to Mosilekatse, the great Chief of the Matebele, who scrupulously forwarded them by the hands of some of his warriors. The latter conveyed them to the south bank of the Zambesi, and called to the Makololo to come over and fetch them. Asked to particularize further, they shouted that the goods were sent by Umtjete (Moffat) to Nake (Livingstone). "Begone," cried the incredulous Makololo, who, not without reason, distrusted Matebele messengers—"you cannot fool us so easily; how could Nake tell Umtjete to send his things here, he himself having gone away to the north?" "Very well," was the reply: "here are the goods; we place them now before you, and if you leave them to perish, the guilt will be yours." The Matebele then went off, and after waiting some time to make sure no trickery was being attempted, the Makololo crossed and took possession of the packages.

Livingstone now eagerly opened them, and was greatly comforted to learn from the contents how solicitously Dr. and Mrs. Moffat had thought of his needs. A good supply of clothing had been sent, most of the undergarments having been made by Mrs. Moffat's own motherly hands, and there was also a quantity of home-made preserves and of tea and coffee. One can imagine how a man so long unaccustomed to such fare would be gladdened by the sight and taste of it.

From the letters and papers enclosed he learned that Sir Roderick Murchison, in an address to the Royal Geographical Society, had advanced the theory that the interior of Africa was of saucer-like formation. Livingstone was slightly chagrined at the news, as he had meant to put forward the same view himself, with observed topographical data to support it, but solaced himself with the reflection that his own discoveries had assisted Sir Roderick to arrive at the conclusion. Sir H. H. Johnston does not agree that the description is very exact, and holds that in the light of fuller knowledge it requires to be carefully modified.[5]

It might naturally be inferred that after a strain so prolonged and severe, and involving so much in the way of persistent ill-health, the persevering pathfinder would now be content to make his way down to Kuruman and recruit in the home of his loyal and kindly father- and mother-in-law. The idea does not seem to have entered his mind. He did not consider that his work was finished; the trail he had blazed, though a possible one for future commercial development, was too lengthy and difficult to afford ready access to the immense areas he had been the first white man to enter. Moreover, he had now viewed with his own eyes the magnificent waterways provided by the Zambesi and its tributaries, and he longed to discover how far and how usefully these might be navigable. Arab traders from Zanzibar met him at Linyanti and told him that a practicable route existed towards the east coast—not wholly by the river, however. He therefore decided to explore possibilities in this direction, but by following the Zambesi as far as he could with a view to ascertaining whether its lower reaches were as serviceable as the upper for the transportation of merchandise.

To this end, after resting for a couple of months, he made a fresh start in November, 1855. There was no difficulty in obtaining volunteers now for the expedition. Sekeletu readily furnished him with everything needful for sustenance and for exchange of commodities on the road—twelve oxen (three of them for riding), butter, honey, meal, beads to pay for transit franchises, and the like. Livingstone gratefully records that he was entirely dependent upon the chief's bounty for the means of carrying out his new programme, for he had nothing of his own left. Nothing is more astonishing in the whole course of the great traveller's achievements than the fact that so large a proportion of his resources was derived from native generosity. He took a much

---

[5] *Livingstone and the Exploration of Central Africa*, p. 179.

larger party with him this time; instead of twenty-seven Makololo, he now had a train of nearly two hundred, all enlisted by the orders of Sekeletu. The chief himself accompanied his guest as far as Sesheke, and treated him not only with courtesy but affection. One little incident during this preliminary march greatly touched the missionary. A storm coming up in the night—mingled lightning, wind, and rain—and the baggage having gone on in advance, Livingstone was obliged to lie down unprotected and try to sleep on the wet earth. Sekeletu rose quietly and covered the shivering man with his own cloak, remaining for the rest of the night without any wrap for himself. "If such men must perish by the advance of civilization," is Livingstone's comment on the unselfish action, "as certain races of animals do before others, it is a pity. God grant that ere this time comes they may receive that gospel which is a solace for the soul in death!" [6]

The incident is the more striking because the missionary had earnestly rebuked the chief for making unprovoked raids against neighbouring tribes, and had denounced in the strongest terms the abominations of slavery, particularly the selling of children away from their parents.

Livingstone's appreciation of the treatment accorded to him at all times by the Makololo tribesmen—including the Barotse and Balonda people, particularly the former—is emphatic. "I felt, and still feel, most deeply grateful, and tried to benefit them in the only way I could, by imparting the knowledge of that Saviour who can comfort and supply them in the time of need, and my prayer is that he may send his good spirit to instruct them and lead them into His kingdom." [7] His personal servant on the journey to and from Loanda, Mashauana, invariably made his own bed at Livingstone's feet, so as to be on hand should his master need anything in the night. "Never on any occasion did I have to call him twice," [8] is the latter's laconic encomium on this unforced devotion. Poor Mashauana, in common

[6] A letter to Thompson (October, 1856) mentions the theft of this cloak, and deplores the loss for sentimental reasons.
[7] *Missionary Travels*, p. 493.
[8] *Ibid.*, p. 430.

with some of his fellow-adventurers of the expedition, found on his
return home after nearly two years' absence that his wife, presuming
herself a widow, had married again. As most of the members of the
party had several wives, Livingstone's answer to their complaint of this
marital inconstancy was that they still had more wives than he. Very
different was the state of things years afterwards when he brought
back, according to promise, the survivors of the expedition now starting
for the east coast. Warned by the too hasty re-marriages that had
taken place during the Loanda expedition, the chief forbade fresh
alliances of the sort unless positive information were forthcoming
from Livingstone himself of the death of the husbands.

Within a few days after leaving Sesheke the party came to the
Victoria Falls, of which Livingstone had repeatedly heard from the
natives. The native name, Mosioatunya, Livingstone replaced in his
maps by that of the Queen of England, the first but not the last time
on which he was to give a European name to an African feature.
Recognizing the importance of the discovery, and feeling a natural
elation at the fact that he was the first white man to make acquaintance with what is now regarded as one of the wonders of the world,
he took pains to inspect it as carefully as his time and defective
apparatus permitted. In keeping with his careful accuracy and avoid-
ance of exaggeration, he formed for the time being only a provisional
estimate of the depth and volume of the Falls. On his return to the
spot in August, 1860, he was able to make more exact measurements,
which confirmed him in the opinion he had previously formed that
they were the largest and most magnificent as well as the most picturesque yet known. They have been so fully described by subsequent
travellers that their main features are now familiar to the public, but
Livingstone's first impressions of them are still worth recalling:

No one can imagine the beauty of the view from anything witnessed in England. It had never been seen before by European
eyes; but scenes so lovely must have been gazed upon by angels in
their flight. The only want felt is that of mountains in the background. The Falls are bounded on three sides by ridges 300 or 400

feet in height, which are covered with forest, with the red soil appearing among the trees. When about half a mile from the Falls, I left the canoe by which we had come down thus far, and embarked in a lighter one, with men well acquainted with the rapids, who, by passing down the centre of the stream in the eddies and still places caused by many jutting rocks, brought me to an island situated in the middle of the river, and on the edge of the lip over which the water rolls. In coming hither, there was danger of being swept down by the streams which rushed along on each side of the island; but the river was now low, and we sailed where it is totally impossible to go when the water is high. But though we had reached the island, and were within a few yards of the spot a view from which would solve the whole problem, I believe that no one could perceive where the vast body of water went; it seemed to lose itself in the earth, the opposite lip of the fissure into which it disappeared being only 80 feet distant. At least, I did not comprehend it until, creeping with awe to the verge, I peered down into a large rent which had been made from bank to bank of the broad Zambesi, and saw that a stream of a thousand yards broad leaped down a hundred feet and then became suddenly compressed into a space of fifteen or twenty yards. The entire Falls are simply a crack made in a hard basaltic rock from the right to the left bank of the Zambesi, and then prolonged from the left bank away through thirty or forty miles of hills.

.   .   .   .

I write in the hope that others more capable of judging distances than myself will visit this scene, and I state simply the impressions made on my mind at the time. I thought, and do still think, the river above the Falls to be one thousand yards broad; but I am a poor judge of distances on water, for I showed a naval friend what I supposed to be four hundred yards in the bay of Loanda, and, to my surprise, he pronounced it to be nine hundred. I tried to measure the Leeambye with a strong thread, the only line I had in my possession, but when the men had gone two or three hundred yards they got into conversation and did not hear us shouting that the line had become entangled. By still going on they broke it, and, being carried away down the stream, it was lost on a snag. In vain I tried to bring to my recollection the way I had been taught to measure a river, by taking an angle with the sextant. That I once knew it, and that it was easy, were all the lost ideas I could recall, and they only increased my vexation. However, I measured the river farther down by another plan, and then I discovered that the Portuguese had measured it at Tete and found it a little over one thousand yards. At the Falls it is as broad as at Tete, if not more so. Whoever may come after me will not, I trust, find reason to say I have indulged in exaggeration.

Before leaving the locality, Livingstone paid a second visit to the island and laid out a little garden there, and planted some fruit and coffee seeds in the hope that the warm moisture from the abyss would nourish them to maturity. This done, he cut his own initials on a tree, together with the date, the only instance, as he says, of his ever indulging in this piece of vanity—more than pardonable in the circumstances. His fear that hippopotami would trample down his little enclosure proved to be only too well grounded, for on his next visit to the scene five years later he found that these animals had destroyed his plantation. The initials remained, but at the present time it is reported that they, too, have vanished, like all things earthly, with the passing of time.

The party now turned away from the Zambesi, following a more north-easterly route through the country of the Batoka tribe. The scenery was glorious and the climate salubrious, but the slave trade had cast an evil spell upon it. Everywhere the harassed people regarded the white man with suspicion until assured of his peaceful intentions; more than once they threatened violence. A frenzied fellow at the first village near which camp was made for the night walked around Livingstone howling, with a battle-axe in his hand, which he shook rather too near to the missionary's head. After enduring the unpleasant demonstration for a time, Livingstone beckoned to the headman of the village and requested him to remove the ruffian. The order was obeyed, and it is amusingly in keeping with Livingstone's character that he should naïvely inform us in his report of the occurrence that he wanted to feel the dangerous threatener's pulse to ascertain how rapidly it was beating, and thus judge whether his ravings were real or simulated; but for the proximity of the battle-axe, the physiological experiment would have been performed. Sekwebu, the faithful and capable head of the escort appointed by Sekeletu, overheard some of the rest of the warriors of this Batoka village counting the numbers of the Makololo and gleefully concluding that they were few enough to be an easy prey. Warned by this token of inimical feeling, the party slept under arms in expectation of a night attack, but managed to get away in the morning without fighting. Here, as everywhere else, Livingstone did not leave without first endeavouring to instil into the minds of the savage population the idea that he represented a mighty people who held the slave trade in abhorrence, and wished all the African tribes to live at peace with each other; nor did he ever lose an opportunity of telling the story of the coming of the Son of God into the world with the message of divine love. The news never failed to produce an impression for good, chiefly because of the bitter experience the hearers had of the dire effects of chronic strife. "We are tired of flight; give us rest and sleep," was their invariable plea in response to the missionary's words of friendliness and hope.

The route now taken led across the Kafue river, a tributary of the Zambesi, whence a course was kept parallel with the left bank of the latter to its junction with the Loangwa. The reception accorded to the party at every stopping-place was cordial, save in one or two instances as they neared the Portuguese frontier. Mburuma the petty chief of a village near the border, sent polite salutations to Livingstone, but was not unjustly suspected of meditating treachery at the crossing of the river. Only one canoe was lent, although others were seen moored at a little distance, and the banks held were by armed men. An entry in the Journal on January 14th, 1856, reveals something of the legitimate apprehensions felt by Livingstone as to the possibility of a tragical termination of his toils:

Evening—felt much turmoil of spirit in view of having all my plans for the welfare of this great region and teeming population knocked on the head by savages to-morrow. But I read that Jesus said, "All power is given unto me in heaven and earth, go ye therefore and teach all nations . . . and lo! I am with you alway, even unto the end of the world." It is the word of a gentleman of most sacred and strictest honour, and there's an end on't. I will not cross furtively by night as I had intended. It would appear as flight, and shall such a man as I flee! Nay, verily, I will take observations for latitude and longitude to-night, though they may be the last.

The one canoe was used to transport both men and baggage to the eastern side of the Loangwa, and though the process was a protracted one, involving many trips and exposing the party to the danger of attack in its divided state, the object was safely accomplished in the end. Livingstone, with his usual unperturbed intrepidity, was the last to embark, remaining on the western bank keeping Mburuma's people amused by showing them his watch, using his telescope lens as a burning glass, and other devices till his men were all safely over. Then, smiling upon his auditors, and expressing a parting wish for their peace and tranquillity, he bade them farewell and was paddled away amid utter quietude. The critical hour had passed.

Zumbo, the farthest outpost of Portuguese influence, was reached the next day, but was found to have been abandoned by its garrison. It has since been reoccupied. In this centre, as in Angola, Livingstone was impressed by the remains of a former Roman Catholic missionary establishment, and viewed with melancholy the relapse into heathenism which had followed the abandonment of Christian propaganda; no trace of permanent good effect could be detected, though a better site than Zumbo, both for missionary work and commercial purposes, could not have been chosen.[9]

At Mpende's village, which they reached several days later, the party encountered the last opposition which was to menace it on the journey. Camp was made to the accompaniment of murderous yells

[9] On p. 764 of the Journal is the entry: "The Governor (of Tete) says frankly that the cause of the decay of this Colony is undoubtedly the slave trade, which withdrew the attention of the colonist from agriculture; and every other branch of industry—cotton, indigo, wheat, coffee, even gold—was neglected for the gambling gains of the hateful traffic. And the ill-will of the natives was engendered as well."

from bodies of armed natives half-hidden in the vegetation around; when three of Livingstone's men went to the village to buy food, they were jeered at and presented with handfuls of chaff. As conflict seemed unavoidable, he directed that an ox should be slaughtered and his men given a good meal to fight on. Tatterdemalions as they were after their long tramp, they were yet more than a match for Mpende's disorderly rabble, and, remarks Livingstone, "had Mpende struck the first blow, he would soon have found out that he never made a greater mistake in his life." [10]

The difficulty was got over by Livingstone showing his hair and the white skin of his breast to some of the villagers whom he induced to approach, thus satisfying them that he was not a Portuguese half-caste. "Ah," was the verdict, "you must belong to the tribe that loves the black men." [11] Mpende then consented to have the party ferried to the south bank of the Zambesi, where a guide was obtained to lead them by a south-easterly track to Tete, avoiding the Kebrabasa rapids, with which Livingstone was to wrestle vainly in years to come.

Here, as in Angola, he received a generous welcome. Major Sicard, the Portuguese commandant, proved to be as good a friend as Lieutenant Canto, Captain Neves, and Colonel Pires had severally done, and insisted on entertaining him at Tete for six weeks until the season should be more healthy on the coast. Arrangements were made for the missionary's Makololo attendants to settle at Tete while their master proceeded to Quilimane and sailed thence for home, the kindly, commandant undertaking to assign them a sufficient amount of land to build homes on and cultivate for their maintenance. The promise was honourably kept to the letter.[12] Livingstone took leave of them on April 23rd, bidding them have confidence that he would return and lead them back to their own land, and, accompanied by eight of their number only, proceeded down stream by launch to the port, every facility being provided by Major Sicard.

He arrived at Quilimane on May 20th, and was at once received with

[10] *Missionary Travels*, p. 592.
[11] *Ibid.*, p. 593.
[12] Though the subsequent undertaking of the Portuguese Government to promote their interests was not fulfilled.

every mark of consideration and respect. Word had come previously both from London and Lisbon that he was on the way, but the news had not been credited; now he was informed that a British brig of war, the *Frolic,* had put in at Quilimane in November to inquire if anything had been heard of him. The sad news was also imparted that a smaller vessel, H.M.S. *Dart,* had called at Quilimane on the same errand, and been wrecked on the bar, with the loss of the Commander and Lieutenant and five seamen; Livingstone was greatly distressed by the tragedy, of which he felt in a measure the cause. As the *Frolic* had gone away again he was detained no less than six weeks on the fever-laden coast, a delay which nullified Major Sicard's well-meant precautions, but which the traveller turned to good account by revising his Journals and writing out his observations. He had heard nothing of his family for three years. Many letters had been sent to him during the period, but only one of these had reached him. Now, to his great joy, a letter from Admiral Trotter, accompanied by some other gifts, which had been left for him with the Commandant, informed him that they were all well. His host, Colonel Nunes, treated him with the same warm-hearted solicitude as all the other Portuguese administrators whom he had met hitherto, and placed him under deep obligation. Livingstone had brought a quantity of ivory from the interior, the gift of Sekeletu, and this he now entrusted to the Colonel for the benefit of his men in case of his own death. The arrangement was explained to the eight Makololo who had accompanied him to the coast, whereupon they replied: "Nay, father, you will not die; you will return to take us back to Sekeletu." They undertook to await his coming, and he on his part assured them that nothing but death would prevent the fulfilment of his compact to rejoin them and lead them home.

The *Frolic* at length reappeared, bringing all needful supplies to Livingstone for the voyage to England, including £150 in money sent by the L.M.S. through Thompson at Cape Town. The gifts were accompanied by a letter from the Society, written by Tidman, stating that the directors "were restricted in their power of aiding plans connected only remotely with the spread of the Gospel, and that the financial circumstances of the Society were not such as to afford any ground of hope that it would be in a position, within any definite period, to enter upon untried, remote, and difficult fields of labour."[13] The tenour of the statement was misunderstood by Livingstone, and the wording wounded him deeply, but as the subject of his subsequent relations with the L.M.S. is one of some importance requiring fuller exposition than it has yet received it can best be considered in the next chapter in connection with developments in England. His own attitude on the question cannot be more felicitously expressed than by an entry in his Journal, repeated by him both in *Missionary Travels* and in his private correspondence: "I view the end of the geographical feat as the beginning of the missionary enterprise."[14] By some strange oversight Blaikie, in the authorized biography of the great explorer, omits the word "missionary," thus missing the main point of the declaration. Livingstone always thought of himself as a missionary first and last, and of his explorations as having meaning and value principally because of their bearing on the spread of the Gospel. He believed intensely that he had been divinely chosen for this special work, and providentially led and guided at every crisis in the prosecution thereof, and it was this conviction that sustained him in the face of almost incredible difficulties and enabled him to bring his plans to a successful issue.

Sekwebu, his loyal and capable second in command on the journey from Linyanti, begged hard to be allowed to accompany his master to England, and with some hesitation the latter granted permission. They sailed together on the *Frolic* to Mauritius on July 12th, but seas were rough and the scenes new and strange to poor Sekwebu's primitive imagination, with the eventual result that he lost his reason and jumped overboard and was drowned, to Livingstone's great sorrow.

This was the last of his troubles in the long series of events that had taken place since he parted with his family four years and a half earlier. By the liberality of the P. and O. Shipping Company he was accorded a free passage to Marseilles, and reached London via Paris and Dover on December 9th, 1856.

[13] L.M.S. archives.
[14] *Missionary Travels*, p. 673; *cf.* Blaikie, *op. cit.*, p. 159.

CHAPTER IX

RECEPTION AT HOME

It was owing to an accident to the ship by which he crossed the Mediterranean that Livingstone landed at Dover instead of Southampton, where Mrs. Livingstone and a large number of friends were waiting to welcome him, so on reaching London the first thing he did was to rush down by train to Southampton to greet his wife and receive the congratulations of his well-wishers there. Nothing astonished him more than to find himself a celebrity; the whole country was ringing with his name. He knew he had done work that would have profound and lasting consequences for good, but he had not anticipated the effect it would produce on the imagination of his contemporaries throughout the civilized world. He had left Loanda in September, 1854, without learning or apparently suspecting that the feat he had accomplished in making his way thither from Cape Town had been acclaimed as a prodigy of endurance and scientific utility; now a still higher achievement stood to his credit, and appetite for details had been rapidly mounting from the moment that tidings of his audacious march through the uncharted wilds of Africa became known.

The first public demonstration in his honour was made at Cape Town, a fact which should not be lost sight of when recalling the scurvy treatment to which he had been subjected there when starting on his great tramp four years before. The change of opinion was overwhelming and found full expression. Sir George Grey, the Governor, presided and spoke first at a great gathering wherein appreciative tributes were paid to Livingstone by various representative men. Sir George said with a prescience the more remarkable because it was the first note struck in a world-wide chorus of approval:

I think no man of the present day is more deserving of honour than Dr. Livingston [1]—a man whom we, indeed, can hardly regard

[1] As the name was still spelt by the public.

as belonging to any particular age or time, but who belongs rather to the whole Christian epoch, possessing all those great qualities of mind and that resolute desire at all risks to spread the Gospel, which we have been generally in the habit of attributing solely to those who lived in the first ages of the Christian era. Indeed, that man must be regarded as almost of apostolic character who, animated by a desire of performing his duty to his Maker and to his fellow-men, has performed journeys which we cannot but regard as altogether marvellous.

The inhabitants of this Colony owe him a double debt—first for what he has accomplished, and secondly, and I think this is the greater debt of the two, for having shown us what great things may be accomplished by a man actuated by the purest and noblest motives.

You will show the rising generation that it is impossible for noble exertions to be made without the whole community coming forward to testify its admiration.

The Hon. Rawson W. Rawson, Colonial Secretary, moved a resolution which was carried in the following terms: "That the eminent services of the Rev. Dr. Livingston, in the promotion of geographical and general science, during his recent heroic journey from the Western to the Eastern Coast of the African continent, which has earned for him the applause and gratitude of the civilized world, merit a special recognition from the inhabitants of this Colony and of the neighbouring States, who have for many years witnessed his energetic labours in the cause of science and of religion."

In the course of his speech commending this resolution to the meeting the mover said: "I am convinced that Livingston's name will live amongst the first heroes and the first benefactors of our race."

None of those present and taking part in the gathering could speak with more authority from special knowledge than the Astronomer Royal, Thomas Maclear, who gave warm praise not only to Livingstone's aptitude as a pupil—for it will be remembered that Maclear had generously given him lessons in taking observations when the explorer was getting ready for his daring venture in 1852—but to the precision with which his valuable finds had been recorded and described. Livingstone had been in the habit of sending to his former instructor such reports as he could of his topographical and other discoveries, and these had been carefully checked by Maclear before publication.

Only one other speaker could lay claim to the same intimacy with Livingstone that Maclear possessed; this was William Thompson, the L.M.S. representative, and his testimony was no less definite:

> I am in a position to express my earnest conviction, formed on long, intimate, unreserved communications with him, personally and by letter, that he has not been actuated by mere curiosity, or the love of adventure, or the thirst of applause, or by any other object less than his avowed one as a messenger of Christian love from the churches, in the privations, sufferings, and dangers he has passed through during the last eight years. If ever there was a man who, realizing the obligations of his sacred calling as a Christian missionary, and intelligently comprehending its object, sought to pursue it to a successful issue, such a man is Dr. Livingston. . . . Whilst so much has been achieved, probably more than by any former explorer, Dr. Livingston's arduous journeys have been carried on unostentatiously, and at the greatest possible economy of means.

The Bishop of Cape Town stressed Livingstone's probable influence in bringing the Spirit of Christ to bear upon regions hitherto afflicted by the twin blights of superstition and slavery. No contribution to scientific knowledge, he said, could compare in beneficence with a blessing so inestimable.

In Great Britain, almost from the moment of landing, he became a focus of national interest and enthusiasm. Within a week of his return to London from Southampton a special meeting of the Royal Geographical Society was convened (December 15th) to welcome him and congratulate him on his achievements. Sir Roderick Murchison presided, and among those present were Mr. Oswell and Colonel Steele, former fellow-travellers of the explorer whose work had now so far transcended the initial endeavours in which they had shared. Professor Owen also attended and warmly seconded the eulogy paid by the chairman to the unparalleled worth of the contributions made by Livingstone to scientific knowledge in the various departments over which his observation had extended. All the speakers acknowledged that they were deeply impressed by the meticulous care and precision wherewith his discoveries had been recorded and made available; it was felt, and rightly, that this exactitude of description and classification was in itself sufficient to entitle Livingstone to a place among the foremost contributors to the world's progress.

He was made a Fellow of the Royal Society a year later, but had left England before his formal admission took place, and consequently did not sign the Charter Book till May 4th, 1865, on his second and final visit home. The manner of his admission was exceptional in that his Certificate of Candidature was signed "Carlisle, P.R." (*Pro Regina*), and that all the other signatories signed with amplifications; the signature following that of the president is "H. Lloyd, Pres. Brit. Assoc." [2] This form of certificate must be almost unique, if not entirely so, and was the Society's way of marking its sense of the special distinction attaching to Livingstone's work, not only, or perhaps chiefly, as a geographer, but as a pioneer in new departments of botany, zoology, and palæontology. These are facts which should not be lost sight of in forming a true estimate of the abiding significance of the additions made by Livingstone to the sum of human knowledge, though it is manifestly impossible to take account of them adequately in a work like the present.

On the day following his reception by the Royal Geographical Society a meeting was held under the auspices of the London Missionary Society in Freemasons' Hall to give him fraternal greeting. Lord Shaftesbury was in the chair, and gave felicitous expression to the gladness and thankfulness wherewith the representatives of an organization which existed solely to spread the Gospel of Jesus Christ to the ends of the earth viewed the astonishing exertions of one of its own accredited agents among the peoples of heathen Africa. In his reply Livingstone was equally appreciative of his connection with the Society and the facilities the directors had afforded him in carrying out what he

[2] The information is furnished by courtesy of the present secretary of the Royal Society in a letter dated January 2nd, 1929.

felt to be a divinely appointed work. No pledges as to the future were given on either side at the time; the assemblage was public, and there was much to discuss with the directors in private before deciding on any important new departure affecting either the missionary himself or the policy to be adopted in respect of the vast territories and numerous populations he had been the means of bringing into touch with Europe.

Concerning Livingstone's relations with the L.M.S. now and later two impressions need correcting: First, that the Society was not willing to follow up his exploratory work; and, secondly, that, to use Blaikie's words, the directors "would have been delighted to let Livingstone work in their service in his own way." [3] Both statements go beyond the facts.

Tidman's communication, to which reference has already been made as having disturbed Livingstone somewhat when it reached him at Quilimane, was not intended to bear the construction which he oversensitively placed upon it, though it might perhaps have been more happily phrased in view of the tremendous task he had accomplished. It is a long letter of six foolscap pages, and dated August 24th, 1855, one copy being sent to Quilimane and another to St. Paul de Loanda. The first three pages consist of an admiring review of Livingstone's unprecedented exploits as a waymaker in lands hitherto untouched by the influence of the Gospel, and gives the information that the writer had received on the explorer's behalf the Gold Medal of the Royal Geographical Society, which was retained at the L.M.S. headquarters pending his arrival to claim it. Then follows the paragraph, part of which has been already quoted in Livingstone's own version, but it should be noted that the words which appear to have hurt him were elaborately and sympathetically qualified. *In extenso* it reads:

> The directors, while yielding to none in their appreciation of the objects upon which for some years past your energies have been concentrated, or in admiration of the zeal, intrepidity and success with which they have been carried out, are nevertheless restricted in their power of aiding plans connected only remotely with the spread of

[3] *Op. cit.,* p. 192.

DAVID LIVINGSTONE IN CONSULAR DRESS
AFTER 1855

the Gospel. Of the important bearing of your researches upon the interests, not only of science, but of general humanity, we have the most entire confidence, and we would also cherish the hope and belief that they will ultimately tend to the diffusion of Christian truth among the populous but yet uncivilized tribes inhabiting the districts to which you have attained access.

But your reports make it sufficiently obvious that the nature of the country, the insalubrity of the climate, the prevalence of poisonous insects and other adverse influences constitute a very serious array of obstacles to missionary effort, and even were there a reasonable prospect of these being surmounted—and we by no means assume they are insurmountable—yet in that event the financial circumstances of the Society are not such as to afford any ground of hope, that it would be in a position, within any definite period, to enter upon untried, remote, and difficult fields of labour.

In view of these circumstances, we should, independently of the pleasure of seeing you amongst us, regard your visit to England as affording a most favourable opportunity for conferring with you fully on your future plans.[4]

A postscript to the letter says: "I have the pleasure to report that Mrs. Livingstone, whom I have seen within these few days, is, together with your children, in good health, but she is of course looking forward with no little anxiety to the termination of your long and perilous journey, and your reunion with your family."

Here is certainly no evidence of lack of friendliness towards Livingstone's comprehensive programme, and his heroic method of developing it—quite the contrary, in fact. But it came into the recipient's hands at an unfortunate moment. Exhausted by toil and sickness, and with the conviction in his mind that he had done something of imperishable value for Christianity and civilization, he was chilled to read that, in the opinion of his superiors, it was "connected only remotely with the spread of the Gospel," and that consequently they felt unable to aid it with the resources at their disposal. It was also unfortunate that the financial statement included in the letter showed a small balance due from Livingstone to the Society. To read this

[4] L.M.S. archives.

when he had stripped himself bare to meet the cost of his terrific journey was a damper, to say the least, and argues a want of tact in Dr. Tidman.[5]

The explanation of the sending of the letter is that 1855 was a depressing year in the history of the L.M.S. It had that year to face a deficit of £12,000, and the Crimean War was still draining all that the benevolent public could spare for the relief of misery and suffering; yet in May of this same year the directors register their resolve "hereafter to extend to the tribes" whom Livingstone had visited, "the blessings of salvation." [6]

By May, 1856, when peace was restored, the L.M.S. had by a great effort cleared the debt and secured a balance in hand of £6,180, of which £3,200 was earmarked for the repair of the missionary ship, and £2,900 was available for other work.

Livingstone spoke at the May meetings of the Society [7] in 1857, being received with overwhelming demonstrations of goodwill, and the stimulus of his presence was so great as to create another forward movement in the Society's operations. It was not until the autumn of that year that the Board was officially informed that he had finally decided not to go out again under its auspices, but was expecting Government support for his plans. Soon after his return home, and following upon the official reception mentioned above, the directors had voted him a special grant of £200 on account of the heavy expenditure he had incurred in their service; but in a letter to Tidman dated April 7th, 1857, he declined this, stating that the publication of the fact had given rise to rumours that he was not in need of money, and adding

---

[5] A letter to Thompson despatched from Mauritius on his way home shows that Livingstone had been irritated by Tidman's words, and foreshadows the severance which afterwards took place. Quoting the phrase "remote and difficult fields of labour," he says: "As these statements are embalmed on some flattering sentence of approbation respecting my late effort to open up the continent to the sympathies of the friends of Christianity, I suppose that it is intended to send me to some of the tried, neat, and easy fields where I can wax fat and kick like Jeshurun. . . . The proposition to leave the untried, remote, and difficult fields of labour as they have been ever since our Saviour died for man involves my certain separation from the L.M.S." (L.M.S. archives.)

[6] L.M.S. archives.

[7] One notable sentence in his speech on this occasion deserves to have emphasis: "I do not think better of the Africans for being black, because if I were not a missionary to them, I believe I should be a missionary to the poor in London."

that he would be obliged if silence were maintained about his supposed financial resources.

Faced with the new openings made by Livingstone in the valley of the upper Zambesi, the Society now resolved upon sending out four married missionaries—two to be under Livingstone's supervision among the Makololo, and two under that of Moffat in Matebeleland. Four good men were found for the projected missions—Mackenzie, Price, Sykes, and Thomas—the decision to appoint them being taken while Livingstone was still on the Society's roll, and in May, 1858, the L.M.S. Report stated that the four new men were on the point of departure, and that though Livingstone was "no longer a missionary," [8] it was confidently expected that he would give the workers kind and valuable assistance. Whether any definite arrangement was made in this sense is not clear. Sir John Kirk's comment, quoted by Coupland, [9] on the unwisdom of sending two inexperienced men into the malarious land of the Makololo without a doctor was probably written in ignorance or forgetfulness of the fact that they were intended to be under Livingstone's direction. Wherever the blame may lie, the omission had a grievous outcome, as we must presently note.

By May, 1858, £7,000 had been raised by the L.M.S. for the new African mission, and altogether in that year the income of the Society from home subscribers was increased by 40 per cent.—an amazing performance, due in great measure to the new missionary zeal awakened by Livingstone's appeals and the diffusion of the knowledge of what he himself had done single-handed. It should be remembered in this connection that the Indian Mutiny had broken out in May, 1857, and threw Britain into paroxysms of horror. Much was said and written about the atrocities committed by the mutinous Sepoys, but the L.M.S. saw in the situation primarily an urgent need for more Christian effort to meet the needs of India, and no less than £11,000 was raised in three months for this definite object. Here again, something must be credited to the influence exerted, though less directly,

[8] That is, on the staff of a missionary society. He never ceased to be a missionary.
[9] *Kirk on the Zambesi*, p. 176.

by Livingstone's name and example; but it would be unjust to say that the Society had not risen to the measure of its opportunities beforehand. A comparison of the dates mentioned will show that the deficit of £12,000 had been turned into a balance of £6,180 eight months before Livingstone landed in England, and the effort towards this end had begun a year before. To secure a total of £18,000 by May, 1858, over and above the ordinary income from home subscribers of £46,000 does not indicate indifference to the new lines of advance that Livingstone had marked out, or any failure to recognize the greatness of the responsibilities thus placed upon the Christian public.

The severance of Livingstone's connection with the L.M.S. was not due to any feeling on his part or on that of the directors that he and they were pursuing dissimilar objects; but as he was now proposing to devote himself to a considerable extent to scientific exploration, he did not think he ought to continue on the pay-roll of a Society which existed solely for Christian propaganda. If the directors had a similar conviction they did not say so, and their actions are proof that they were ready to support to the full the new spiritual enterprise he had made possible.

The year 1857 was Livingstone's *annus mirabilis*. His personality caught the popular imagination, and he was applauded and worshipped to a degree that at times he found exceedingly irksome. He could scarcely appear on the street without being surrounded by admiring crowds; his appearance in church was the signal for an indecorous rush in his direction; and his rugged face was displayed in the pages of most of the illustrated prints of the day.

Honours of a more serious kind poured upon him. The Prince Consort, with some other members of the royal family, received him personally soon after his arrival in London, and showed a keen and well-informed interest in his doing and purposes. A few weeks later he was presented with the Freedom of the City of London, a compliment repeated by the cities of Glasgow and Edinburgh, and the little town of Hamilton, which had been the scene of some of his earliest associations. The speech of the City Chamberlain on the admission of the new Freeman to the distinguished company of honorary citizens of

London, was notable for the eloquent comparison it instituted between the recipient of the City's favour that day and many of his predecessors in the same rôle. After speaking of the military heroes who had been made Freemen, the orator said:

> Your calling, on the contrary, has led you to seek the honour of your country and the moral elevation of mankind by the peaceful triumph of the missionary, by the expanding influences of scientific discovery, by preparing the way for that intercommunion and commerce between alienated races, the tendency of which is to make a corporate guild of all nations, to unite all the tribes of the earth in a bond of universal brotherhood, to hasten that grand millennium of the whole civilized world "when nation shall not lift sword against nation, neither shall they learn war any more." [10]

Glasgow's pride in her now famous son was shown not only by the grant of honorary citizenship, but by the gift of £2,000 raised by public subscription as a testimonial to the worth of the services he had rendered to industry and commerce; the degree of LL.D. was conferred upon him by his University, and other Universities, including Oxford and Cambridge, took a similar method of recognizing his merits. His speech at Cambridge on the occasion of his reception by the University made a deep impression, not because of its charm of language or ease of delivery—as a fact, it was lacking in both—but because of its utter sincerity and moral force. Its immediate result was the creation of the Universities Mission to Central Africa, which, after a disastrous beginning, has become one of the most fruitful and influential missionary organizations in the world.

Livingstone's personal appearance on this occasion has been well described by J. W. Clark, the Registrar, speaking at a Jubilee Meeting of the U.M.C.A. in the Senate House, December 4th, 1907. "He appeared in company with the veteran Professor Sedgwick, Dr. Whewell, and other distinguished persons. In marked contrast to them, we saw a man of moderate height, very plainly dressed, his face tanned to a dark brown by long exposure to sun and wind, and furrowed by deep lines which spoke of anxiety, hardship, and disease, endured and over-

[10] Record of the Court of Common Council.

come. I think I never saw any man whose appearance told its own tale as Livingstone's did. We all felt that we were about to hear a wonderful narrative of personal experiences, and that every word would come true.

"The lecture which followed when the cheers which greeted his entrance had subsided enough to allow him to begin was not a lecture in the ordinary sense of that word. It was a series of notes on the physical features of Africa; on its inhabitants; on their language; on the way to deal with them, and on the 'open path for commerce and Christianity' which he had himself been permitted to make.

"His language, for which he apologized on the ground that for seventeen years he had spoken the native languages of Africa, and had in consequence almost forgotten his own, was peculiar to himself.

"He used short, jerky sentences, expressive of thoughts which he could not arrange in set periods, but which he did not wish his hearers to lose. But the most carefully ordered speech would have been far less effective, and when he suddenly shouted: *'Do you carry on the work which I have begun. I leave it with you,'* and sat down, there was silence for a few seconds, and then came a great explosion of cheering never surpassed in this building." [11]

He was invited to address the British Association meetings in Dublin, an opportunity which he turned to good use by outlining what might be done in the fertile district of the lower Zambesi, whereupon a movement was immediately started to secure Government support for the development of trade in this direction. The Manchester Chamber of Commerce, attracted by his description of the cotton-growing possibilities of the region and the mineral wealth in which it abounded, took up the idea, as did Leeds, Sheffield, Liverpool, and Birmingham. Many religious bodies and learned and philanthropic institutions presented him with addresses, and his native village of Blantyre received a special visit from him, and joined in the chorus of pride and satisfaction that everywhere greeted the tidings of his endeavours in the cause of God and humanity.

All this was very tiring, and he longed to have done with it; his shy-

[11] U.M.C.A. Report.

ness and inexperience of the ways of society made the constant lionizing a weariness to him, and he would have avoided it altogether if
he could consistently with his duty to the cause of Christianity in
Africa; he only endured it in the hope of directing enlightened attention to the urgent needs of the mission field there. Writing to his
friend Maclear towards the close of this period of crowded engagements, he says: "I finish my public spouting next week at Oxford. It
is really very time-killing, this lionizing, and I am sure you pity me in
it. I hope to leave in January. . . . I shall rejoice when I see you again
in the quiet of the Observatory. It is more satisfactory to serve God
in peace. May He give His gracious blessing to us all! I am rather
anxious to say something that will benefit the young men at Oxford." [12]
Mr. Frederick Fitch, with whose family he and Mrs. Livingstone stayed
for a time, observes that they were an extraordinarily simple and unpretentious couple, sensible and quiet in manner, and with no taste at
all for the social milieu into which they had been plunged. Their
natural dignity and reserve protected them to some extent from the
fussy intrusions of strangers. They had a sense of humour which
showed itself on occasion in an undemonstrative mutual perception of
some absurdity, and the twinkle in Livingstone's eye instantly communicated itself to his wife. "Neither of them cared for grandeur; it
was a great trial to Dr. Livingstone to go to a grand dinner." [13] When
he did go, he sometimes startled his company by disagreeing with them
on current matters of opinion, his blunt honesty asserting itself, as it
had been wont to do in earlier days when he came to the Metropolis
a raw and unpolished student from the north.

There were some critics of his deeds and utterances who considered,
after the narrow-minded fashion then prevalent in certain religious
circles, that he had not shown himself sufficiently in earnest about the
conversion of souls, and that he had forgotten his evangelistic vocation
in his passion for discovery. Echoes of the same accusation are still to
be heard, though seldom, and time has shown that Livingstone was
right in giving to evangelization a wider meaning than up till then it

had received. But the criticism stung him, and he resented it. To one such fault-finder he replied: "Nowhere have I ever appeared as anything else but a servant of God, who has simply followed the leadings of His hand. My views of what is *missionary* duty are not so contracted as those whose ideal is a dumpy sort of man with a Bible under his arm. I have laboured in bricks and mortar, at the forge and carpenter's bench, as well as in preaching and medical practice. I feel that I am 'not my own.' I am serving Christ when shooting a buffalo for my men, or taking an astronomical observation, or writing to one of His children who forget during the little moment of penning a note, that charity which is eulogized as 'thinking no evil.' " [14]

What time he could snatch from the exacting public functions forced upon him was devoted to the writing of his book, *Missionary Travels and Researches in South Africa.* This work had been projected long before, for the news of his successful journey to Loanda had led the publishing house of John Murray to approach him through Sir Roderick Murchison with the proposal that he should put his experiences into volume form and give them to the world. It should not be overlooked that Livingstone was already well accustomed to the use of the pen. He had written freely and at length both to private correspondents and to various publications from the beginning of his acquaintance with conditions in South Africa, and, as we have seen, his Journals and smaller note-books were in constant use and carefully posted. As some of these lie before the present writer, they are striking examples of methodical and laborious usage, and if the total of Livingstone's entries therein were added to his published material, the output of his brain thus represented would be enormous, though it has to be remembered that much of the content of his letters and printed writings was transcribed from the diaries he carried about with him. It will thus be seen that he was not an unpracticed writer, though he never considered himself to be a gifted stylist. He knew well the value of publicity for his work, and he took care to avail himself of it. He had been in the habit of sending articles to his friend Watt and others for insertion, if possible, in the leading reviews from time to time in

[14] Blaikie, *op. cit.,* p. 181 *f.*

the hope of ventilating opinion on African affairs in Great Britain and securing sympathy for the natives and for the economic development of the interior. His communications to the Royal Geographical Society of course appeared, but his efforts through other channels were seldom acceptable until he acquired a national reputation. The *Quarterly Review* printed at least one of his contributions while he was still unknown, and several others appeared in recognized missionary organs.

The writing of the *Missionary Travels* he found to be a heavy and uncongenial task, which raised his respect for the craft of authorship very considerably. He would rather cross Africa again, he said, than write another book. Yet the fact that it is still a living literary production, constantly read and studied both for the human interest of the narrative and the permanent importance of the information it conveys, stamps it as a classic of its kind. Its unstudied simplicity of expression has a grace of its own which a more ornate literary form seldom attains in works which are intended to be at once *ad populum* and technical. Its one conspicuous defect is bad arrangement, and this is due to the haste with which it was put together, and to the method of transcribing from voluminous notes above mentioned.

Though the book was issued at a guinea, which in those days was considered a high price, as it would be still for a work designed for general circulation, it had an instant and immense vogue. It was what would be called a best seller in the twentieth century, but in the nineteenth was a phenomenon of the book trade. A first edition of twelve thousand was sold out before publication, and the second went almost as quickly. For the first time in his life Livingstone was now supplied with ample funds of his own earning, but he did not remain in affluence for very long. A good half of his literary profits went towards financing his next African venture, and the rest, which he deposited in an Indian bank for the benefit of his family, disappeared in the failure of that institution.

It has hitherto been taken for granted that Livingstone's withdrawal from the service of the London Missionary Society and engaging in that of the British Government was due to the initiative of the latter. Such statements on the subject as have appeared hitherto are to the effect that, in consequence of representations from various influential quarters, as indicated above, the Foreign Secretary, the Earl of Clarendon, approached Livingstone on behalf of the Cabinet with the offer to send him out again with a special commission, authorized and defined by the Government, to explore the region of the lower Zambesi with a view to ascertaining the nature of its resources as a field for settlement and commerce.

The belief is incorrect. It was Livingstone himself who took the first step in making the connection, as a copy of his letter to Lord Clarendon, dated May 22nd, 1857, preserved in his private Journal,[15] now reveals. In this letter he states his intention of devoting himself to further work in Africa, and shows how his future efforts will tend to the benefit of trade and the enhancement of his country's good name. He outlines a policy which he thinks will not offend or encroach upon the rights of Portugal, and expresses the hope that this will meet with the approval of Her Majesty's Government. The statement is followed by the definite suggestion that he should undertake the work as an accredited representative of the Government, and adds: "As I do not intend to accept gratuity from my former employers, the London Missionary Society, I venture to accept such a salary as your Lordship may deem suitable, should you approve of my suggestion and think me worthy of employment in a public capacity."

This document throws new light on the subject of Livingstone's relations with the Government. A charge of parsimony and want of consideration for the needs of its agent has since been made against the Cabinet of the day, not without some justification, but there is no trace of such a tendency at this stage. Lord Clarendon told Livingstone to ask for whatever he might deem necessary and it should be supplied. Instructions to this effect were given to the Admiralty, and it was Livingstone, not the department, that cut down the estimates and decided upon the modest equipment finally available. He was given the rank of Consul for the east coast of Africa to the south of Zanzibar, and for the unexplored interior, and appointed commander of an expedition with wide discretionary powers to survey and report

15 Lent by D. Wilson.

upon the country watered by the lower Zambesi. He appears to have been proud of his new status, and for the rest of his life was scarcely ever seen without the peaked cap with a gold band, which was the outward mark of it. The other members of the expedition detailed to serve under his direction were Commander Bedingfield, R.N., as navigating officer, Dr. John Kirk as botanist and physician, Richard Thornton as geologist, Thomas Baines as draughtsman and storekeeper, George Rae as engineer, and Livingstone's brother Charles as secretary and general assistant.

Whether it was wise for Livingstone thus definitely to detach himself from missionary service and become a Government official with a purely secular commission may be doubted in view of later events. There were not a few of his best friends who had misgivings about it at the time, and these did not diminish in force as news of the vicissitudes through which the expedition subsequently passed began to filter through to the public. But none of this was anticipated by any of the promoters of the scheme, and it was amid a chorus of national approval that the party received its send-off. On February 13th Livingstone was received in audience by Queen Victoria, who gave him her best wishes for his success, and at a great public dinner in his honour on the same day distinguished representatives of almost every section of the national life expressed confident expectation that the venture would prove to be the beginning of great things for Africa and the world. The prophecy was fulfilled, but not for many years, nor without much suffering and sacrifice on the part of the man upon whom the principal responsibility rested. Many disappointments were in store for him, and the course of the expedition was to be marked by failure and disaster at every stage, though now, in looking back upon what it accomplished, we see that it was the crown of Livingstone's labours, and the piece of work of most lasting benefit to mankind of all that he was divinely enabled to do. That he himself had some prevision both of the end to be attained and the price to be paid for it is indicated by the closing sentences of his address at Cambridge on December 3rd, 1857: "I beg to direct your attention to Africa. I know that in a few years I shall be cut off in that country, which is now open;

do not let it be shut again. I go back to Africa to try to make an open
path for commerce and Christianity; do you carry out the work which
I have begun. I leave it with you." [16]

Professor Sedgwick says that the effect of the last five words upon
the cultured academic audience was tremendous. The previous part
of the speech had been somewhat haltingly delivered and without
rhetorical embellishment of any sort, but at the end the speaker suddenly raised his voice to a shout and instantly stopped. It was as
though he had thrown a bomb into the midst of the assembly—as indeed he had. No single utterance has ever had more far-reaching
results, not even that of Abraham Lincoln on the field of Gettysburg.

[16] *Cf.* Clark, *ut sup.*, p. 197.

CHAPTER X

BACK TO THE ZAMBESI

LIVINGSTONE and his new colleagues sailed from Liverpool on March 10th, 1858, on board H.M.S. *Pearl.* They carried with them the sections of a steam-launch, built to Livingstone's own specifications, and called the *Ma-Robert,* the native name for Mrs. Livingstone, in allusion to the name of her eldest son. The component parts of this small vessel were so designed that they could be screwed together when a suitable point was reached for commencing the navigation of the river, a prospect which proved deceptive. Not the least of Livingstone's tribulations from the beginning to the end of this ill-starred endeavour was the inefficiency of the *Ma-Robert,* upon which he animadverts with severe disapprobation of the conduct of the man who had built her, and who had professed to be doing so as a special favour "for the good of the cause." Not unwarrantably, he stigmatized the claim as savouring of hypocrisy.[1]

Mrs. Livingstone accompanied her husband, taking with her their youngest child, Oswell. The others had to be left behind, greatly to the concern of both parents, a concern which would have been greater had they known that the children would never see their mother again. She bore the voyage badly, and was so ill on arriving at Cape Town, where Dr. and Mrs. Moffat met them, that it was deemed advisable for her to go back with them to Kuruman and rest for a time before rejoining her husband at a rendezvous in the delta of the Zambesi. The arrangement was the more necessary as she was expecting to be confined. Her youngest daughter, Anna Mary, was born in the fol-

[1] An entry in the locked Journal under date August 26th, 1858, reads: "Engine pump would not work. It ought to have been a ball valve instead of an Indian rubber one. Mr. Laird has served us very ill, and now we feel the effects of his greediness in saving £100 or so by giving us an old cylinder and bad boiler. The tubes are too few, and placed on the bottom and one side instead of all round." This was at the very beginning of the expedition's experiences with the *Ma-Robert. Cf. Narrative of an Expedition to the Zambesi,* pp. 92 f. and 149.

lowing November, but it was nearly a year before the father could be apprised of the event, owing to the difficulty of locating him or establishing reliable communication.

A great public welcome was given to Livingstone at Cape Town. The Governor, Sir George Grey, took the lead in arranging this demonstration, as he had done in connection with that of November, 1856, which, though the man honoured thereby was then far away on his voyage to England and home, struck the first note in the universal symphony of admiration that was to sound around him during the ensuing twelve months. At this second gathering he was received with an enthusiasm which must have impressed him as in curious contrast with the treatment accorded him on his last previous visit to the same city. Then he had been thwarted and baffled at every point, viewed with unfriendliness and mistrust; now he was applauded as one of the outstanding international figures of the day. A gift of eight hundred guineas, subscribed for by the inhabitants of Cape Town, was presented to him in a silver box by the Governor himself; and a day or two later he and all the members of the expedition were entertained at a public banquet, on which occasion the chief speaker was the missionary's tried and true friend, the Astronomer Royal, Thomas Maclear. It must have been a proud hour for both, and an ideally complete vindication of the aims of the one and the faith of the other.

The *Pearl* and her complement arrived at the mouth of the Zambesi on May 15th, and spent some time in attempting to find and chart the best of the several entrances to the main channel. Concluding that the Kongone was, on the whole, the most accessible, they managed to penetrate as far as what is now called Expedition Island, and there disembarked and transferred their stores to the assembled *Ma-Robert*. Serious disharmony now arose between the leader and Commander Bedingfield, and culminated in the latter's resignation. Into the culpability or otherwise of this officer it were profitless to inquire at this distant date, but we have the authority of Dr. (better known as Sir John) Kirk for stating that Bedingfield was not working well with his chief, and Livingstone's report of the whole circumstances to the Foreign Office was accepted, after consultation with the Admiralty, as a

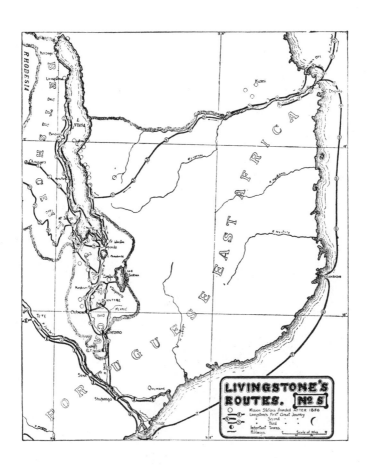

RHODESIA

BRITISH CENTRAL AFRICA

PORTUGUESE EAST AFRICA

PORTUGUESE

L. NYASA

TETE

LIVINGSTONE'S
ROUTES. Nº 5
○ Mission Stations founded AFTER 1856
Livingstone's First Great Journey
‚‚ „ Second „
„ „ Third „
◉ Important Towns.
Railways.   Scale of Miles

true account of the facts. Kirk's private diary censures Bedingfield but hints that he had some provocation. Both of the Livingstone brothers, in his judgment, but especially Charles, were lacking in *savoir faire* and the art of mixing agreeably with others. He states that David Livingstone was not a good administrator,[2] however great his other gifts, and this would appear to be true. He could get on with natives better than with white men, and the inference is reasonable that his disputations with Bedingfield and others sprang in a measure from an inability to adjust himself easily to the habits and predilections of men of different social antecedents from his own. Bedingfield, on the other hand, evinced some amount of professional snobbery. He resented being under the orders of a man whom he felt to be at once his social inferior and less experienced than himself in the technique of seamanship. Tension ensued, and ultimately became intolerable, and when, as Kirk says, Bedingfield's resignation became necessary if the further disorganization of the expedition were to be avoided,[3] Livingstone became his own navigating officer, a plan which would have worked well enough had the *Ma-Robert* been equal to what was required of her.

This was for Livingstone but the beginning of sorrows. Looking back now on the work he did in the Zambesi expedition, those most competent to judge are of opinion that it was of even greater value than the brilliant and spectacular feat which brought him fame. But it did not seem so then either to himself or to the world; it was regarded as a grievous failure and disappointment to all concerned, and went far towards breaking the leader's indomitable spirit. The constant bickering and squabbling that went on between the European members of the expedition gradually became known at the Cape and in England, and, spreading widely elsewhere, exposed Livingstone to some amount of misjudgment. But this was the least of his trials; far greater was the crushing of his hopes of opening up a commercial path by water all the way from the ocean to his beloved Makololo people. The impassable Kebrabasa gorge gave the *coup de grâce* to this fervent

[2] Coupland, *Kirk on the Zambesi*, p. 181.
[3] *Ibid.*, p. 117.

expectation, which he had long held and confidently expressed to the
British Government and the public, and he did not surrender it until
its utter futility was demonstrated by tests that even he could not ignore. Then blow followed blow, as we shall see, in the disasters that
overtook the missions he was the means of founding, and in the frus-
tration of his efforts, through no fault of his own, to fulfil the programme entrusted to him by his superiors. But let us follow the story.

Bedingfield resigned in July;[4] Tete was reached in the *Ma-Robert*
on September 8th, to the almost frenzied delight of Livingstone's
Makololo followers, who for more than two years had remained on
this spot expecting him to return and take them home to their own
country. But they were not to be taken home just yet; the river had
to be explored thirty miles above Tete to see if the great Kebrabasa
rapids might be navigable. With this purpose Livingstone made two
journeys overland, as the *Ma-Robert* could not be coaxed sufficiently
near to the crucial point for accurate observations to be made. But
learning on the second return journey that there was still a cataract
higher up which he had not seen he retraced his steps, and accompanied only by Kirk and four Makololo made his way to it. The district
traversed was so rough and the heat so intense that the party could
only progress at the rate of one mile an hour, with frequent stoppages
for rest, and so severe was the strain even upon the native attendants
that they begged and implored Livingstone to have mercy upon them
and give up the project. His description of the scene in *A Narrative
of an Expedition to the Zambesi* has in it an element of sardonic
humour:

> The Makololo told Dr. Livingstone they "always thought he had
> a heart, but now they believed he had none," and tried to persuade
> Dr. Kirk to return, on the ground that it must be evident that, in
> attempting to go where no living foot could tread, his leader had
> given unmistakable signs of having gone mad. All their efforts of
> persuasion, however, were lost upon Dr. Kirk, as he had not yet

---

[4] One of Bedingfield's least offensive peculiarities appears to have been a desire that the
expedition should be successful in doing something towards finding the lost ten tribes of Israel.
"As if," caustically observes Livingstone in an early note in the locked Journal, "we hadn't
enough Jews already."

learned their language, and his leader knowing his companion to be equally anxious with himself to solve the problem of the navigableness of Kebrabasa, was not at pains to enlighten him.[5]

But the result of the investigation was heart-breaking to Livingstone himself, though he tried hard not to believe the evidence of his senses. He wrote home to Lord Russell that he considered the Kebrabasa rapids to be navigable at flood time, and not till he and his companions had been nearly drowned subsequently in a desperate attempt to shoot the worst of the cataracts by canoe did he give up the idea. Even then he still talked of the possibility of blasting away the rocks and making the passage safe, but with his private Journal before us we can realize how racked in spirit he was by the conclusion he was now forced to face that this immense natural barrier had shattered his plans for opening the interior of the continent to the humanizing influences of Christian civilization. The discovery was bitter, and the mortification it caused him is only now revealed to the world. In the following extracts from the Journal of this period—his own solitary communings with God and never meant to be inspected by other human eyes than his own—we are privileged to look more deeply into the noble heart of David Livingstone than in the reading of anything he ever saw fit to give to his contemporaries:

September 1st, 1858.—We shall succeed, but I feel concerned about our companions down the river. The Lord look in mercy on us all. It is His work we are engaged in. The high position I have been raised to was not of my seeking. Nor was the éclat which greeted me at home a matter of my choice. I therefore commit all to the care and help of Him who has said, "Commit thy way unto the Lord, trust also in Him, and He shall bring it to pass." I do so from the bottom of my heart, and pleasant it is to cast one's cares on Him who careth for us. Lord, take Thou the guidance of all my affairs, and let them all tend to the promotion of Thy glory.

October 17th, 1858.—If we can blast away the rocks which obstruct the passage, how thankful I shall feel. It will be like opening wide the gates which have barred the interior for ages. Will the good

[5] P. 60.

Spirit of the Lord grant this honour unto us, His servants, of this expedition? If it is to promote the good of my fellow men, I will turn quarryman next.

End of November, 1858.—Things look dark for our enterprise. This Kebrabasa is what I never expected. What we shall do if this is to be the end of the navigation I cannot now divine, but here I am, and I am trusting Him who never made ashamed those who did so. I look back to all that has happened to me. The honours heaped on me were not of my seeking—they came unbidden. I could not even answer the letters I got from the great and noble, and I never expected the fame which followed me. It was Thy hand that gave it all, O Thou blessed and Holy One, and it was given for Thy dear Son's sake.

It will promote Thy glory if Africa is made a land producing the articles now raised only or chiefly by slave labour. O grant me the honour to begin the great work here, but whatever Thy Will may be, I do hereby submit to it as the best. Only punish me not as my grievous lack of service and unprofitableness deserve. Spare me, good Lord, spare me, whom Thou hast redeemed with Thy most precious blood. The good Lord look upon me. Thou hast raised me. I trust in Thee if Thou throwest me down. Spare me, dear Jesus. Dear Lamb of God, do not utterly despise the work of Thy hands. I am all the work of Thy hands.

December 3rd, 1858.—Came to a dead halt, urging everything we could think of to induce the guides to go on. They at last said they would go to die with me. The Makololo declared . . . that I had become insane surely, for they showed me the broken blisters on their feet in vain. . . . To make it permanently available for commerce the assistance of a powerful Government is necessary, and a company of Sappers would soon clear out the channel. This is perhaps the most favourable circumstance connected with the affair, for it would be difficult to induce the Portuguese to give up their pretensions if they could take all the trade into their own hands without.

He was greatly depressed for a time by the disillusionment he had undergone, though, if he had but known, it had one great beneficial

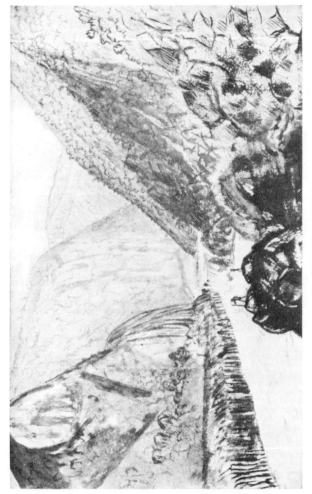

THE KEBRABASA GORGE

From a sketch by Sir John Kirk

outcome: it forced him to turn north and lay bare to the world the arterial roads of the slave trade.

The first thing Livingstone did after returning to Tete was to make application to the British Government for a more suitable boat, giving as a reason that the *Ma-Robert* had not sufficient engine power for the work that had to be done. This was to state her defects mildly; he did not yet know the worst of which she was capable, but was soon to find out. While awaiting an answer from London he decided to explore the Shiré river in the hope of discovering the great lake which the natives said was its source. A beginning was made with this enterprise in January, 1859, when the party succeeded in pushing up the Shiré for two hundred miles before their progress was arrested by the rapids which Livingstone named the Murchison Cataracts, after his friend Sir Roderick Murchison. The *Ma-Robert*—henceforth nick-named the *Asthmatic*—revealed her true character in a variety of ways on this preliminary excursion into a part of Africa hitherto unvisited by Europeans. She had a voracious maw; a day and a half of hard work was regularly required to cut sufficient wood to keep her boiler going for a day. The delay and waste of time and energy thus caused were vexatious enough, yet frequently recurring breakdowns were still more annoying, and, to crown all the drawbacks, she was so far from being watertight that nothing could be kept dry and the labour of baling her out was excessively wearisome. The strain on all concerned was unremitting, and did not conduce to cheerfulness and amiability.

Returning to Tete for repairs, they tried to ascend the Shiré again in mid-March, landing this time at the village of a chief named Chibisa, a man of some originality and force of character with whom Livingstone made friends. The explorer's opinion of Chibisa was favourably influenced by the fact that, like Katema, he had a jolly laugh—"which is always a good sign in a man." It is but just to add that Chibisa's opinion of himself was still higher than that of his white visitors, for, as he said, he was conscious of being endowed with far superior natural powers to those of most other men. He certainly was a person of proved capacity and a useful friend to the party then and later.

Here, leaving the steamer in charge of two English sailors, Walker and Rowe, Livingstone and Kirk struck overland with the object of finding Lake Nyassa, of which they had heard much. The journey was a trying one, owing to sickness and native hostility, and its only trophy was the discovery of the small brackish Lake Shirwa. The two explorers rightly felt that this was but a minor reward of their toils, but the beauty and luxuriance of the surrounding country led them to form the well-founded conviction that it would be a promising field for colonization. Both men adhered firmly to this view for the rest of their lives, and, as already mentioned, Livingstone made a liberal offer to help in financing any pioneer group of settlers who would be prepared to come out and see what could be done in the way of developing the resources of one of the most naturally productive regions in the world. As a result of the Zambesi expedition he realized that the Shiré and Nyassa region provided the best means of access to the great fertile interior of Africa, and his vision in this respect has been amply confirmed by events, as the prosperous centres of Blantyre and Livingstonia, not to mention others of importance, bear living witness.

Making their way back to the *Ma-Robert* after this experimental trip, Livingstone and Kirk sailed with the rest, first to Tete and then to Kongone, for the repairs which were seen to be imperative if any further effort to reach Lake Nyassa by water were to succeed. Livingstone had already written home to his friend, James Young, asking him to have a boat built and sent out at the explorer's own expense, and constructed according to his directions, which might be able to do what the *Ma-Robert* had so far failed in doing. The order was more efficiently complied with than that effected through the Government, but its execution had to be awaited for some little time longer.

They arrived at Kongone again in their leaky boat on June 23rd, 1859, and here another schism took place, Baines and Thornton being dismissed. Thornton rejoined the expedition later, but died soon afterwards; Baines departed permanently, protesting against the treatment he had received and which he vainly petitioned the Foreign Office to inquire into and rectify.

It would appear that in the case of these two men Livingstone acted more harshly than he ought to have done. His manner of reinstating

Thornton and granting him full payment for the period of his absence was almost equivalent to an apology. Whether his reasons for discharging Baines were well founded will perhaps never be completely known. Sir H. H. Johnston [6] warmly espouses Baines' cause and says it is more than time that justice were done to this man's memory. Kirk liked him and says he worked harder than any other member of the expedition, but does not profess to adjudicate on the matter chiefly at issue between him and his leader, the improper use of some of the Government stores which had been placed in his care. [7]

The same impartial and reliable witness suggests that Livingstone may have been influenced by prejudice in this, as in some other instances, through listening to the complaints of his brother Charles. The time came when Livingstone seems to have suspected this himself, for when differences came to a head between the two brothers, as they did before long, the older man reminded the younger of the accusations made by the latter against his fellow-members. Commenting on the incident Kirk observes that, although Livingstone may have known the real value of his brother's insinuations against other men, he had unfortunately allowed them to exercise a powerful influence upon his own mind. [8]

This statement is the more trustworthy because of the character of the man who makes it. Next to Livingstone himself Kirk was the most competent member of the expedition, and his equable temper, proved loyalty, and high integrity cannot be impugned. His admiration for his chief finds constant expression in his diary, notwithstanding his perception of some rather trying peculiarities in Livingstone's disposition and ways of conducting himself in relation to others. His opinion of Charles was very different. "The character of the two brothers," he says, "is in no respect alike—Dr. L. straightforward, honest, rather shy, unless engaged in his great scheme of opening

[6] *Op. cit.*, p. 250.
[7] Coupland, *op. cit.*, pp. 114 and 158-162.
[8] *Ibid.*, p. 181. But writing to Horace Waller a decade later (a hitherto unpublished letter), Livingstone says: "He (Baines) offered to pay me—confessed his theft twice *to me*—then gammoned the soft-heads on dismissal by saying I was always kind but was led by my brother! I am just the weakling to be so led!"

Africa; Mr. C. L.—" Kirk's biographer does not finish the quotation, but adds that "it is only fair to its other members to state the clear fact that the mainspring of those quarrels was the mischief-making of the expedition's 'Moral Agent.'" [9]

Livingstone's locked Journal, above mentioned, contains an entry which shows that angry words spoken to him by his brother when remonstrated with sank deep into his affectionate heart and rankled there. The entry is dated May 13th, 1860. "My brother informs me that the members of the expedition did not get orders what to do, and were always at a loss how to act; that so far as it has failed, I am to blame in having rejected the Bann.[10] . . . As he seems to let out in a moment of irritation a long-pent-up ill-feeling, I am at a loss how to treat it. As an assistant he has been of no value. Photography very unsatisfactory. Magnetism still more so. Meteorological observations not creditable, and writing in the Journal in arrears. In going up with us now he is useless, as he knows nothing of Portuguese or the native language. He often expected me to be his assistant instead of acting as mine. This ebullition happened because I found fault with him for destroying my pillow. It was, he said, all my fault. I rejected the Bann, and every evil followed that as a matter of course. He was perfectly blameless, as if my act had destroyed his individual responsibility. He allowed £100 of magnetical instruments to be completely destroyed by damp, but must not be blamed."

Another note is dated June 11th of the same year. It is recorded in a little memorandum book and bears the appearance of having been hastily jotted down immediately after the occasion to which it refers. "Manners of a cotton spinner—of the Boers—didn't know how to treat men—seemed intent on a row—would be but a short time in the expedition—regretted that he was on this journey—would rejoice when he could leave it. So far my brother Charles."

The childishness of the remarks here reproduced does not obscure the pain they caused to him against whom they were directed. The restraint wherewith they are set down—not a petulant or resentful

[9] Coupland, *op. cit.*, p. 181.
[10] A boat rejected on Bedingfield's advice.

ejaculation accompanying them—is a sufficient indication of Christian forbearance and fraternal feeling on the elder Livingstone's part. His magnanimity was further demonstrated when the *Narrative of an Expedition to the Zambesi* came to be written and published. David Livingstone wrote it himself at Newstead Abbey, and spent eight months in the task, but on the title page the book is described as by David and Charles Livingstone. The only part that Charles had in it was that David drew upon his brother's diary to some extent for details included in the work; for this Charles was allowed the credit of part authorship and to receive the American profits on the sale. Charles left the expedition in April, 1863, owing to being much reduced by repeated attacks of fever. Through the influence of Sir Roderick Murchison he was later appointed British Consul at Fernando Po, and died a few months after his illustrious brother in 1873. Kirk was in frequent consultation with David Livingstone during the writing of the *Narrative,* and although Professor Coupland doubts whether any part of the book is actually from his pen there are pages wherein his influence can almost certainly be traced, and the quotation in the following paragraph is one of them.

In mitigation of the apparent wrong-headedness and misbehaviour of the younger Livingstone, and probably at times of all the other members of the expedition, too, the now well-known fact has to be allowed for that the maladies which assail white men in a tropical climate tend to induce chronic irritability. The description here given of the psychological as well as physical results of continued malarial poisoning could only have been written by one who knew them well both in himself and others, and may quite possibly have been the outcome of intimate exchange of reminiscences between Kirk and David Livingstone concerning the difficulties they had had jointly to struggle with on the banks of the Zambesi.

Very curious are the effects of African fever on certain minds. Cheerfulness vanishes, and the whole mental horizon is overcast with black clouds of gloom and sadness. The liveliest joke cannot provoke even the semblance of a smile. The countenance is grave,

the eyes suffused, and the few utterances are made in the piping
voice of a wailing infant. An irritable temper is often the first symptom of approaching fever. At such times a man feels very much
like a fool, if he does not act like one. Nothing is right, nothing
pleases the fever-stricken victim. He is peevish, prone to find fault,
and to contradict, and thinks himself insulted, and is exactly what
an Irish naval surgeon before a court-martial defined a drunken man
to be: "a man unfit for society." If a party were all soaked full of
malaria at once, the life of the leader of the expedition would be
made a burden to him.[11]

Charles Livingstone was new to tropical Africa and never free from
fever from the first week of landing there. The same may apply to
Bedingfield, Baines, and the rest, and perhaps explains everything.
Kirk alone kept his head and stood gallantly by his chief, though often
very ill and ultimately obliged to go home about the same time as
Charles Livingstone, and for the same reason.

In August, 1859, the third and this time successful attempt to reach
Lake Nyassa was made by way of the Shiré river. Leaving the *Ma-
Robert* as Chibisa's village once more, the Livingstone brothers, together with Kirk and Rae and thirty-eight native attendants, the
majority of them Makololo, set out to reach the much-desired goal on
foot. The route taken led them by the beautiful Shiré heights and
through some of the most magnificent scenery and salubrious country
they had yet seen. Its one appalling affliction was the slave trade, of
which plenty of cruel evidence abounded on every hand, and their
own movements were viewed with suspicion and hostility by the Manganja natives, through whose territory they had to pass. The Manganja were an unattractive tribe, as unpleasant to look upon as they
were treacherous, and their unfriendly attitude was due to their experience of the ruthless methods of the slave raiders; they could not believe
that the new-comers meant well by them or were to be trusted. Livingstone and his followers had consequently to proceed cautiously and

---

[11] *Narrative of an Expedition to the Zambesi*, p. 73 f. Since the above was written, the
author's inference has been corroborated in a letter from Dr. Wilson, who states that his Uncle
Charles was in reality an amiable man, a lover of children, and a great favourite with the
younger members of the Livingstone family.

maintain unceasing vigilance against attack, a mode of progression which they felt to be wearing in the extreme.

Lake Nyassa was finally discovered in the morning of September 16th, and was hailed with a gladness the more intense because mingled with relief that their hopes had not been in vain, that here, indeed, at last they had come upon something that justified the authorization and despatch of the expedition itself, even if no further tangible gains were to be added.

Hastening back to Chibisa's, which they reached in an exhausted condition, the party divided, Kirk and Rae undertaking to make their way to Tete by land, while Livingstone and the rest took the *Ma-Robert* to Kongone once more to be patched up. The first-named pair nearly died *en route* through constant exposure to the scorching rays of the sun and being parched with thirst. The others reached Kongone at the end of the year, only to find that the mails that had been brought from England for them by H.M.S. *Lynx* had been lost at the bar by the capsizing of the boat which was bringing them ashore; the same fate attended the stores, to whose arrival they had been almost as eagerly looking forward. Part of the mails was subsequently recovered and sent after them to Tete, where they were received several months later, but most of the stores perished.

Rae was now sent home to England to superintend the building of the vessel which was to take the place of the *Ma-Robert* in navigating the Zambesi, and as the *Ma-Robert* was now virtually useless, Livingstone decided that he must no longer defer the execution of his engagement to conduct his Makololo adherents back to Linyanti.[12] As might be expected, some of these had no longer any wish to return to their former habitations; they had settled down in the neighbourhood of Tete, cultivating the patches of ground that had been assigned to them by the Portuguese commandant, and had acquired new wives and families. Between thirty and forty of them had died of the prevalent local fever, and several had been murdered by raiders. With those remaining and willing to go, Livingstone started for Makololo land

[12] Had he done so sooner, as seems to have been possible, he could probably have saved the lives of the members of the Makololo mission by using his influence to induce Sekeletu to allow them to fix their residence in a non-malarial district (see below, pp. 223 *ff*.).

in March, 1860, proceeding by canoe as far as the Kebrabasa rapids and then going on foot. At the crossing of the Kafue river news reached the travellers of the arrival of the L.M.S. mission in Matebeleland. It was reported to be prospering, and this filled Livingstone with cheerful expectations concerning what he should hear of the corresponding mission to the Makololo. Little did he anticipate the sad reality.

On every side, as in the Shiré valley, they were surrounded as they went by horrible evidences of the fell activities of the slave trader, the smiling land through which the missionary and his Makololo band had passed four years before being now in process of conversion into a vast charnel house. One of the most wicked and exasperating accompaniments of the traffic as it had developed since the earlier day was the fact that the Portuguese half-castes who directed it did not scruple to shelter themselves under Livingstone's name and reputation, calling themselves his children, and declaring that they had his authority to take what they pleased. To his great grief he now realized that one effect of the world-wide publicity given to his achievement in traversing this vast region had been to attract the spoilers into it and reduce it to ruin.

They arrived at the Victoria Falls on June 9th, to the great interest of Kirk and Charles Livingstone, who were now privileged to behold the majestic natural phenomenon of which they had heard through their leader's reports to the public and to scientific bodies in England. Measurements of precision were taken to check Livingstone's earlier figures, and as more efficient means were now available for this purpose than he had had with him on the former occasion, it was found that the dimensions of the Falls were much greater than he had stated.

At Sesheke they found Sekeletu living in strict seclusion as a victim of what was supposed to be leprosy.[13] He had developed into a superstitious and cruel tyrant on account of his affliction, and caused a num-

---

[13] Livingstone's note-book shows that the history, symptoms, and treatment of the disease were all inconsistent with its being leprosy. He told Sekeletu that he was unacquainted with leprosy. The probability is that the chief was suffering from an unpleasant eruption on the skin. It was serious enough to infect Livingstone and Kirk on the backs of their hands through touching their patient, and lunar caustic had to be applied to get rid of it. It troubled them for some time afterwards.

ber of persons to be put to death on the accusation of having bewitched him. Much discontent had been aroused, and there were rumblings of the tribal revolts which, within a comparatively short time, were to shatter the Makololo dominion to pieces. Livingstone and Kirk treated him successfully for his ailment at some risk to their own health, and the chief recovered temporarily from the disease, but did not live long afterwards.[14] He took a fancy to Kirk, and made liberal offers to him in the hope of inducing him to remain as friend and adviser to a weak and troubled autocrat round whom the clouds were gathering. Had Kirk seen his way to do so, the Makololo State might have lasted longer, but that he was right in refusing can hardly be questioned; the work on which his great reputation rests was of another kind.

The journey from the Kafue river to Sesheke resembled a triumphal procession, says the Zambesi narrative. The joy of the tribes at seeing Livingstone again found exuberant expression everywhere, all the more so because of the sufferings experienced by the poor creatures on account of the slave trade. The route followed was not precisely that of Livingstone's first great journey to the coast, but was sufficiently near to it for his reputation to be well known, and there were many of the inhabitants who had come under his influence on the previous occasion. He and his companions were now welcomed with the most lavish hospitality at every stopping place. "The natives sent to our sleeping-places generous presents of the finest white meal, and fat capons to give it a relish, great pots of beer to comfort our hearts, together with pumpkins, beans, and tobacco, so that we 'should sleep neither hungry nor thirsty. . . .' We entered and left every village amidst the cheers of its inhabitants; the men clapping their hands, and the women lullilooing, with the shrill call, 'Let us sleep,' or 'Peace. . . .' When we halted for the night it was no uncommon thing for the people to prepare our camp entirely of their own accord; some with hoes quickly smoothed the ground for our beds, others brought dried grass and spread it carefully over the spot; some with their small axes speedily made a bush fence to shield us from the wind; and if, as occasionally happened, the

14 He died in 1864.

water was a little distance off, others hastened and brought it with firewood to cook our food with." [15]

All this argues that the crafty lies of the half-caste Portuguese slave traders had not imposed on the population to the extent of making them believe that their former friend had become their enemy, and it was touching evidence of their hope that he had now returned to protect them and give them guidance and security. To this his invariable reply was that others had come and were coming to take his place and tell them more about the God who loved the black man and would have all tribes to dwell together in amity.

Alas for the expectation! Rumours were already reaching the party to the effect that the members of the L.M.S. mission to the Makololo had perished. At the Victoria Falls the vague assertions became definite information; all the European missionaries had fallen victim to that malignant foe of the white man, African fever.

This was a painful shock to Livingstone, to be succeeded later by the equally tragic collapse of the initial establishment of the Universities Mission in the unhealthy Magomero region, as will be related presently. For both of these disasters Livingstone was held by many to be in a measure responsible, and the fact detracted somewhat for a time from public confidence in his judgment. He himself appears to have felt that this might be so, and in the case of the Makololo mission he cannot be entirely acquitted from blame, as the enterprise had been undertaken in reliance upon his advice and co-operation. He had pressed upon the Society the desirability of following up without delay the influence he had acquired among the Makololo people, and offered to defray out of his own salary as Government Consul some portion of the expenditure involved, up to half if necessary.

Robert Moffat, with his ripe experience, viewed the venture with some misgivings, to which he gave expression in a letter to Tidman from Cape Town on July 20th, 1858. The letter is here quoted *in extenso* as giving the clearest and wisest statement of the case that has yet appeared, and as weighed and considered at the moment of the

[15] *Narrative of an Expedition to the Zambesi*, p. 234.

party's arrival by the man best qualified to express an opinion upon the dangers to be met.[16]

MY DEAR BROTHER,

It was with unfeigned pleasure and gratitude to God that I met the missionary brethren and their wives on board the mail steamer last Wednesday.

For some years past the signs of the times seemed to indicate that your missionaries in southern Africa were being left to die out. Our fears on that score have been now removed, and I, for one, cannot help taking renewed courage in the resolution of the directors to dash at once into the interior regions now that favourable openings seem to invite.

Glad as I am of the arrival of so many of our liberal recruits to fill up the thinned ranks of the mission band, I have my fears and feel my mind beset with difficulties connected with the mission to the Makololo which I cannot overcome.

.   .   .   .

Livingstone's expedition has succeeded in getting up the Zambesi a considerable distance. . . . The Governor informs me that Dr. Livingstone had sent a message to the effect that he intended to be down at the mouth of the Zambesi on Christmas Day. Now before that time he may or may not have surveyed the country between the Kafue and Zambesi, the supposed sanatorium of that part of the country.

The same may be said with respect to his reaching Linyanti to prepare the Makololo for the probable arrival of the missionaries. Without there be a considerable degree of certainty of their removing to a more healthy situation, the inhabitants of Linyanti will not feel willing to leave their swamps and rivers, especially until they have been assured that they will not be molested by the Matebele.

This they will require to know through a source upon which they can place the fullest reliance—*i.e.*, either from Livingstone or myself.

That they will break up their town and remove some hundred miles immediately on the arrival of the missionaries without some such assurance, we can hardly expect.

[16] L.M.S. archives.

Now all this makes it rather a serious matter to recommend three missionaries and their wives to proceed at once to Linyanti. In summer this might prove fatal to some, if not all.

Moffat then goes on to say that in his belief it would be better to house the new-comers at Kuruman until about May of the following year (the beginning of winter), to allow time for the removal of Sekeletu's people and the establishment of more healthy conditions.

He had heard from a traveller that the Matebele chief had sent a party of men to the Zambesi below the Victoria Falls to superintend the erection of some large canoes. Sekeletu had also heard of this, and fearing that hostilities were intended, sent warriors to attack the Matebele and drive them away. The attack failed, and the fact probably accounts for Sekeletu's change of attitude towards the project of moving his town to a higher and healthier location. Livingstone had assured the L.M.S. that the chief was willing to order such a removal in the event of missionaries coming to work among his people.

The consequent exposure of the missionary party to the inroads of the prevailing disease in a marshy and low-lying district, on the score of which Moffat had expressed some anxiety, soon developed. Mr. Helmore with his wife and four children, and Roger Price with Mrs. Price and one child, left Kuruman for Linyanti on July 8th, 1859. There had been much earnest discussion as to the wisdom of leaving the wives and children at Kuruman for a time, but the women resolved that they would share the difficulties of the journey with their husbands rather than follow them at a later date It was expected that Livingstone would meet them at Sekeletu's and introduce the whole party to the chief. They arrived at Linyanti spent by the fatigue of more than ordinarily arduous travel,[17] to find themselves suddenly domiciled in the midst of fever-haunted swamps. Livingstone was not there, nor was there any message to say when he was coming. The chief refused either to remove himself or to allow the members of the newly arrived mission to remove to a healthier site.

[17] Helmore had had to walk thirty miles daily to fetch water for the party.

Tragedy came swiftly. Helmore and Price made a gallant effort to commence work, preaching in the open air under a hot sun, and surrounded by rank and steaming vegetation. Two of the Helmore children succumbed to fever; then the infant daughter of Mrs. Price; then Mrs. Helmore; Helmore and Mrs. Price were the last victims. Six deaths out of a party of nine.

Roger Price and the two Helmore orphans alone remained to struggle back to Kuruman and health. But even as they went Sekeletu robbed them of food, clothing, and bedding, riding the while in Helmore's waggon, which he had already appropriated. Yet this was the same chief who was still keeping Livingstone's waggon and stores guarded and intact, awaiting their owner's return.

Blaikie only refers briefly to this capital disaster, the worst that had befallen the London Missionary Society for more than a generation. He states positively that although Livingstone had been consulted by the directors about the sending of the mission, and his advice taken thereon, he was "not a little hurt" that not a word had reached him concerning the movements of the party[18] It is hard to see, in the light of his own movements as recounted above, how any word could have reached him. Blaikie's further statement in a footnote, that there was no foundation for the belief that Livingstone had promised to meet the party at Linyanti, goes beyond Livingstone's own admissions. Writing to Tidman on November 10th, 1860, he says:[19]

On reaching the country of the Makololo in August last, I learned to my very great sorrow that our much esteemed and most worthy friends, the Helmores, had been cut off by fever, after a very short residence at Linyanti.

Having been unexpectedly detained in the lower parts of this river until May last, my much-longed-for opportunity of visiting the upper portion was affected only by performing a march on foot of more than six hundred miles, and then I was too late to render the aid which I had fondly hoped to afford.

[18] *Op. cit.*, p. 231.
[19] L.M.S. archives.

Dr. Tidman, in his reply, joins in the regret that Livingstone's "presence and aid" had not been available for the members of the Makololo mission, as expected.

There is a discrepancy between Livingstone's repeated assurances of the friendly disposition of Sekeletu and the latter's bad treatment of the missionaries who had come to settle at Linyanti on the former's recommendation. It is explained by Livingstone's own note in the *Narrative of an Expedition to the Zambesi:* [20] "But if the Doctor and his wife," said the chief and counsellors, "would come and live with us, we would remove to the highlands at once, as Moselekatse would not attack a place where the daughter of his friend, Moffat, was living." That condition was not fulfilled, and Sekeletu would not place reliance on the presence of the new missionaries, who had not the same value to him as hostages against his enemy.

The Makololo mission was projected by Livingstone, and its direction committed at Livingstone's suggestion to his friend Helmore, a man well acquainted with the language and qualified for the task by twenty years of experience in South Africa. Helmore and the rest found their graves at Linyanti, because the well-founded expectation of settling the mission on a healthy site was frustrated by Sekeletu, who compelled them to remain in a pestilential spot because they were not the particular guests he desired. When Livingstone went on to Linyanti from Sesheke to visit the graves of the unfortunate mission party, he found there intact the waggon he had left in charge of the tribe in 1853, together with packages sent later by Moffat for his use. [21] The whole had been covered in carefully to screen them from the weather, and were in as good condition as could be expected after so long an interval. In reporting upon this gratifying fact, Livingstone takes the opportunity of drawing a contrast between the trustworthiness of the Makololo and the want of conscientiousness in the English trader to whom his two manuscript volumes of notes had been committed by the tribesmen with the request that he should deliver them to Moffat,

[20] P. 282.
[21] *Ut sup.,* p. 197.

THE MA-ROBERT

From a sketch which Livingstone sent to Wm. Crosfield in 1858

as the sender wished. [22] Not for a long time did the trader do as he had promised, and then only in part. But Roger Price could have told a different tale about the obliging nature of these natives and their regard for the white man's property as illustrated by the behaviour of their chief.

This was the end of all concerted attempts to evangelize the Makololo as such. The break-up of their composite State, which soon followed, created an entirely different condition of things, and blotted out the tribe as a dominant people.

Livingstone and his companions left Sesheke on the return journey to the coast on September 17th, 1860, Sekeletu sending with them a new guard commanded by Pitsane and Leshore, who were furnished with authority to requisition any supplies that might be needed from underchiefs within Makololo territory *en route*. On the whole these were forthcoming without demur, though signs were manifest that obedience to Sekeletu's orders was not a strong motive for showing courtesy to the travellers in the majority of cases. One Batoka chief, Moshobotwane, was openly contemptuous of the message of his overlord, but generous in extending hospitality to the white men. Sinamane, of the same tribe, but with a more powerful following, was equally so. His forceful personality impressed Livingstone, who describes him as one of the ablest of the native chiefs he had met and a good, though not very scrupulous administrator. He willingly lent all the canoes required to transport the party farther down stream and exhibited a lively interest in their proceedings. He had never seen white men before, and asked many questions about their beliefs and mode of life, listening with marked respect to Livingstone's preaching when the latter held his usual Sunday service and told the story of the Son of God who had come down from heaven to bring love to men. Tidings of this service having reached a neighbouring chief, Moemba, who was the next to entertain the party, he came to Livingstone of his own accord asking that he and his people might be "Sundayed" too. The petition was gladly complied with. Livingstone

[22] *Narrative of an Expedition to the Zambesi*, p. 297.

never allowed an opportunity to slip of delivering the Gospel message; this, as all associated with him throughout the period of the Zambesi expedition and later, Kirk especially, have borne emphatic witness, he still counted as his primary vocation, and was unswervingly faithful to it.

One amusing minor incident is chronicled. At a point below the village of Mpande a large canoe was purchased for the party and a good price given, but before the bargain was clinched the seller said plaintively that his bowels yearned for his boat and that he must have a little larger payment to stop their yearning. Livingstone—or is it Kirk?—says the plea was irresistible and secured its object.[23] The manner in which the small extra gain was sought would certainly appeal to Livingstone's grave susceptibility to the comic side of things in his dealings with primitive human nature, but to Kirk's genial benevolence and smiling tolerance of human weaknesses it would seem too naïvely guileful to be denied. We know now that these qualities in Kirk, together with an all but inexhaustible patience, were needed to the full before the expedition terminated.

He almost lost his life a few days later, and did lose what to him was all but equally precious, the elaborate notes he had painstakingly recorded of the journey, in addition to valuable drawings and botanical specimens. It was a grievous loss that nothing could make good. Eight volumes containing the results of his laborious observations vanished, as did his surgical case and other instruments, his revolver, bedding, clothes—all he possessed, in fact, except one small bag, which he grabbed in the act of sinking. The scene of the accident was the higher reach of the Kebrabasa rapids. It is feelingly referred to in the *Narrative of an Expedition to the Zambesi*,[24] but Kirk himself gives us a better account of it in his diary. Livingstone's persistence in attempting to navigate the dangerous waters was the direct cause of what might easily have been the complete destruction of the entire company and their goods. Kirk's canoe had managed to paddle into comparative safety when he suddenly perceived that Livingstone's was

[23] *Narrative of an Expedition to the Zambesi*, p. 321. The paragraph is in Kirk's style.
[24] P. 334.

in imminent peril of being dashed to pieces on a big rock round which the flood swirled and tore irresistibly. He says: [25]

> Every second we expected to see it upset and all in the boiling water. To make things worse, Mr. C. L.'s canoe was running as if into them; both would be upset. The only hope was from us. We all looked. Had we paddled on we should have saved ourselves easily, but had the others capsized there was no hope of saving them, for the water boiled up and curved in eddies, so that no man could survive. We lost a few strokes of the paddles while thus looking at the almost inevitable destruction of the others.
>
> The next thing I saw was the water rushing over our canoe. We were upset and all in the water. The others told me after that we struck with a loud crack. I heard nothing, the thing was instantaneous. Dr. L., occupied with his own danger still, heard the crash and looked up. The thing was over before he could direct his eyes and we were all under water or clinging on. It is a great thing when these accidents happen suddenly; there is no danger of any one losing presence of mind. The men behaved admirably.

The devotion and courage of these same men had been well illustrated shortly before, when Livingstone himself had been saved from immersion and perhaps drowning in the tempestuous current of a gorge formed by the Mburuma mountains.

> In going down it, the men sent by Sekeletu behaved very nobly. The canoes entered without previous survey, and the huge jobbling waves of mid-current began at once to fill them. With great presence of mind, and without a moment's hesitation, two men lightened each by jumping overboard; they then ordered a Batoka man to do the same, as "the white men must be saved." "I cannot swim," said the Batoka. "Jump out, then, and hold on to the canoe"; which he instantly did. Swimming alongside, they guided the swamping canoes down the swift current to the foot of the rapid, and then ran them ashore to bale them out. A boat could have passed down safely, but our canoes were not a foot above the water at the gun-

[25] Coupland, *op. cit.*, p. 178.

wales. Thanks to the bravery of these poor fellows nothing was lost, although everything was well soaked. [26]

Livingstone appears to have had good reason for his high opinion of the Makololo, whom he esteemed as the finest specimens of the native Africans of whom he had any knowledge. They were an eclectic race, created by the genius of Sebituane and destined like the Normans in Europe to infuse a new vitality into others rather than to achieve a permanent national existence of their own.

After Kirk's mishap the rest of the journey to Tete was made by land. The town was reached on November 23rd, and a month later almost to the day witnessed the end of the abominable *Ma-Robert*. All the members of the expedition, the two sailors who had been left in charge of her included, embarked in her on December 3rd, and were stranded on a sandbank on the 21st. The vessel filled with water, and could not be floated again. The Christmas of 1860 had to be spent in discomfort on an island near Senna, but two days later a courteous Portuguese merchant, Senhor Ferrão,[27] sent canoes for the accommodation of the whole party and had them conveyed to his residence on the mainland, where they were kindly and bountifully entertained until the new year, when they were sent on to Kongone by the same timely helper.

The fortunes of the expedition now seemed at their lowest. The British members thereof and their attendants were dependent on the local Portuguese officials for lodging and food, both of which were ungrudgingly proffered, a fact which should not be forgotten in forming a judgment upon the conduct of the latter when they and Livingstone later became at variance. Stores were exhausted; the explorer's clothing was worn out; they were in poor physical condition; tempers were

---

[26] *Narrative of an Expedition to the Zambesi*, p. 329.

[27] "Senna has one redeeming feature: it is the native village of the large-hearted and hospitable Senhor H. A. Ferrão. The benevolence of this gentleman is unbounded. The poor black stranger passing through the town goes to him almost as a matter of course for food, and is never sent away hungry. In times of famine the starving natives are fed by his generosity; hundreds of his own people he never sees except on these occasions; and the only benefit derived from being their master is, that they lean on him as a patriarchal chief, and he has the satisfaction of settling their differences, and of saving their lives in seasons of drought and scarcity." (*Narrative of an Expedition to the Zambesi*, p. 35 f.)

frayed; no news had come from home, and their spirits were at zero.

But on January 31st the sun broke through their clouds for a time. The new steamer, the *Pioneer*, which had been constructed in England under Rae's superintendence to replace the *Ma-Robert*, arrived and anchored outside Kongone, though unable to cross the bar until the river rose five days later. With her came two cruisers conveying the members of the new Oxford and Cambridge mission under Bishop Mackenzie. Livingstone's heart was greatly cheered by the advent of these new volunteers for Christian service in the Nyassa region he had so lately visited, and he rightly felt their presence and the spirit of their fine leader to be something of a counteractive to the tragical issue of the attempt to plant a mission station in the Makololo country. The Bishop and his fellow-missionaries were eager to begin operations at once, and to this end pressed that they might be taken in the *Pioneer* to some suitable location in the neighbourhood of the Shiré river; but as instructions had come for Livingstone and his assistants to explore the Rovuma river on the northern frontier of the Portuguese sphere of influence in the hope of finding access to Lake Nyassa thereby, he did not feel able to assent to the proposal. After some discussion it was agreed that the mission party should be accommodated on the island of Johanna for the time being, the Bishop accompanying Livingstone to the Rovuma as a guest and to acquire experience of the kind of conditions amid which he might expect to labour. The association thus established, brief as it was, engendered in the two men a mutual respect that was never dimmed by the smallest disagreement. It seems necessary to say this in recollection of the sharp criticisms later directed against Livingstone in connection with the Bishop's untimely death. Mackenzie was one of the noblest servants of God who have ever consecrated themselves to service in the foreign field, and the shock of his martyrdom, for it was nothing less, stunned the church at home, though ultimately, like that of Livingstone himself, proved to be the means of calling forth an amount of zeal and self-sacrifice in the same cause greater than either of them dreamed of when they first clasped hands at Kongone. The Rev. Horace Waller, who at the instance of the great missionary explorer himself edited

Livingstone's *Last Journals* when these reached England so dramatic-
ally in 1874, was another member of the Bishop's party of whom Livingstone thought highly. The personnel of the party was excellent in
quality, but in Livingstone's opinion the number was too large for
a convenient beginning and laboured under the same fatal disadvantage as the Makololo mission, the lack of efficient medical resources. [28]

Mackenzie took his men to Johanna and then joined Livingstone
and the rest of the members of the Government expedition who were
awaiting him in the *Pioneer* at the mouth of the Rovuma. Here on
March 9th, 1861, they commenced their task of ascertaining if and to
what extent the river were navigable, and whether it did or did not
issue from Lake Nyassa. The main purpose of this effort was, if possible, to obtain an accurately charted waterway to the great inland sea
which the expedition had been the means of discovering and reporting
to the world, for by now the Portuguese authorities had taken alarm
at Livingstone's activities and were endeavouring to close the Zambesi
to others than traders of their own nationality. Livingstone had re-
luctantly come to the conclusion that Portuguese trade consisted chiefly
in human flesh, and that legitimate commerce was not only in a lan-
guishing condition, but rapidly disappearing, killed by the slave trade.
Portuguese control was ineffective, and did not correspond to the extensive claims that were made for it. He found that the officials were
borrowing his charts and soundings without acknowledgment, and
asserting a priority of knowledge both of the Zambesi mouths and the
interior which they did not really possess. A hasty but futile attempt
had been made to forestall him at the Rovuma by the Governor of
Mozambique, who had sent an agent to the Sultan of Zanzibar to try
to persuade this potentate to consent to the Rovuma being made the
boundary of Portuguese territory. Of Lake Nyassa, the upper reaches
of the Shiré, and of the Zambesi above the Kebrabasa rapids they had

---

[28] He writes to Waller after the failure of the initial effort: "The clerical portion of the
mission—all good and pious men I believe—had not previously been specially educated for
the work. Bishop Mackenzie was the only missionary, and Scudamore would in time have
become a first-rate one; but simply because it was not known what other missions have had
to endure a most precious opportunity of planting the gospel was lost."

known nothing before the publication of Livingstone's discoveries; nor had they ever heard of the Victoria Falls.

The hopes based on the exploration of the Rovuma were speedily frustrated, however. The *Pioneer* only succeeded in penetrating for about thirty miles from the entrance to the river. The season was too late and the water too low to admit the passage of a vessel of as deep a draught as four feet—or, rather, it might have done so, but, unfortunately, four feet represented the draught of the *Pioneer* when unladen; with stores and fuel added it was more. Realizing this, Livingstone would fain have left her at the highest point reached and pushed on over land to the lake, but an outbreak of fever among his officers, coupled with the Bishop's strongly expressed desire not to delay longer the initiation of the work for which he and his fellow-missionaries had come to Africa, left no alternative but to turn back. This they did, Livingstone once more acting as navigating officer, owing to the fact that nearly everyone else was ill, and he alone capable of undertaking the job. After picking up the members of the Bishop's party at Johanna they steered for the Zambesi and the Shiré, the same drawback of the too deep draught of the *Pioneer*, an otherwise excellent vessel, delaying them very considerably; the Bishop and his colleagues toiled as manfully as the more seasoned members of the Government expedition in hauling the ship over shoals by means of ropes. It was not until July 8th that they reached Chibisa's village.

The task of finding a suitable location for the Universities Mission had now to be faced, and though it hindered the prosecution of the work of the official expedition somewhat, Livingstone consented to accompany the Bishop in exploring the Shiré heights with the more immediate object in view.

This was the turning-point in Livingstone's relations with the Portuguese, for it now became fully evident that the local authorities, if not the Lisbon Government itself, were behind, or at least encouraging, the nefarious operations of the slave traders. War was raging in the Manganja country, which lay on either bank of the Shiré below Chibisa's, and a tribe known by the name of the Waiao or Ajawa was harrying the villages far and near, and carrying off great numbers of the inhabitants to be sold into bondage. Terrible and revolting were the spectacles to be met with in the track of the marauders. The population of the district was dense, but was rapidly being decimated. Skeletons lay everywhere, and the stench from the putrefying bodies of the recently slain offended the nostrils of the horrified missionaries and sickened their souls; the river itself was encumbered by floating corpses, which were washed against the sides of the anchored *Pioneer* and the borrowed canoes in which members of the party paddled their way farther up stream. The dead in the raided districts outnumbered the living, the invaders seeming to take a pleasure in killing for killing's sake. Little children and aged persons of both sexes were as ruthlessly murdered as any of the able-bodied men who showed resistance, and it was no uncommon thing for infants to be torn from their mothers' arms and dashed to pieces in order that the women should be freer to march without having to carry their offspring or otherwise care for them on the way. It was Livingstone's opinion that not more than a fifth of the poor creatures captured survived, and not more than a tenth ever reached the coast, the overwhelming majority either dying or being butchered in cold blood.

At a village in the hills, ruled over by a petty chief, Mbame, with whom Livingstone possessed some previous acquaintance, the party received information that a slave gang was shortly to pass, and the question at once arose whether it would be legitimate to interfere therewith on behalf of the wretched victims. Livingstone decided that he was morally justified in so doing, because for some time past he had been in possession of positive proof that the scoundrels engaged in the traffic were deliberately following the trails blazed by himself and availing themselves, for their own wicked purposes, of affiliations he had made. Scarcely had his resolves been taken—the Bishop was absent at the moment, having gone some little distance to bathe—when the opportunity presented itself for putting it into practice.

A few minutes after Mbame had spoken to us, the slave party, a long line of manacled men, women, and children, came wending their way round the hill and into the valley, on the side of which the village stood. The black drivers, armed with muskets, and be-decked with various articles of finery, marched jauntily in the front, middle, and rear of the line; some of them blowing exultant notes out of long tin horns. They seemed to feel that they were doing a very noble thing, and might proudly march with an air of triumph. But the instant the fellows caught a glimpse of the English, they darted off like mad into the forest; so fast, indeed, that we caught but a glimpse of their red caps and the soles of their feet. The chief of the party alone remained; and he, from being in front, had his hand tightly grasped by a Makololo! He proved to be a well-known slave of the late Commandant at Tette,[29] and for some time our own attendant while there. On asking him how he ob-tained these captives, he replied, he had bought them; but on enquiring of the people themselves, all, save four, said they had been captured in war. While this enquiry was going on, he bolted too. The captives knelt down, and, in their way of expressing thanks, clapped their hands with great energy. They were thus left entirely on our hands, and knives were soon busy at work cutting the women and children loose. It was more difficult to cut the men adrift, as each had his neck in the fork of a stout stick, six or seven feet long, and kept in by an iron rod which was riveted at both ends across the throat. With a saw, luckily in the Bishop's baggage, one by one the men were sawn out into freedom. The women, on being told to take the meal they were carrying and cook breakfast for themselves and the children, seemed to consider the news too good to be true; but after a little coaxing went at it with alacrity, and made a capital fire by which to boil their pots with the slave sticks and bonds, their old acquaintances through many a sad night and weary day. Many were mere children, about five years of age and under. One little boy, with the simplicity of childhood, said to our men, "The others tied and starved us, you cut the ropes and tell us to eat; what sort of people are you? Where did you come from?" Two of the women had been shot the day before for attempting to untie the thongs. This, the rest were told, was to prevent them from attempting to escape. One woman had her infant's brains knocked out, because she could not carry her load and it. And a man was

[29] So spelt by Livingstone at this period.

despatched with an axe, because he had broken down with fatigue. Self-interest would have set a watch over the whole rather than commit murder; but in this traffic we invariably find self-interest overcome by contempt of human life and by bloodthirstiness. [30]

The dramatic episode above described has been dwelt upon in detail because it had untoward consequences which to this hour have involved both Livingstone and Mackenzie in some measure of hostile criticism. The former did not have to use force on the occasion to effect his object of setting slaves at liberty, but from his own words it is clear that he was prepared to do so, and when the Bishop arrived on the scene, he in turn cordially approved of the action taken. No formal protest was made by the local Portuguese officials, but as the leader of the slave gang was an agent of the local commandant, there could not be much doubt that he had his master's tacit or overt sanction for what he was doing; a hint to this effect was afterwards given in a remark of the Governor-General of Mozambique, brother of the Governor of Tete, that further action of the kind on Livingstone's part or that of other British missionaries in territory over which Portugal claimed suzerainty would not be permitted. [31] Complaint was subsequently made to the British Government that Livingstone was using geographical exploration and missionary zeal as a mere excuse for encroaching upon Portuguese commercial and territorial rights in the interest of his own country. Unquestionably this was one main reason for the recall of the expedition, though unconfessed as such by the British Cabinet. The Prince Consort [32] intervened privately in the matter because of his consanguinity with the Portuguese royal family, and as British statesmen took the view that Livingstone had not adhered to his undertaking to refrain from embroiling himself with Portuguese officials and merchants, it was deemed politic to cancel his commission. This was not yet, however; it took time for the new feeling of

---

[30] *Narrative of an Expedition to the Zambesi*, p. 356 f.
[31] To Kirk. *Cf.* Coupland, *op. cit.*, p. 233; and *Narrative of an Expedition to the Zambesi*, p. 420.
[32] The Prince, as is well known, was a man of humane and philanthropic principles, but in this instance Livingstone's action had been misrepresented both to him and the King of Portugal.

antagonism between the explorer and his former Portuguese friends
to mature; but here we have the overt act which marked the beginning of it.

Writing to Horace Waller on February 12th, 1863, he takes a more
sanguine view of British Government action in the matter than events
were to justify for years to come. It does not seem to have occurred
to him at this juncture that fault could be found with what he had
done, or that there could be any doubt about its receiving the sanction
of Her Majesty's ministers.

> Between ourselves, Earl Russell gave me a warm touch of appro-
> bation for our doings when last up, and sent orders to our ministry
> at Lisbon to make a strong representation to the Portuguese Govern-
> ment about the deeds of the Tettites. I have been following up my
> former statements by giving an account of the sad depopulation that
> has gone on by means of Mariamo.[33] We have counted thirty-one
> bodies floating down; and I have taken good care to point out to
> Lord Palmerston the causes of the failure of his policy on the East
> coast which has been so triumphant on the West. . . . I trust that
> by the blessing of the Highest, this may lead to an alteration of
> policy. But this, of course, is only among ourselves to be talked of
> for the present. A canoe load of ammunition, wines, etc., for Mari-
> amo was caught at the mouth of the Shiré coming up *in the name of
> the Mission.* Oh, the scamps! And His Excellency of Quilimane
> has been writing to the other of Mosambique, saying that so much
> merchandise as powder, arms, and calicoes are introduced for the
> scientific and exploring expeditions under Dr. L. and Bishop M. that
> the commerce of the country is injured.

A further regrettable result of the decisive action above recorded
was its bearing upon the immediate future of Bishop Mackenzie and
his mission. Fifty more slaves were freed by Livingstone and the
Bishop together on the next day but one after what had happened at
Mbame's village. This also was done without striking a blow, but
a further pursuance of the same methods by the Bishop was not at-

---

[33] The most notorious of the Portuguese half-caste slave raiders, stigmatized as a rebel, but
suspected by Livingstone to be operating with the connivance of the Portuguese officials.

tended with the same good fortune. In response to the invitation of a local chief, Chigunda, Mackenzie fixed upon Magomero in the Shiré region as the site for his missionary station. In proceeding thither, he and his party were attacked by a party of Ajawa raiders, who fired upon them, compelling them to return the fire in self-defence. The Bishop had been vainly attempting to parley with his assailants and use moral suasion. Livingstone was still present, and in his report of the occurrence states that this was the first occasion on which he had ever come into armed conflict with African natives. He earnestly advised the Bishop to keep rigidly clear of tribal quarrels in time to come if the mission were to prosper, and after seeing him and his colleagues established at Magomero, took leave of them and returned to the *Pioneer*.

No sooner was he gone than the Bishop was confronted with the perplexing problem of the attitude he must take towards the murderous Ajawa, who were burning and slaying without mercy among the very people the mission aimed to benefit. Appeal was made to him to come to the deliverance of prisoners the raiders had seized, and after consultation with his fellow-labourers he yielded to the petition and went with an armed force—firstly in the hope of persuading the aggressors to restore the captives and retire, but, failing this, to compel compliance. The Ajawa, remembering Livingstone's action at Mbame's now knew that they were dealing with British missionaries instead of Portuguese traders, and instantly showed fight rather than release their prey. A sharp skirmish ensued, in which the Ajawa were routed.

Mackenzie's action in engaging in hostilities in this manner was severely commented upon in the press, both of the Cape and Great Britain, and Livingstone came in for a predominent share of the blame. At the time he defended the Bishop, but later excused himself for so doing on the ground that he had felt it right to stand by a friend who was being unfairly treated, but that he had not really approved of what had been done; the Bishop had acted, he said, in direct opposition to his wishes and counsel.

One cannot help feeling that in taking this ground Livingstone does not exhibit himself at his best; he is a little over-anxious to exonerate himself from complicity in a course of conduct not so very different from that which he had himself adopted a little while before. It might fairly be said that he had set the example, although he had not gone so far as the Bishop in employing force to free an oppressed neighbourhood from brigandage and massacre. The affair is fully dealt with in Goodwin's *Memoir of Bishop Mackenzie,* chap. xi., wherein the view is taken that the forcible liberation of slaves at Mbame's village by Livingstone fixed the character of sturdy champions upon Mackenzie's party. Goodwin writes: "The foundation of this pacific policy (Mackenzie's) was destroyed before the entire responsibility of the conduct of the party devolved upon the Bishop." On the other hand, Mackenzie himself, quoted by Goodwin, says:[34] "Livingstone was right to go with loaded gun, and free the poor slaves; and, there being so few English here, we are right, though clergymen and preachers of the Gospel, to go with them, and by our presence, and the sight of our guns, and their use if necessary (which may God avert) to strengthen his hands." The plain fact is that the indignation excited in the honest and compassionate hearts of these two Christian men and their associates rendered it impossible for them to stand idly by while unspeakably vile atrocities were being committed in their proximity. Their spontaneous action on behalf of the victims needs no laboured defence.[35]

Towards the end of January, 1862, a further accession of strength seemed to be vouchsafed to Livingstone in the arrival of H.M.S. *Gorgon* with Mrs. Livingstone on board, accompanied by Bishop Mackenzie's sister; Mrs. Burrup, wife of one of the Bishop's colleagues; the Rev. E. Hawkins and other recruits for the Universities Mission; and the Rev. James Stewart of the Free Church of Scotland, who had been sent out by his denomination to ascertain what was possible in the

[34] P. 238.
[35] The letter to Waller quoted above, February 12th, 1863, is explicit in regard to Livingstone's attitude towards the militancy of the members of the mission in this case, whatever he may have felt or said when trouble supervened about it afterwards. "I thought you wrong in attacking the Ajawa till I looked on it as defence of your poor orphans. I thought that you had shut yourselves up to one tribe, and that the Manganja, but I think differently now, and only wish they would send out Dr. Pusey here. He would learn a little sense—of which I suppose I have need myself." A characteristic gibe at the Tractarian leader, and an equally characteristic confession.

way of instituting missionary operations in the part of Africa where
Livingstone was now engaged. The *Gorgon* had also a brig in tow,
which was bringing the admirable little boat Livingstone had had
built for himself through the good offices of James Young at a cost of
£6,000. Fortune seemed to be smiling upon the expedition at last.

Yet scarcely had the new arrivals been transferred to the shore
and afterwards to the deck of Livingstone's new boat, the *Lady Nyassa*,
for the voyage up the Shiré to join the mission at Magomero, when the
terrible tidings broke upon them that the Bishop and Mr. Burrup were
both dead, having succumbed to exposure and virulent attacks of the
usual scourge, malarial fever. The blow was as paralyzing to Livingstone as to the bereaved women, and he did not overestimate the extent
of the calamity when he said to his companions, "This will hurt us
all." He knew what the first effect of the news would be in England,
and his forecast was correct; it was felt that the attempt to push into
the interior was premature, and that the work, if renewed, should proceed more cautiously. In consonance with this general opinion, Bishop
Tozer, who came out to succeed Bishop Mackenzie, removed the headquarters of the mission to Zanzibar, despite Livingstone's protest,[36]
and Mr. Stewart reported to his committee in Edinburgh that it would
be wise to defer establishing a Free Church mission on the mainland
until conditions were better understood in a country so unhealthy
for Europeans. These decisions were very disappointing to the great
originator of the new missionary advance that had been made, all the
more so because his heart was set on suppressing the slave trade, which
was daily assuming larger proportions; but there is little doubt that
in the circumstances the policy adopted was sound. The tide only
receded for a time, to flow with greater volume in years to come.
Livingstone would see of the travail of his soul and be satisfied if he

[36] Livingstone and Tozer were not mutually attracted, and the former delivers a shrewd
thrust at the latter's prudential withdrawal from Magomero by remarking that "the Mission,
in fleeing from Morambala to an island in the Indian Ocean, acted as St. Augustine would
have done, had he located himself on one of the Channel Islands, when sent to Christianize
the natives of Central England" (*Narrative of an Expedition to the Zambesi*, p. 574).
    An undated letter to Horace Waller contains the sardonic passage:
    "Tozer is trying the effect of gaudy dresses, banners and crosses as mission agencies. If he
succeeds it will be interesting to find Mohammedans bowing down to red crosses and red
flags, not to mention Tozer's red hair, though they think all these are idols."

could view the results of his labours and sacrifices in the Shiré and Nyassa districts to-day. [37]

How deeply he felt what to his heroic spirit was nothing less than a cowardly abandonment of a great opportunity is well illustrated by the following striking paragraph in a letter to Horace Waller, dated August 13th, 1863:

> The great teacher commanded His missionaries to begin "at Jerusalem" with those who had committed the worst murder the world ever saw. As to their conduct neutralizing the effect of the teaching of the missionaries—my dear fellow, if wickedness even *in* the churches *could* have done that Christianity would long ago have been banished from the world.

We may reasonably anticipate at this point his outburst to the same friend when he learned that he himself was to be deprived of official countenance and support for the work he was doing for the deliverance of a helpless and down-trodden race. All his hopes and plans were falling in ruin about him, and in his generous rage at what was happening he cries out defiantly:

> I guess that I shall work alone in Africa yet. £100 a year would do to support one. . . . I don't know whether I am to go on the shelf or not. If so, I make the shelf Africa. If *Lady Nyassa* is well sold I shall manage, though I be not so rich as you. . . . A mission without difficulties would be to me like a man without a shadow.
>
> Think of Moffat running away from a difficulty—a lion from a turkey cock—no! no!

Hard fate had not done with him yet. The next life to be exacted as part of the price of the deliverance of Africa from heathen darkness and cruelty was that of his own beloved wife. Mrs. Livingstone had only rejoined him for a few weeks, to pass away from him for ever in this world. She died at Shupanga on April 27th, 1862, after a brief illness engendered by enforced delay in that disease-ridden

---

[37] There is scarce a mission in Nyassaland to-day that is not a direct result of the ringing call to service that issued from David Livingstone." (J. N. Ogilvie, *"Africa's Sunny Fountains"*: *Travel Notes of a Visit to the African Mission Fields of the Church of Scotland,* 1920.)

spot. This was the crowning tragedy of Livingstone's whole experience, as has already been indicated in an earlier chapter. The cry that issued from his breaking heart in the hour of bereavement was heard by none but God; it was in his private diary that it found most poignant expression; not even to Dr. and Mrs. Moffat could he reveal the uttermost depths of his sorrow. Those who had most to do with him from this time forward have stated that he never was the same man again. The succession of calamities he had sustained within a comparatively short period robbed him of some of his resiliency. Henceforth he was graver, more silent, aloof and self-contained than before, but, if possible, more dogged, single-minded, and concentrated in purpose. He lived now but for one thing, to claim Africa for Christ and make an end of the slave trade.[38]

As soon as the *Lady Nyassa* could be fitted together and launched, he and the remaining members of the expedition returned to the Rovuma river to continue the exploration that had been abandoned when the current failed the *Pioneer*. The party was subjected to continual harassment from hostile natives, and only succeeded in confirming what they had previously suspected, that the Rovuma did not flow out of Lake Nyassa. They were only able to sail for a hundred and fifty miles inward ere they found themselves blocked by cataracts, as on the Shiré and Zambesi; it was therefore deemed best to make their way back to these, which were now perceived to be the main arteries east of the great central watershed. This done, they embarked in the *Pioneer* on January 10th, 1863, and with the *Lady Nyassa* in tow steamed up to the Murchison Cataracts. There they landed, took the *Lady Nyassa* to pieces, and began the bold engineering enterprise of constructing a forty-mile road along which the sections of the boat might be carried to the upper reach of the Shiré, whence unobstructed access to the lake was to be expected. Before the work could be completed a despatch was received recalling the expedition. Obscuran-

---

[38] Writing to his trusted friend, Horace Waller, April 28th, 1863, he permits himself to break silence for a moment on a subject to which his references were as rare as they were dolorous. "Last night was the anniversary of my Mary's death. That bitter sorrow is somewhat healed, and I think of her as looking down with her wonted interest in my work."

tism and diplomatic expediency had triumphed for the moment, and Livingstone and his schemes of evangelization and commerce were to be eliminated from a scene where they had become an inconvenience to sinister ruling interests. [39]

This was at the beginning of July, and as some months must intervene before there would be a sufficient depth of water to render it possible to take the *Pioneer* down to the ocean, Livingstone decided to make good use of the time in exploring the shores of the lake. It was hopeless to proceed with the scheme of transporting the *Lady Nyassa* thither, the Government order to leave being too definite to permit of the continuance of a work it would take long to complete. This was another grievous disappointment to him. He had reiterated again and again through various channels his belief that even one small armed steamer on the lake would be sufficient to scotch, if not to destroy, the slave trade; is it, then, illegitimate to suggest that if he could have put his own small ship on that great inland sea he would not have hesitated to use it in the cause to which all the moral force of his nature was now devoted? [40] As it was, all he could do was to have a small sailing boat borne past the rapids in the hope that he might be able to explore at least some portion of the northern and western shores of the lake to ascertain if any large river flowed into it from that side. The boat was lost, together with the greater port of the stores intended for the trip, through the awkwardness of the native bearers; yet, undaunted, this extraordinary man, accompanied only by Rae and five Makololo attendants, tramped on foot round the south and southwestern side of Nyassa, covering a total of seven hundred and sixty miles in fifty-five days, and getting to within ten days' march of Lake

[39] "I had come to the conclusion," he writes to Horace Waller on April 30th, "that no good could be done by this expedition while the subjects of His Most Faithful Majesty were allowed to follow on our footsteps and spoil all by their slave forays, and told Earl Russell this distinctly. He does not refer to this in his instructions to withdraw, as it would perhaps be impolitic in a statesman to do so."

[40] To Horace Waller, November 3rd, 1866, he writes: "Instead of a steamer that I did my best to get on the lake, two Arab dhows ply their calling as slavers. The owner of one has swept a large tract of the western side clear of people—at least, so say his own people. They kept their craft out of my way lest I should burn them. No one can estimate the amount of good Bishop Mackenzie's mission would have effected; but it has gone for our day."

Bangweolo. But for the obligation laid upon him to get back to the
Pioneer and hand her over to the British naval authorities at Mozambique before the end of the year, he would have done much more.

What to do with his own little *Lady Nyassa* was something of a
problem for him. He had not unreasonably hoped that the Government might reimburse some portion of his outlay upon her, a sum
that had swallowed nearly the whole of his fairly considerable literary
profits. Had he been allowed to go on with his work the boat would
have proved more serviceable than the larger vessel, but as he was not,
and as the Government made no offer to relieve him of her, he was
forced to dispose of her on his own responsibility. Sell her on the
African coast he would not, lest she should fall into Portuguese hands
and ultimately be used for the harrying of defenceless people and the
conveyance of slaves. Concluding that there was but one alternative
left to him, he undertook one of the most amazing feats of his whole
amazing life, that of sailing the tiny vessel across two thousand five
hundred miles of ocean and docking her in Bombay. He navigated her
himself, and with a crew of three white men and a handful of natives,
managed to bring her safely into harbour after one of the most thrilling voyages on record. He entered Bombay unnoticed, and it was
not until the port officials boarded the battered midget and examined
her papers that the identity of her daring commander was discovered.
Then, indeed, the warmest of greetings was extended to him. Sir
Bartle Frere, the Governor, received him with much respect and insisted on entertaining him during his stay; the entire British community rose to do him honour, and merchants and representatives of
every commercial and manufacturing interest showed themselves
fully alive to, and anxious to co-operate with, his designs for the proper
development of tropical and semi-tropical Africa. This well-informed
and intelligent friendliness did not cease with the occasion on which it
was first manifested, but took practical form later, as will be mentioned in its place.

But Livingstone did not remain long on Indian soil. He was anxious to get home and deliver his soul to the British nation on the
burning subject of African slavery and the moral responsibility of

Christendom in relation thereto; therefore, without delaying to negotiate with a possible purchaser of the *Lady Nyassa,* he laid up the boat, made arrangements for his men, took leave of his distinguished host, who had now become a closely attached friend, and embarked for England by the first available steamer. He arrived in London on July 23rd, 1864.

CHAPTER XI

THE LAST VENTURE

His reception in England on this occasion was not at first as enthusiastic as the previous one; there was less excitement about it and more disposition to be critical. The Government was not cordial—he speaks of the coldness of Lord Russell's manner to him—and London Society, as is the way of London Society, did not find him quite such a sensation as it had done eight years earlier, and now had other lions in view to share attention with him.

But the country at large took him to its heart again, and listened to what he had to say with, if possible, added respect. His address to the British Association at Bath, on the iniquities of the slave trade, produced a profound impression and stirred the public conscience to such effect that the Portuguese authorities at Lisbon felt themselves constrained to answer it, and forthwith instituted an anti-Livingstone propaganda, accusing him of misrepresentation and ulterior motives. But the facts he had supplied could not be explained away, and Lord Palmerston, as guardian of British foreign policy, openly showed that his sympathies were with the returned explorer's protest against the barbarities of an evil system carried on under the ægis of a European power. Nor was there any hesitation on the part of the churches and of the nation generally in accepting his statements as true, and an agitation at once began for stricter measures to be taken for the patrol of the East African coast by British warships for the purpose of suppressing the traffic in human beings, as had already been done with comparative success in the west. In the provinces there was as great an eagerness to see and hear the famous missionary as formerly, and had he felt disposed to spend the whole of his time in addressing meetings and giving lectures he would have been furnished with ample opportunity for doing so. There was no diminution of interest either in his personality or his work.

But feeling that he could better serve the cause he had at heart by putting the story he had to tell into narrative form, he accepted the invitation of his friend, W. F. Webb, of Newstead Abbey, to make that noble residence his home while writing his recollections of his six years' service as the head of a British Government mission of exploration in Africa. He and Webb were no strangers to each other; they had met while the latter was big game hunting on African soil some years before, and each had at once discerned in the other a kindred spirit. The members of the Webb family became greatly attached to Livingstone, and regarded him with a reverence and affection that the eight months of his sojourn under their roof deepened and intensified in the familiarity of daily intercourse, and he on his side responded to their kindness with warm gratitude, for one of his most marked characteristics at all times was his sensitiveness to human sympathy; he expanded in its atmosphere, and was as thankful for it as he was easily wounded and repelled by harsh and unfair treatment. His generous hosts insisted on inviting his daughter Agnes to be his fellow-guest for the whole period of his stay, and she and they in concert helped him with his work as capable and willing amanuenses.

The book was finished on April 15th, 1865, and he was then free to consider a proposition which had been made to him by the Royal Geographical Society through Sir Roderick Murchison some months earlier, that he should return to Africa to endeavour to settle a question which had long been a subject of much speculation among travellers and scientific geographers, namely that of the central watershed of the continent. For ages the mystery of the source or sources of the Nile had been one of the commonplaces of discussion. The mystery had already ceased to be a mystery, although this neither he nor anyone else knew positively at the time, and the suggestion of clearing it up once and for all fascinated him. Sir Roderick could not have dangled a more seductive temptation before his mind, and it derived added force from being combined with the larger programme of

defining the watershed of the three great river systems of Africa—
the Nile, the Congo, and the Zambesi. It may with truth be said that
Livingstone has done more towards solving this problem than any
other single investigator.

He consented to go, and Government sanction and support were
obtained for the project, but on far from advantageous terms. Indeed,
the details of Livingstone's financial arrangements at this time both
with the Government and the Royal Geographical Society reflect no
credit upon either of these bodies. Lord Palmerston sent a message
to him at Newstead Abbey to inquire what he could do for him. Had
Livingstone been more worldly-minded he would have asked for some
distinction for himself in addition to a pension and a satisfactory provision for his family. Instead of this he merely asked for free access
to the highlands by the Zambesi and Shiré to be secured by a treaty
with Portugal. In the end, after much negotiation, the Government
agreed to sending him out with the status of Consul for that portion
of the African coast lying between the Portuguese sphere of influence
and Abyssinia. The sum of five hundred pounds was granted towards
his equipment, but he was to have no salary, and was explicitly informed that he must expect no pension. For sheer meanness this arrangement would be hard to beat, considering what Livingstone had
already done to add to the world's knowledge and to the power and
reputation of Great Britain. The fact was that at the moment he
was somewhat of an embarrassment to an administration that wanted
to keep on friendly terms with Portugal and was not prepared to
spend money to preserve African aborigines from slaughter and servitude. The terms of Livingstone's new commission carefully shut him
out, so it was believed, from all possibility of giving trouble to the
Portuguese and their slave-hunting satellites.

Rigorous and parsimonious as the conditions were, they seem to have
disturbed Livingstone less than his instructions from the Royal Geographical Society. The latter annoyed him, for an inadequate grant
of five hundred pounds was accompanied by the most detailed directions as to what he was expected to do and the reports he was to
furnish. In his private correspondence he gives vent to some amount

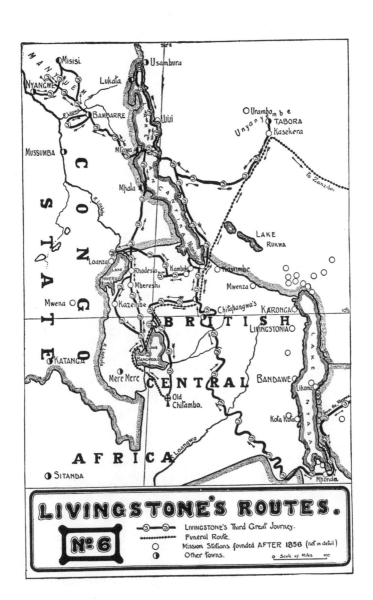

MANYUEMA

Misisi.

NYANGWE

Lukala.

Usambura

BAMBARRE

Mfawa

Uiui

Uramobombe

Unyanyo

TABORA

Kasekera

MUSSUMBA

CONGO STATE

Mhala

To Zanzibar

LAKE RUKWA

Loanza

LAKE MWERU

Rhodesia

Kambde

Mwena

Mberesh

Kazembe

Kawimbe

Mwenza

Chitahangwa's

KARONGA

BRITISH

LIVINGSTONIA

Mere Mere

CENTRAL

BANDAWE

Mwena

KATANGA

LAKE BANGWEOLO

Old Chitambo.

Likoma

Kota Kota

AFRICA

SITANDA

Mponda

LAKE NYASA

LIVINGSTONE'S ROUTES.

Nº 6

LIVINGSTONE'S Third Great Journey.
Funeral Route.
Mission Stations founded AFTER 1856 (not in detail)
Other towns.
Scale of Miles

of irritation in respect to these requirements, and very reasonably inquires what the personages who drafted them really knew of the expense of African travel and what they expected in return for the meagre donation they had contributed towards carrying out the programme assigned him. Had it not been for the munificence of his friend, James Young, who gave as much as the British Government and the Royal Geographical Society put together for the purposes of the expedition, it is inconceivable that it could have been organized at all. But as Livingstone wrote to this ever-loyal and dependable helper: "I would not consent to go simply as a geographer, but as a missionary, and do geography by the way, because I feel I am in the way of duty when trying either to enlighten these poor people, or open their land to lawful commerce." [1]

A few weeks before he sailed he had the mingled sorrow and consolation of taking a last farewell of his mother. He had known that she was dying for some time before the end came, and had been spending time with her in intimate and loving exchange of experiences, but he was not actually present at the final scene; the fulfilment of necessary engagements at Oxford detained him in the south, but he was able to reach her home in time to fulfil her dear wish that one of her boys should lay her head in the grave. Her last words were a benediction upon his youngest child, Anna Mary, who had been lifted up for her to see.

He left England for Bombay in August, and on arriving lost no time in disposing of the *Lady Nyassa* and getting together what he held to be the necessary minimum of equipment for what proved to be his last work in and for Africa. The British residents of Bombay subscribed nearly a thousand pounds for the undertaking, an action in marked contrast with that of the official promoters of the scheme at home. He did not obtain a high price for his boat—£2,300 for what had originally cost him £6,000. He was not a good man at business, and never understood finance; hence the step he next took, of depositing the small amount thus obtained in an Indian bank for the benefit of his children, was a mistaken one. The bank failed a short time after-

[1] Blaikie, *op. cit.*, p. 295.

wards, and every penny was lost. His expenditure on the *Lady Nyassa*
was from first to last a bad bargain for himself, and an almost total
sacrifice of what were at the best but slender means. It may with
truth be said that virtually all he was ever able to earn was freely expended on his work; neither he nor his dependents derived any profit
therefrom. He gave far more in this way than he ever received in
salary.

On the present expedition he took with him a number of African
boys, mostly emancipated slaves, who had been trained at the Nassick Mission near Bombay, and a detachment of thirteen Sepoys. The
latter were included because they were supposed to be accustomed to
marching and discipline, but in practice they proved to be lazy and in-
subordinate, as well as cruel to the animals under their care. Sir Bartle
Frere helped by giving the explorer and his company free passage in a
Government steamer to Zanzibar. The steamer was to be handed over
to the Sultan as a gift, together with a letter commending Livingstone
to that potentate's good offices, an introduction which smoothed the
way considerably in the provision of further facilities. At Zanzibar
ten Johanna men were engaged as an addition to the company brought
from India, so that Livingstone's total following now consisted of
thirty-six men, several of whom had served with him previously.
Among these were Susi and Chuma, whose names will ever be held
in honour for their fidelity to their great leader in his hour of direst
need, a fidelity which extended to treating his remains as a sacred
charge after his death and bringing them in safety to the coast—
one of the most wonderful feats on record, never surpassed by
Livingstone himself. Chuma was one of the slaves liberated by Livingstone and Bishop Mackenzie in 1861, and had spent some time
afterwards in the care of the Universities Mission. An amusing reference to him appears in an undated note to Horace Waller: "Chuma
is a very sharp fellow—never got into any quarrel at school. I suspect his appearance put the fear of death into the Hindoos, but Dr.
Wilson thinks it is his goodness." Evidently this is early in their
relationship. To the same correspondent a letter from Ujiji, dated
November 3rd, 1871, passes a strong encomium on this man: "I see I

have said nothing of Chuma, though he has most character and he is likely to turn out the most influential of all the *libertos* I know—a boisterous, roaring, laughter-provoking boy—some modesty and reads frequently." How well this discerning judgment was deserved the near future was to prove.

Six camels were purchased in Zanzibar, four Indian buffaloes, two mules, and four donkeys. It was hoped that these might be immune from the ravages of the tsetse fly, but the experiment did not prove successful. The camels and buffaloes were as viciously attacked by the pest as the draught oxen had been in the explorer's previous experience; the mules and donkeys fared better, but observations on their utility were vitiated by the drivers' callousness and neglect.

Furnished with letters of recommendation from the Sultan to the Arabs of the interior, the expedition started from Zanzibar for the Rovuma river on March 19th, 1866, the animals and stores being towed in an Arab dhow by H.M.S. *Penguin*. Owing, however, to the formation of new sand-banks at the mouth of the Rovuma, entrance there was found to be impracticable, and a landing was effected instead at the bay of Mikindany, twenty-five miles farther north. The *Penguin* then left and the march began. It is almost pathetic to read at this stage with what exhilaration and high hopes Livingstone faced the task before him. An entry in his Journal dated March 26th states:

> The mere animal pleasure of travelling in a wild, unexplored country is very great. When on lands of a couple of thousand feet elevation, brisk exercise imparts elasticity to the muscles, fresh and healthy blood circulates through the brain, the mind works well, the eye is clear, the step is firm, and a day's exertion always makes the evening's repose thoroughly enjoyable.
>
> We have usually the stimulus of remote chances of danger either from beasts or men. Our sympathies are drawn out towards our humble, hardy companions by a community of interests, and, it may be, of perils, which make us all friends. . . . The effect of travel on a man whose heart is in the right place is that the mind is made more self-reliant: it becomes more confident in its own resources—there is greater presence of mind. The body is soon well-

knit; the muscles of the limbs grow as hard as a board, and seem to have no fat; the countenance is bronzed, and there is no dyspepsia. Africa is a most wonderful country for appetite, and it is only when one gloats over marrow bones or elephant's feet that indigestion is possible. No doubt much toil is involved, and fatigue of which travellers in the more temperate climes can form but a faint conception; but the sweat of one's brow is no longer a curse when one works for God: it proves a tonic to the system, and is actually a blessing. No one can truly appreciate the charm of repose unless he has undergone severe exertion. [2]

This cheery avowal is almost identical in substance with the radiant descriptions he sent home of his first experiences of African travel when journeying from Algoa Bay to Kuruman by ox-waggon twenty-five years before. The veteran explorer is of the same mind as the missionary neophyte totally unacquainted with the perils and perplexities of the path he has chosen. Here is clear demonstration, if such were needed, that Livingstone was a born wanderer, and could never have settled for very long in any one spot or routine occupation; he must be for ever on the move, learning, scrutinizing, achieving, revealing; it was his destiny, and he could no more have escaped it than he could have remade his temperament. It is idle to speculate whether he might have become equally celebrated in another line of life; no other line of life was possible for him.

But the joyous anticipation of high adventure here confessed did not last long; a very different story was soon to be told. From the first day after the overland march to Lake Nyassa commenced, the Sepoys and Johanna men outvied each other in shirking and untrustworthiness. They were unscrupulous liars and thieves, ever ready to avoid duty on the smallest pretext and to abuse their leader's kindness and forbearance to the farthest limit. By June 18th Livingstone is committing to his Journal his conviction that the Sepoys are "an utter nuisance," and they have had to be warned that physical chastisement will be inflicted upon them if they do not mend their ways. On July 7th comes the significant entry, absolutely unique in Livingstone's memo-

[2] *Last Journals*, vol. i., p. 13 *f.*

DAVID LIVINGSTONE AND ANNA MARY, HIS YOUNGEST
DAUGHTER

ries of his relations with subordinates, that in fulfilment of the warning
he had given, he administered corporal punishment with a cane to two
defaulters. The note is added: "I felt that I was degrading myself,
and resolved not to do the punishment myself again." [3] Within a few
weeks all the animals were dead of ill-treatment and underfeeding; in
more than one instance there was good reason to believe that they were
purposely killed by the rascals to whose charge they had been committed. How it was that Livingstone's mastery of these fellows was
so much less thorough than the moral sway he had been wont to exercise over his Makololo and other native helpers on his previous and
equally arduous expeditions must remain unexplained; probably it was
due to failing vitality; partly, also, it may be accounted for by the intensity of his absorption in his objective. From this time forward
there is evidence that he became increasingly obsessed by the urge to
keep on at all hazards, ever looking for something ahead, ever hun-
gering for fresh prospects, and unwilling to halt or turn aside; the
craving to discover had become insatiable with him, an end in itself,
not to be moderated nor denied.

Ere the month was out the Sepoys had to be paid off and sent back
as utterly useless and worse; they were an actual danger to himself, and
quite capable of murdering him. Unfortunately, their bad example
and obscene habits and conversation left an evil moral legacy behind
in the debasement of the Johanna men and some of the Nassick porters. In September the former deserted through fear of the fierce
Mazitu, a Zulu tribe whose country they were entering, and their
leader, Musa, on returning to Zanzibar, spun a tale so circumstantial
of Livingstone's death by violence at the hands of natives that the world
believed it, and did not learn the truth till some months later. Lieutenant E. D. Young, who had left the *Gorgon* to work with Livingstone
in the latter part of the Zambesi expedition, was commissioned by the
Royal Geographical Society to verify or disprove Musa's statements.
This he did, ascending in his boat, the *Search,* as far as the upper Shiré,
and completely establishing the fact that the explorer was still alive
and continuing his progress, though at too great a distance for com-

[3] *Ibid.,* p. 70.

munication with him to be possible for some time. This was the first
of the several organized attempts that were made during the next five
years to satisfy public solicitude for Livingstone's safety by seeking
news of him and taking measures for his relief. It was an excellent
piece of work, and reflected great credit upon the man chiefly responsible for it.

Livingstone remained in ignorance of Musa's fiction, the consequent
anxiety, and the efforts put forth on his behalf.[4] By the time Young
reported he was steadily plodding his way along between Lakes Tanganyika and Bangweolo, amid incredible difficulties and privations.
He had reached Lake Nyassa within four months of the departure
from Zanzibar, but found himself unable to hire or purchase boats for
crossing it; the slave traders placed a positive embargo on all negotiations for transit facilities in the hope of turning him back; they had
no mind to assist him to make closer acquaintance with their perform-
ances. He was therefore reduced to going on foot round the south end
of the lake, and thence striking north-west towards Lake Moero (or
Mweru), which he had reason to believe might mark the main line of
division between the sources of the great central river systems of the
continent. In this theory he was not far wrong, though, as he later
learned, Lake Moero forms only a part, and not the most important
part, of the chain of sources of which he was in search.

The daily horrors he encountered on his progress along the shores
of Lake Nyassa filled him with sadness. Since he had last visited this
region and been struck by its grandeur and illimitable natural wealth,
the blight of civil war and slavery had fallen upon it and converted it
into a wilderness; food was almost unobtainable, the land was becoming depopulated, ruin and desolation abounded; charred habitations,
the inhabitants driven away or abducted, many dead from starvation
or sheer wanton blood lust, were common sights. The spectacle excited ineradicable melancholy in his heart. "Many hopes have been
disappointed here," he writes. "Far down on the right bank of the

---

[4] "I did not know of Young's trip up after me nor of Musa's lies till now" (letter to Horace
Waller from Bambarre, February 5th, 1871).

Zambesi lies the dust of her whose death changed all my future prospects; and now, instead of a check being given to the slave trade by lawful commerce on the lake, slave dhows prosper!" [5]

His line of advance lay through a depleted territory, amid almost impassable swamps, torrential rains, and persistent floods. Hunger menaced him and his little band; he rarely had enough to eat, and then of unsuitable diet. Gone were the delighted comments on the abundance of provisions to be expected; instead there appear in his daily jottings remarks on the remembrance of dreams of enjoying an unrestricted meal of good English roast beef and the like wholesome sustenance for his wasting frame. To crown all, on January 20th, 1867, two of his now very small band of bearers bolted with his medicine chest. The gravity of this misfortune can scarcely be exaggerated. As he himself says, "I felt as if I had now received the sentence of death," [6] This was exactly the state of the case, for to being left without medicines is directly attributable the complication of disorders from which he cumulatively suffered henceforth and ultimately succumbed. Unquestionably he ought to have turned back as soon as he knew of the robbery and sent to the coast for fresh supplies; it was folly to persevere in the absence of remedies for the ailments that, as he very well knew, always beset African travel; only his immovable determination to reach his goal at all hazards could have carried him on, and he solaced himself with the consideration that what had happened might be overruled for good by divine Providence.

All the other goods I have divided in case of loss or desertion, but had never dreamed of losing the precious quinine and other remedies; other losses and annoyances I felt as just parts of that undercurrent of vexations which is not wanting in even the smoothest life, and certainly not worthy of being mourned over in the experience of an explorer anxious to benefit a country and people—but this loss I feel most keenly. Everything of this kind happens by the permission of One who watches over us with most tender care; and this may turn out for the best by taking away a source of suspicion among

[5] *Last Journals*, vol. i., p. 100.
[6] *Ibid.*, p. 177.

more superstitious, charm-dreading people further north. I meant it as a source of benefit to my party and to the heathen.[7]

In the midst of his trouble of mind at realizing the probable extent of the calamity that had befallen him, he finds it possible to make allowance for the ignorance and moral crudity of the men who had robbed him. The passage is characteristic of Livingstone, both in its simple piety and compassionate feeling:

> We returned to Lisunga, and got two men off to go back to Chafunga's village, and intercept the deserters if they went there; but it is likely that, having our supply of flour, they will give our route a wide berth and escape altogether. It is difficult to say from the heart, "Thy will be done"; but I shall try. These Waiyau had few advantages: sold into slavery in early life, they were in the worst possible school for learning to be honest and honourable; they behaved well for a long time, but, having had hard and scanty fare in Lobisa, wet and misery in passing through dripping forests, hungry nights and fatiguing days, their patience must have been worn out, and they had no sentiments of honour, or at least none so strong as we ought to have; they gave way to the temptation which their good conduct had led us to put in their way. Some we have come across in this journey seemed born essentially mean and base—a great misfortune to them and all who have to deal with them, but they cannot be so blamable as those who have no natural tendency to meanness, and whose education has taught them to abhor it. True; yet this loss of the medicine box gnaws at the heart terribly.[8]

Three days later we come upon an entry eloquent of a distress which was to remain almost a normal condition with him for long to come:

> We all feel weak and easily tired, and an incessant hunger teases us, so it is no wonder if so large a space of this paper is occupied by stomach affairs. It has not been merely want of nice dishes, but real biting hunger and faintness.[9]

On March 10th the Journal records:

[7] *Last Journals,* vol. i., p. 178.
[8] *Ibid.,* p. 178.
[9] *Ibid.,* p. 179.

I have been ill of fever ever since we left Moamba's; every step I take jars in the chest, and I am very weak; I can scarcely keep up the march, though formerly I was always first, and had to hold in my pace not to leave the people altogether. I have a constant singing in the ears, and can scarcely hear the loud tick of the chronometers. The appetite is good, but we have no proper food. Chiefly maëre meal, or beans, or mapemba, or ground-nuts, rarely a fowl.[10]

There is little left of him by now except concentrated will; yet, despite his desperate physical condition, his daily observations are as carefully made and chronicled as heretofore, the route mapped and described with exactitude, and every natural object of importance, organic or inorganic, noted, and in some instances pictured for reference. He had no skill as an artist and pretended to none, but in the smaller notebooks which he carried about with him and from which his Journal was posted up at every stopping-place are many rude sketches of scenes, plants, and living creatures, preserved apparently for the refreshment of his own memory and the information of naturalists at home, should the reports ever get there. As some of these sketches lie before the present writer they exhibit tokens of experiments in colour continued until the exact shade required had been obtained. Where did the colour come from? It could only have been derived from squeezing out and mixing the juice of plants as the traveller passed along with dragging feet and aching frame. Was ever scientific observation conducted more conscientiously or at greater strain?

The party reached the southern end of Lake Tanganyika on April 4th, 1867, but by this time Livingstone was so weakened by continuous attacks of illness that he could go no farther for several weeks, and lay prostrate and unconscious in an improvised shelter with no other attention than could be provided by the best of his simple-minded native adherents. His account of their devotion at this crisis in his fortunes and theirs is very touching:

After I had been a few days here I had a fit of insensibility, which shows the power of fever without medicine. I found myself flound-

10 *Ibid.*, p. 200.

ering outside my hut and unable to get in; I tried to lift myself from my back by laying hold of two posts at the entrance, but when I got nearly upright I let them go, and fell back heavily on my head on a box. The boys had seen the wretched state I was in, and hung a blanket at the entrance of the hut, that no stranger might see my helplessness; some hours elapsed before I could recognize where I was.[11]

His intention after recovering sufficiently to be able to take the road again was to follow the lake round to the north-west to see if it discharged in that direction, but the headman of the tribe inhabiting the district surrounding his camp earnestly advised him not to do so, as the Mazitu were in force on the route he proposed taking and would infallibly attack him. At the moment Livingstone was inclined to disbelieve this counsel, though deeming it prudent to comply therewith, but he learned later that it was correct. On the strength of it he turned westward to pursue his search for the watershed of the great river systems. Everywhere he came upon the usual grim traces of slave-hunting activities; one in especial made a deep impression on his mind because of the pathos of it. A mother and child were among the captives in a slave gang guarded by Arabs with whom he came into touch. The child was only three years old, but knew well enough that he was to be parted from his parent, and clung to her crying bitterly; the price asked for him was four yards of cotton cloth. The poor little fellow's feet were raw and blistered from being compelled to tramp long distances in the sun. Livingstone never became inured to such sights.

Yet, notwithstanding, these same Arab slave drivers were friendly and courteous to him, the fact of his being a white man leading them to assume a certain kinship. He came in contact with the ruthless marauder, Tipu Tib (Tipo Tipo in the Journal), who, instead of being hostile, showed himself helpful to the worn and impoverished traveller and furnished him with the means of reaching Lake Moero. It is startlingly incongruous to think of Livingstone marching in company with professional slave catchers and beholden to them for food and such little comforts as were obtainable—probably even for his life, for

[11] *Last Journals*, vol. i., p. 205.

CHUMA AND SUSI

he could hardly have endured much longer the unsuccoured state of physical want and pain to which he had been reduced.

At Casembe's town, to the south-east of Lake Moero, he stayed a month, making use of the time to prepare the letters and reports he meant to send home by Arab traders at the first opportunity. These despatches were never received; the messengers destroyed them as telling too much to the outside world to be compatible with their inhuman slave-seizing interests. This destruction of his correspondence was repeated at intervals, and was no doubt a deliberately adopted policy; as such it had the effect of causing much anxiety to the explorer's friends and the public, and, as will be seen presently, some amount of misunderstanding in which Kirk was involved.

He would have turned here towards what was then the fairly important trading station of Ujiji on the north-eastern shores of Lake Tanganyika in the hope of obtaining some news from home, but learning that there was a larger lake (Bangweolo) not far south, he decided to go there first. The immediate result of announcing this plan to his men was a mutiny. Whether through Arab instigation or not, all but five of the attendants who had remained with him hitherto refused point blank to accompany him farther. This fresh desertion was enough to dismay the most stout-hearted and experienced of African travellers, and Livingstone does not minimize the seriousness of the prospect it presented him with, but it could not avail to divert him from his purpose; on he went with his now grievously attentuated following, almost entirely without resources of any kind except what he could hope to obtain from the goodwill of the inhabitants of the country through which he might pass; for self-defence against possible assault he had nothing worth depending upon at all, yet everywhere the same ghastly spectacles of misery and death confronted him that he had now become accustomed to expect in the track of the slave raider. Long lines of wretched creatures chained together or, in the case of the men, fastened two and two with a forked stick bolted round the neck of each were frequently encountered, and he chafed at being unable to help them in any way. On June 24th, 1868, the Journal records a striking incident which came under his notice when in contact with a melancholy procession of this kind:

> Six slaves were singing as if they did not feel the weight and degradation of the slave sticks. I asked the cause of their mirth, and was told that they rejoiced at the idea "of coming back after death and haunting and killing those who had sold them. . . ." Then all joined in the chorus, which was the name of each vendor. It told not of fun, but of the bitterness and tears of such as were oppressed, and on the side of the oppressors there was a power; there be higher than they! [12]

Still more moving, however, to a British reader is the entry that follows the above. Little did the lonely traveller suspect how near he was to the end of all his earthly toils and that his bones would be laid with high honour under the roof of his own nation's most historic shrine. We have already noted his presentiment that he would die in Africa, but here we come for the first time upon the explicit statement of a desire that his remains might rest there. The sentiment, though with greater simplicity, resembles that of another mighty son of Britain whose life was spent for Africa, Cecil Rhodes; but the tenderer note is Livingstone's.

> We came to a grave in the forest; it was a little rounded mound as if the occupant sat in it in the usual native way: it was strewed with flour, and a number of the large blue beads put on it: a little path showed that it had visitors. This is the sort of grave I should prefer: to lie in the still, still forest, and no hand ever disturb my bones. The graves at home always seemed to me to be miserable, especially those in the cold damp clay, and without elbow room; but I have nothing to do but wait till He who is over all decides where I have to lay me down and die. Poor Mary lies on Shupanga Brae "and beeks fornent the sun." [13]

He and his faithful five were in imminent danger once on this extraordinary journey. On July 13th a horde of savages, under the influ-

[12] *Last Journals,* vol. i., p. 306.
[13] *Ibid.,* p. 307 *f.*

ence of the potent native intoxicant to which reference has been made in an earlier chapter, surrounded and threatened them with poised spears, battle-axes, and bows and arrows. One indiscreet movement would have resulted in the instant massacre of the whole party, but Livingstone, with his usual self-command, sat quite still, displaying not the smallest symptom of nervousness, and this probably saved them from destruction. In giving details of the scene he says:

There is usually one good soul in such rabbles. In this case a man came to me, and, addressing his fellows, said: "This is only your pombe. White man, do not stand among them, but go away." And then he placed himself between me and a portion of the assailants, about thirty of whom were making their war-like antics. While walking quietly away with my good friend they ran in front and behind bushes and trees, took aim with bow and arrow, but none shot: the younger men ran away with our three goats. When we had gone a quarter of a mile my friend told me to wait and he would bring the goats, which he did: I could not feel the inebriates to be enemies; but in that state they are the worst one can encounter, for they have no fear, as they have when sober. One snatched away a fowl from our guide; that too was restored by our friend. I did not load my gun; for any accidental discharge would have inflamed them to rashness. We got away without shedding blood, and were thankful. The Mazitu raid has produced lawlessness in the country: every one was taken as an enemy.[14]

Lake Bangweolo was discovered on July 18th, 1868, and Livingstone spent some time in exploring the peculiar marshy districts around its shores—oozy sponges through which he could only force his way with extreme difficulty and with the added discomfort of being preyed upon by blood-sucking aquatic creatures. He began to entertain the theory that these curious sponges were probably the head sources of the Nile, and was long buoyed up with the belief that the solution of this ages-old problem now stood to his credit. He writes a long dissertation upon it, with suggestive remarks on the changing features of a country due to variations of climate and sea level, illustrating his views by in-

14 *Ibid.*, p. 311 *f.*

teresting references to the Biblical account of the passage of the children of Israel through what were probably at that period the fordable marshes at the northern end of the Red Sea. Henceforward the passion to win complete confirmation of his claim to have thus achieved what no previous explorer in all recorded history had been able to do possesses him almost exclusively; he recurs to it again and again, and it is in the hope of placing it beyond dispute, as we shall observe as we proceed, that he finally refuses to avail himself of the means of deliverance when it comes, and turns back to die in the heart of the African forest. A grand illusion, but a sad one! He perished in the pursuit of one objective while God was using his perseverance and self-sacrifice in the attainment of another.[15]

The postponed journey to Ujiji to pick up the stores and correspondence which he believed to be awaiting him there was undertaken in company with an Arab slave party commanded by Mohamad Bogharib, and again we have the glaring incongruity of assiduous attention being paid to Livingstone by the very men who were treating barbarously the wretched African captives whom they dragged along in their train. The station was reached on March 14th, 1869, but to Livingstone's great disappointment he found that the greater number of the packages he expected had either been lost or left at Unyanyembe. The little he was able to obtain possession of included a change of clothing, for which he was unspeakably thankful, but as the remainder was inaccessible at the moment owing to a war that was going on between Arabs, Mazitu, and local tribes, he turned north-west with the object of proving that the Lualaba river was either the head waters of the Nile or of the Congo. With his usual magnanimity he re-engaged some of the faithless porters who had deserted him at Lake Moero, but these and others added at Ujiji proved so unsatisfactory *en route* that he had to leave them behind and, attended only by Susi, Chuma, and Gardner, made two bold but unsuccessful attempts to reach the river. He got no farther than Bambarre, an Arab settlement in the Manyuema (or

---

[15] In a lengthy letter to Horace Waller from Bambarre, February, 1871, he enunciates his programme thus: "My work leads me down the Lualaba in canoes till it touches the head of the Nile, probably near the eastern arm followed down by Speke, Grant, and Baker. Then double back up the western line of drainage to the fountains on the watershed" (*sic*).

Manyema) country, where he was held up for many weeks by heavy inundations and the obstacles placed in his way by the lying and churlishness of the people. He says of the tribe: "The Manyuema are the most bloody callous savages I know," [16] yet he overhears some of them telling others that he is the "good one," and adds the laconic observation, "I owe this character to the propagation of a good name by the slaves of Zanzibar who are anything but good themselves." [17]

He had forwarded to Zanzibar from Ujiji an order for a fresh supply of stores and a reinforcement of native bearers to carry them, and these were duly sent by Dr. Kirk, who at the time was acting British representative at Zanzibar. The new party arrived on February 4th, 1871, at Bambarre, but turned out to be a graceless lot. Ten of them were Banian slaves, whose first action was to demand higher wages and strike work until they obtained them. They then declared and stuck to the statement that their orders were not to go forward, but to compel Livingstone to return immediately. The falsehood was accompanied by threats which would quickly have been executed but for their fear of being shot by Mohamad Bogharib. An odd situation truly: Livingstone's treacherous servants kept in order by a slave-hunting Arab chief! The support afforded may not have amounted to more than saving the missionary from actual violence at the hands of these knaves; it could not turn them into honest men, and Livingstone blamed Kirk severely for not having furnished him with human material of a better quality. How far Kirk was responsible for the unfortunate selection has never been made very clear. The explanation afterwards given was that he himself had been imposed upon by the contractors with whom he had stipulated both for men and goods. [18]

Be this as it may, the result was to bring Livingstone as near to despair as his great heart ever allowed. After a fresh outbreak of trouble with the Banian men he enters in his daily record the gloomy confession: "It is excessively trying, and so many difficulties have been

[16] *Last Journals*, vol. ii., p. 95.
[17] *Ibid.*, p. 105.
[18] Writing to Horace Waller immediately after the arrival of the caravan, Livingstone expresses appreciation of the service rendered. "Ten men have come from Kirk, who, like the good fellow that he is, worked unweariedly to get them and the goods off in the midst of disease and death." The bad quality of the recruits had yet to be experienced.

put in my way I doubt whether the Divine favour and will is on my side." [19]   There is no parallel in his whole history for such a questioning of the reality of the spiritual guidance of which he ever felt himself to be the subject; his faith in regard to this was sublime; no servant of God was ever more fully persuaded that he was a chosen instrument for the doing of an appointed work than David Livingstone.   It was this conviction that carried him through the dark and dreary hours of depression and weakness that were his constant portion in the last three years of his life, for with everything to discourage and nothing to hearten him, except the one bright experience of Stanley's visit to which we must come presently, the thoughts he commits to his Journal are in the strain of a child-like confidence in the validity of his vocation. Thus, October 25th, 1870, he writes:

> In this journey I have endeavoured to follow with unswerving fidelity the line of duty.   My course has been an even one, turning neither to the right hand nor to the left, though my route has been tortuous enough.   All the hardship, hunger and toil were met with the full conviction that I was right in persevering to make a complete work of the exploration of the sources of the Nile.   Mine has been a calm, hopeful endeavour to do the work that has been given to me to do, whether I succeed or whether I fail.   The prospect of death in pursuing what I knew to be right did not make me veer to one side or the other.   I had a strong presentiment during the first three years that I should never live through the enterprise, but it weakened as I came near to the end of the journey.[20]

In the same connection he records his longing to accomplish the object here stated and then retire.   "I pray that it may be to my native home" [21]—the only instance, so far as the present writer is aware, of the expression of any definite wish or intention on his part to end his days near the place of his birth.   As we have already seen, he had previously had another thought in mind, that of finding his grave in the same soil as the wife he had never ceased to mourn.

[19] *Last Journals,* vol. ii., p. 110.
[20] *Ibid.,* p. 72.
[21] *Ibid.,* p. 73.

A touching paragraph in a long letter to Horace Waller dated September 2nd, 1872, shows how wistfully his thoughts were turning towards his native land at this time, and the relief and rest of quiet domesticity. After thanking Waller for a most welcome gift of foot gear—he had long been almost shoeless—he adds: "I beg your aid to secure lodgings for me—say anywhere near Regent's Park—comfortable and decent but not excessively dear. Agñes will come up and will need accommodation at the same place—one sitting room will do for both. . . . Kindly think of the lodgings and artificial teeth when you hear of my coming home." The remark about the teeth is not without relevance. His teeth were in a very bad state, as Stanley reports, a fact which alone would account for much of his now chronic ill-health.

Seeing nothing for it but to make his way back to Ujiji for better men and whatever stores consigned to him from Zanzibar might succeed in getting through from Unyanyembe, he joined the slave party of another Arab chief, Dugumbé. This personage had acquired a grisly reputation for the ruthlessness of his methods in raiding the Manyuema territory, and Livingstone came in for a share of the enmity thus aroused. Not unnaturally he was judged, as he says himself, by the company he kept, but there was no help for it; either he must keep with this well-armed slaver or perish by the way, for his depraved Banians had been overheard plotting to lure him into a Manyuema trap and then run away and leave him to be killed. This danger, at least, was obviated by keeping near Dugumbé, who treated him with unremitting kindness and respect, even causing him to be carried in a litter when his strength gave out, and providing him with such rude remedies for his ailments as were obtainable in the circumstances. But for an appalling massacre of Manyuema women and children and old people perpetrated by three miscreants of Dugumbé's following, Livingstone's gratitude would have been warmer; as it was, the necessity of witnessing an atrocity of such magnitude induced in him an uncontrollable anger which brought on an attack of sickness and made him resolve to get away from the neighbourhood of his sinister associates at all risks. He would have pistoled the murderers with his own hand in the first impulse of his righteous rage, had not Dugumbé dissuaded him from starting a blood feud which might have interminable consequences.

The retreat through the Manyuema land was terrible. Three times in one day Livingstone escaped death by the narrowest margin. A spear grazed his back and would have transfixed him had he not happened to stoop as it was thrown; another hurled from an ambuscade missed him by a foot; a gigantic tree fell as he passed and crashed to earth a yard behind him as he ran from under it with all the speed of which he was capable. His own comments on the succession of perils need no embellishment to convey a just idea of the gruelling to which he was exposed without cessation:

> I became weary with the constant strain of danger, and—as, I suppose, happens with soldiers on the field of battle—not courageous, but perfectly indifferent whether I were killed or not.[22]

This was on August 8th, and by September 23rd, as he is drawing near the end of the journey, his harassing experience is summed up in still more pungent terms:

> I was sorely knocked up by this march from Nyañgwé back to Ujiji. In the latter part of it, I felt as if dying on my feet. Almost every step was in pain, the appetite failed, and a little bit of meat caused violent diarrhœa, whilst the mind, sorely depressed, reacted on the body. All the traders were returning successful: I alone had failed and experienced worry, thwarting, baffling, when almost in sight of the end towards which I strained.[23]

It is not of slight importance to observe that the very next entry in the Journal, ten days later, is a single sentence: "I read the whole Bible through four times whilst I was in Manyuema."[24] The solitary pilgrim, whose daily companionship is that of assassins and slave drivers, never for a moment free from the shadow of violent death, with shrunken and enfeebled frame, slowly dying on his feet as he advances

[22] *Last Journals,* vol. ii., p. 147.
[23] *Ibid.,* p. 153.
[24] *Ibid.,* p. 154.

or while being borne along by savage hands, yet undeviating in purpose and with single eye to the fulfilment of the will of God through his efforts and sufferings, finds his chiefest solace and inspiration in the Scriptures. This one fact is worth a whole volume of description of his opinions and achievements.

He arrives at Ujiji on October 23rd, 1871, "a mere ruckle of bones," to be smitten by fresh calamity. "A moral idiot," [25] the Arab "Shereef" in charge, had sold his stores. Dismayed and helpless, he sat down to consider what was to be done, but no clear way out of his plight suggested itself. He could but send to Zanzibar again for help and wait in destitution until it arrived.

Thrillingly dramatic came the change in his fortunes. Within five days after the crushing disaster here briefly described his loyal and devoted Susi came running to him at the top of his speed with the excited ejaculation, "An Englishman! I see him!" and immediately rushed off again to meet the stranger. All the world knows who the rescuer was. Henry M. Stanley, at the head of an expedition initiated and financed by James Gordon Bennett of the *New York Herald*, had arrived in the nick of time to put new life into the veteran explorer and give to Europe and America the most entrancing epic of that generation.

It is easy to understand the feelings of lively gratitude wherewith the spent and isolated Livingstone would welcome the young journalist who had come so many thousands of miles to find him and render him the assistance he so urgently needed. [26] He was at the end of his resources, and had been so long cut off from communication with the outer world that he was totally ignorant of the march of events and might well be excused for imagining himself abandoned and forgotten by his countrymen. [27] This was far, indeed, from being the fact; Stan-

---

[25] *Ibid.*, p. 155.

[26] Referring to Stanley's treatment of himself, Livingstone writes to Horace Waller, September, 1872: "He behaved as a son to a father—truly overflowing in kindness. The good Lord remember and be gracious unto him in life and in death. Oswell was told by Kirk that Stanley would make his fortune out of me; if so he is heartily welcome, for it is a great deal more than I could ever make out of myself."

[27] "The successful laying of the Atlantic Cable I inferred from my Canadian brother, saying: 'Last cable news told us you were alive, and we put off our mourning' "—(to Waller, February, 1871, from the Manyuema country).

ley had merely been more fortunate and not more expeditious than others who had been despatched on the same errand. As noted above, Livingstone had not long heard of E. D. Young's exploit,[28] nor did he know that at that very moment a well-equipped party, under the command of Lieutenant Dawson, was on its way from England to Zanzibar to afford him the relief which had now reached him from another quarter, and, not knowing, he could hardly avoid drawing a contrast between American interest on his behalf with apparent British indifference. That the American interest was in part actuated by motives of business enterprise did not lessen its value for him, and in his personal expressions of indebtedness to Mr. Gordon Bennett he uses a warmth of language, albeit restrained and dignified, that was fully deserved.

It was natural, too, that the injuries which he had endured at the hands of the vile squad of Banian slaves whom Kirk had sent should have rankled in his mind and led to his saying some things implying depreciation of his former comrade, which hurt Kirk, and for a little time chilled the admiration the latter entertained for his old chief. Nor did Stanley help matters in this respect. As one main object of his quest was to obtain a good advertisement for the *New York Herald,* he had refrained from disclosing its nature to Kirk when the two met at Zanzibar, and Kirk, in consequence, was somewhat non-committal in replying to Stanley's questions about Livingstone's movements. This created in Stanley a prejudice against Kirk to which he gave unmeasured utterance, both in his reports to his paper and in his book, *How I Found Livingstone.* That he did nothing to soften any feelings of resentment that may have possessed Livingstone on account of what the latter fancied to be Kirk's neglect of his welfare we can hardly doubt. Stanley reiterates the charge of neglect *ad nauseam* against Kirk in *How I Found Livingstone,* though he virtually withdraws it in the appendix. Professor Coupland states that his next book will completely exonerate Kirk and modify Stanley's statements. One regrettable outcome of Stanley's intercourse with Livingstone was the au-

---

[28] The following sentence appears in a letter to Horace Waller from Unyanyembe on February 19th, 1872: "I have just seen Young's book. He did his work right nobly and well, and I feel grateful to him as I mention in a despatch of thanks to the F.O."

thorization given in writing to the one by the other to turn back at his discretion any slave caravan he might meet bringing further stores. This was interpreted as a slight upon Kirk, as perhaps it was intended to be, and had for one of its effects—not on Stanley's initiative, however—the stoppage of the British expedition which Stanley met on his way back to the coast. It is gratifying to read in Livingstone's last despatch to Lord Granville, dated July 1st, 1872, that he had no grudge against Kirk, and was sorry to learn that his protest against the employment of Banian slaves had been so construed.

> I regret very much to hear incidentally that Dr. Kirk viewed my formal complaint against Banians as a covert attack upon himself. If I had foreseen this, I should certainly have borne all my losses in silence. I never had any difference with him, though we were together for years, and I had no intention to give offence now. But the public interest taken in this expedition enforces publicity as to the obstacles that prevented its work being accomplished long ago.[29]

The acerbity of Stanley's references to Kirk and other British officials was not lessened by the ungenerous attitude taken towards himself by a large section of British public opinion when the news of his success reached Europe. Deep chagrin was felt that it should have been reserved for an American to do what the British people wanted to see done for Livingstone. Frank disbelief in Stanley's story was widely avowed, and when its truth could no longer be denied, the facts were either grudgingly admitted or given a distorted presentation. The spirit thus shown was far from universal, however, and ample amends were made in after years for its temporary manifestation. The time was to come when this man of British birth but American upbringing was to receive full honour as Livingstone's successor in the exploration of the Congo basin and the opening of Uganda to humane influences. That his brief contact with Livingstone gave a new direction to his life and made him the man he ultimately became was not the least of the fruits of the bold endeavour which owed its inception to the alert and vigorous mind of James Gordon Bennett.

[29] Quoted in appendix to *How I Found Livingstone.*

Why did not Livingstone go home with Stanley? The question is often asked, but the answer to it is not obscure if we have regard to Livingstone's plain words—both those that were intended for publication and those that were not. The two men were together for four months and a half, and explored the northern end of Lake Tanganyika before returning to Ujiji and parting at Unyanyembe. Stanley did his utmost to persuade the missionary, for whom he now experienced an attachment amounting to veneration, to return to England in his company and take the rest which seemed to be, and indeed was, imperative if his hopes were to be fulfilled. But Livingstone was immovable. He wanted another six or seven months, he said, to complete the task assigned him by Sir Roderick Murchison and the Royal Geographical Society; then he would gladly doff his armour:

Writing to Horace Waller from east of Lake Tanganyika on September 2nd, 1872, he says he had first suggested Kirk to the Royal Geographical Society and the Government as leader of the expedition. Kirk refused it.

It was only after this that I consented to take it myself and *unsalaried;* but I have Lord Russell's letter saying that he fully intended to give me £500 a year if I settled anywhere. A most desirable place of settlement offered at Mataka's, but I should not then fulfil the task laid on me by Sir Roderick, whose wish to me was law, for I loved him with very great affection. I thought that I could finish all in two years, and elected to give £500 twice told by a non-settlement.

A previous letter to the same correspondent expresses a like determination, but with a misgiving that his endurance is being sapped.

I am terribly knocked up, but this is for your own eye only—in my second childhood, a dreadful old fogie—doubtful if I live to see you again. I stick to my work in spite of everything because most of my friends will say as my good daughter does, "Much as I wish to have you home, I would rather that you finish your work to your own satisfaction than come merely to gratify me." There's a good brave girl, I guess—a chip of the old block and no mistake.

These are sufficiently plain statements of his intention and the reason for it. He would go on for what he thought would be the comparatively short time required to delimit the watershed of the Congo and the Nile. On June 14th, 1872, he enters in his Journal the sentence: "In February or March, 1874, please the Almighty Disposer of events, I shall complete my task and retire."

In the meantime he would entrust Stanley with the responsibility of organizing for him a reliable band of native helpers at Zanzibar efficiently equipped with supplies; Stanley was also to take home and deliver his locked Journal to his daughter Agnes, and to see that his belated reports and correspondence reached the persons to whom they were addressed. All these commissions were duly executed, and brought the younger traveller friendly commendation from everyone immediately concerned, and ultimately from the public. Queen Victoria was among the first to express definite appreciation of the service rendered, and the members of the Livingstone family were equally ready with grateful acknowledgment of their obligation. One of the most felicitous expressions of this sentiment emanated from the great explorer's brother John in a letter written to the *New York Herald* from his Canadian home. There is a distinction and moral wholesomeness in the terms of this communication worthy of David Livingstone himself.

Livingstone's work was ended now, though he did not realize it. For five months he waited wearily for the reinforcements that Stanley had undertaken to send. They arrived on August 14th, 1872, a well-selected body of fifty-seven men, including Jacob Wainwright, the educated native to whom we owe the first-hand written account of the last months of Livingstone's life and the details relating to his death. There were no more discoveries of any importance to be made. This closing period is mainly one of painful and profitless but heroic meandering in pursuit of an illusory goal. In a letter to John, written from the littoral of Lake Bangweolo in December, 1872, he says:

If the good Lord above me gives me strength and influence to complete the task in spite of everything, I shall not grudge my hunger and toils. Above all, if He permits me to put a stop to the enormous evils of this inland slave trade I shall bless His name with all my heart. The Nile sources are valuable to me only as a means of opening my mouth with power among men.

In a previous letter to John, written from the Manyuema country in the midst of the trying experiences already narrated—the date being approximately April, 1870—he says:

As soon as I shall have ascertained where the western arm [of the Nile] joins the eastern I shall retire and pray that the Almighty may lead me safely home. . . . Had I known all the toil, hunger, hardship and time involved in getting a clear idea of the drainage, I might have preferred a strait waistcoat, the head shaved and a blister on it, to undertaking the task.

During the last few months of his tramping to and fro in the swampy environment of Lake Bangweolo, as Horace Waller has told us, every scrap of paper, even old newspapers yellow with African damp, had to be used for his notes, sewn together and the notes written across the type with ink made from the juice of a tree. These were all conscientiously preserved by his faithful followers Susi and Chuma, in co-operation with Jacob Wainwright and others of Stanley's contingent. It was with the help of these excellent fellows that the Journals were afterwards deciphered and published. They reveal that towards the end he began to be haunted by the misgiving that he had been following a will-o'-the-wisp and tracing the course of the Congo instead of the Nile, which was precisely the state of the case and could not fail to depress his spirits. On February 14th appears the entry:

If the good Lord gives me favour, and permits me to finish my work, I shall thank and bless Him, though it has cost me untold toil, pain, and travail; this trip has made my hair all gray.

   .   .   .   .

April 6th.—It is quite impossible at present to tell where land ends and lake begins; it is all water, water everywhere, which seems to be kept from flowing quickly off by the narrow bed of the Luapula,

which has perpendicular banks worn deep down in new red sand-
stone. It is the Nile apparently enacting its inundations, even at its
sources.

. . . .

April 10th.—I am pale, bloodless and weak, from bleeding pro-
fusely ever since the 31st of March last; an artery gives off a copious
stream, and takes away my strength. Oh, how I long to be permitted
by the Over Power to finish my work!

. . . .

April 18th.—Very ill all night, but remembered that the bleeding
and most other ailments in this land are forms of fever.

. . . .

April 19th.—It is not all pleasure, this exploration. No observations now, owing to great weakness: I can scarcely hold a pencil,
and my stick is a burden.

There is little more to record. The dying man is now unable to do
more than enter in his small pocket diary the dates as they pass. He
has no longer strength to ride, much less to walk, and his men carry
him in an improvised litter.

Towards the end of April they halted at Chitambo's village, Ilala,
and here it was evident that the sufferer had reached the limit of physical endurance and could no longer bear the strain of movement. The
last part of the journey had been made by canoe on the river Lulimalo,
spelt by Livingstone "Molilamo" in the final sentence he was able to
write in his note-book. "Knocked up quite," runs the brief statement,
with the date, April 27th—David Livingstone's unconscious farewell to
the world; he could lift pen no more. His agonies in the last few stages
of his progress had been dreadful, chiefly owing to dysentery and constant hæmorrhage. He could neither stand nor sit up, and had to be
laid on his back in the canoe when ferried across to Chitambo's side
of the river. A hut was hastily prepared for him outside the village
by some of his thoughtful attendants who had gone on ahead of the
slowly advancing procession that conveyed the prostrate form of their
master to the spot chosen for encampment. The next day, April 30th,

Chitambo called to give a friendly welcome to the party, but was requested to come again on the morrow, as the white man was too exhausted to converse with him. On the morrow Livingstone was dead. At four o'clock in the morning he was found kneeling by his bedside with his head resting on his hands as if in the attitude of prayer, but life had evidently been extinct for some time, as the body was cold.

Thus fitly passed one of the moral giants of our race at the very heart and centre of the strange and troubled land he had done his best to deliver from the twin curses of heathenism and slavery. Had he himself thought out and carefully fixed upon the manner in which his lifework should end, he could not have made more effectual use of the solemn event for the furtherance of his most cherished object. Had he died in his own homeland, and in the enjoyment of comfort and honour, he would not have accomplished as much as he did by dying in want and loneliness and pain, surrounded only by a group of the big black children who had learned to love and revere him because they felt that he loved and understood them. At the closing scene not even these were present; it was better so. "And he was not, for God took him."

Concerning the rude embalmment that followed and the amazing resolution so intrepidly carried out by these same black men there is no need to say more. It is one of the most inspiring stories ever told, and still helps to enhance our faith in human nature. In the divine order it did much, when it became known, to intensify the reverence attaching to Livingstone's memory; the civilized world felt it to be wholly in keeping with the worth of the man the reverent sepulture of whose mortal remains was thus treated as a sacred trust to be fulfilled at all hazards; no finer tribute could have been paid by Africans to one who was to them a spiritual father and the herald of hope and peace. That the dust of David Livingstone lies in Westminster Abbey to-day is more the doing of Susi and Chuma and their brave companions than of the British nation itself, which with united voice acclaimed their fidelity as sublime, and crowned their deed by according

INSCRIPTION CARVED BY THE "IMMORTALS" ON THE
TREE AT CHITAMBO UNDER WHICH LIVINGSTONE'S
HEART WAS BURIED

to the illustrious dead the greatest homage in its power to bestow.[30] When they buried their master's heart at Ilala before setting out on their tremendous journey to the coast, they undesignedly performed an action as poetically right in its way as the rest of their historic achievement. As such it holds a place in the roll of gracious things that exercise a beneficent influence on the imagination of mankind.

Near to Unyanyembe these faithful men with their precious burden heard of a second relief expedition sent out by the Royal Geographical Society under the command of Lieutenant Cameron to seek for news of Livingstone and make contact with him if possible. This expedition was partly financed from the resources unused by the earlier one under Lieutenant Dawson, which had turned back on learning of Stanley's success. To the equipment of the Dawson expedition the Government had contributed a thousand pounds in addition to the amounts furnished by the promoters. It is much to be regretted that Dawson and his colleagues did not push on to join Livingstone after meeting Stanley, especially as the explorer's son, Oswell Livingstone, was with them; the decision to abandon the project was one of those unfortunate mistakes which later developments magnify. It was soon seen to be such, and Lieutenant Cameron's expedition was expressly organized to do what could be done in making up for lost time. Another expedition promoted and paid for by James Young was simultaneously attempting to penetrate to Livingstone from the west. Both were too late.

On learning of Lieutenant Cameron's advance, and erroneously believing that Livingstone's son was accompanying him, Jacob Wainwright wrote the famous letter containing the first authentic news of the explorer's death, and Chuma hurried forward with it on October 20th to meet the caravan and report what he and those with him had done for the preservation of the remains with the intention of delivering them into the hands of persons who would undertake to convey them to England. The quaint phrasing of this communication adds to its pathos when the heroism of the messengers is realized.

[30] "Chitambo said: 'Why not bury him?' 'Oh, no; very big man; cannot bury here'" (deposition of Susi and Chuma to Horace Waller).

UKHONONGO,
October, 1873.

SIR,

We have heared in the month of August that you have started from Zanzibar for Unyenyembe, and again and again lately we have heared your arrival—your father died by disease beyond the country of Bisa, but we have carried the corpse with us. 10 of our soldiers are lost and some have died. Our hunger presses us to ask you some clothes to buy provision for our soldiers, and we should have an answer that when we shall enter there shall be firing guns or not, and if you permit us to fire guns then send some powder.

We have wrote these few words in the place of Sultan or King Mbowra.

The writer JACOB WAINWRIGHT.
Dr. Livingstone Exeped.

Cameron cannot fairly be blamed for not immediately grasping the full significance of the facts thus naïvely stated. He and his companions would have buried Livingstone's body there and then but for the firm resistance of the men who with so much difficulty and risk to themselves had borne it in safety for five months through forests, swamps, and rivers, exposed to ceaseless harassment from hostile tribes and possible slave hunters, and with an insufficiency of food and protection from the weather. Nor was the march over now. It had to be continued to the coast with two sick white men in train—Lieutenant Murphy and Dr. Dillon—while Cameron went on to Ujiji to take possession of any of Livingstone's effects which might have been left there. Arrived at Zanzibar, no further notice was taken of the brave black men who had performed a feat so unique in the annals of exploration or mission work. They were relieved of their charge without thanks or other overt recognition of the great thing they had done, and but for the thoughtful and liberal action of James Young in having the principals sought for and brought to England, the world would perhaps have heard no more of them and been deprived of the particulars of Livingstone's last days, which only Susi and Chuma were qualified to relate.

Livingstone was interred in Westminster Abbey on April 18th, 1874, and it was by a happy and appropriate arrangement that among his pall-bearers should be Jacob Wainwright, the writer of the letter above quoted, and who had read the Prayer Book burial service over the body of his great master when the heart was taken therefrom and reverently committed to the ground in the depths of an African forest. The other pall-bearers were Stanley, Kirk, Waller, E. D. Young, William Oswell, Sir Thomas Steele, and William Webb—all men who had enjoyed Livingstone's intimacy, and most of whom, like himself, had borne themselves as paladins amid scenes of conflict and peril, with death never far away.

CHAPTER XII

THE HARVEST

It would have been of some comfort to Livingstone in his last hours if he could have known of the active interest that was being exhibited by his countrymen on his behalf. The thrilling news Stanley had brought had quickened the imagination and added to the pride already felt by all persons of British nationality in Livingstone's manifold achievements performed at a cost in toil and strain so heavy for a man of his years. Mingled with the admiration was some measure of shame at the shabbiness of the treatment he had received hitherto from the authorities at whose bidding he had gone forth on his latest and most exacting enterprise. Some amends had been made, as we know, both by the Government and the Royal Geographical Society for earlier omissions by the despatch first of Young and then of Dawson to ascertain the fate of the explorer and afford him succour. Public opinion had insisted upon these measures. Now it did more. Can we be mistaken in inferring that to the stimulus imparted by Stanley to public feeling concerning the imperativeness of giving worthier recognition to Livingstone's services must be credited the fact that in June, 1873, the British Government voted him a pension of three hundred pounds per annum? This was a marked change from the policy of sending him out with no salary, but it was no longer needed: he was already dead. In the following year small pensions were allotted by the Treasury to each of his surviving children.

But far more significant was the outburst of earnest desire to emulate him and carry on his work. Stanley himself, as we have seen, found his real vocation through coming under the influence of Livingstone, and the same may be said of the succession of famous travellers who in the last quarter of the nineteenth century addressed themselves to clearing up the problems he had left unsolved. The desire of his heart was granted in the suppression of the slave trade on the Zanzibar side of south central Africa, a consummation directly brought about by the firm action of his old friend and comrade, Sir John Kirk. Commerce began to extend its ramifications through every part of the enormous area he had trodden with a valour and determination the more magnificent because unattended by any display of the resources of a conqueror. The partition of Africa among the great powers of Europe had yet to come.

He had some prevision of Kirk's success, for in a long communication to Horace Waller, difficult to decipher except with a magnifying glass because written across and across on an old report of the Royal Geographical Society, he says—the date appears to be somewhere about the beginning of February, 1871: "I am truly thankful that there is some prospect of the suppression of the East African slave trade as carried on by the Sultan's subjects. I have heard but little of the details, but I believe a great deal is owing to the exertions of our friend Kirk, on whom for my share may heaven's rich blessings descend. The sights I have in this journey seen of slaving make my blood run cold, and I am not easily moved or very sentimental. . . . It is an awful traffic, and can be congenial only to the devil and his angels. If our statesmen stop the frightful waste of human life in this region, and mitigate the vast amount of human woe that accompanies it, they will do good on the large scale and cause joy in heaven."

Of specific Christian missionary advance the tale is still more impressive. Within a few years of Livingstone's death, a wave of missionary energy began to roll over the African continent. There was no lack of volunteers, and all the great missionary societies not only planned the invasion of new fields whose very names were hitherto unheard of, but found themselves encouraged so to do by the increasing number of their supporters. The lonely passing of a mighty spirit in the heart of Africa, so like to that of a Moses or an Elijah, wrought upon the faith of many men and women in the churches of the English-speaking nations and even far beyond, and they came forward in ever-growing numbers to offer themselves as messengers of Christ to the heathen. The following conspectus may serve to give some idea of the

direct results up to the present of the current thus set flowing. The
figures show the state of Protestant missions in the countries opened
up by Livingstone. If the influence of his life and example upon missions in the rest of Africa and other parts of the world were taken
into consideration, the statistics would have to be multiplied.

Area	*Societies*	*Foreign Staff*	*Native Staff*	*Christian Community*
Belgian Congo	24	653	4,528	108,000
Rio Mini	2	15	27	2,872
Bechuanaland	4	12	31	22,380
Southern Rhodesia	13	202	1,593	23,109
Northern Rhodesia	12	194	1,519	21,515
Portuguese East Africa	12	109	627	30,755
Nyassaland (Protestant)	9	245	1,589	107,388
Tanganyika	10	176	939	41,832
Kenya	11	252	979	1,308
Uganda	3	112	4,275	146,617
Angola	10	186	940	35,000
Total	110	2,156	17,047	540,776

The numbers given above are taken from the *Statistical Atlas of
Missions,* 1925 (Edinburgh House Press). Later surveys show marked
increase, but do not cover the whole area. The figures for South Africa
alone, and relating to missions begun before 1840, also show a great
expansion in the same period. There are 58 Societies, 1,934 Foreign
Staff, 11,332 Native Staff, and 947,229 members of the Christian Community.

What manner of man was Livingstone in his mature years when
placed in comparison with the earlier period wherein he had not
yet found himself or determined his vocation? The glimpses we
have had of his most private and secret self-communings reveal him
as a good man of essentially simple mind, and this accords with the
impression he produced on those who succeeded in winning his confidence. He has been accused of egotism, and, judged by present-day
standards of good form, there might seem to be some colour for the

charge. A fastidious reader might be repelled by the frequent use of the expression "my work" or "my great work" in his writings—*e.g.*, the entry in his diary on May 31st, 1862, expressive of his feelings at the loss of his wife: "I know her prayer was that she might be spared to be a help and comfort to me in my great work." Again: "By the failure of the Universities Mission my work seems vain." In his relations with Bishop Mackenzie, Bishop Tozer, Dr. Kirk, and Dr. Stewart (who recommended a pause before attempting to plant a Free Church of Scotland Mission near Lake Nyassa), he was over-anxious to show himself in the right, as we have seen reason to believe.

If these facts seem to indicate self-centredness, it should be remembered that the man to whom they attach was no braggart, and we have the overwhelming evidence of his own self-revealing colloquies with God, never intended to be profaned by circulation among his contemporaries, to prove that he was utterly consecrated to what he believed to be his mission in life, and pure from all self-seeking. His was a humble heart, and in ordinary society he was shy and diffident except when his opinion was called for on matters on which he felt deeply. Then he became formidable, for he was too single-minded to care what people thought on any subject once he saw his way clear. Hence his perspective on life was different from that of most men; like the greatest way-makers of the race, he had a profound conviction that he was not his own, but divinely chosen and set apart for the doing of a specific work. His ruling conviction was that nothing must be allowed to stand in the way of this, and if anything threatened to do so he was apt to show irritation. He often amazed those who wrought with him by the lengths to which he would proceed when a definite purpose took possession of him and he saw himself balked of its accomplishment. It was this that led him to sacrifice all family ties to the necessities of the task to which he had put his hand; and it was this that at times made him behave with what appeared to be a strange indifference to the feelings of those about him. He would go on his way without taking them into his confidence or pausing to consider their needs. This peculiarity, as we have seen, had sad consequences in the persistence wherewith he carried out his design of transporting his entire household across the Kalahari and attempting to effect a settlement with Sebituane in 1851, and a still more tragical outcome in the collapse of the Makololo mission in 1860.

Kirk's diary is illuminating from this point of view. The attempt to find a way to Lake Nyassa via the Rovuma river in 1862 was a failure for the sufficient reason that the river did not flow out of the lake, but of this Livingstone could hardly be persuaded, though the fact was glaringly obvious to every one else. So obstinately determined was he to force an entry to the Nyassa region through other than Portuguese territory, and thus strike a deadly blow at the slave trade, that he disregarded as long as he possibly could all evidence that told against his hopes. Neither the sickness of his colleagues, nor the hostility of the natives, nor the drying up of the river itself sufficed to deter him until it became a physical impossibility to go another step unless he went alone and unattended to meet certain death. He had already shed most of his responsible colleagues, and even Kirk had become aware that he would be sacrificed without mercy to his chief's obsession if he ventured to go counter to it in any way. "Dr. L., though kind and considerate to me," he remarks, "still is not to be depended on; and any day, if a misunderstanding should take place, all former services would be lost sight of." [1] A whimsical entry on August 23rd states: "Dr. L. is uncomfortable at sea, and looks so. When the weather gets foul or anything begins to go wrong, it is well to give him a wide berth, most especially when he sings to himself. But the kind of air is some indication. If it is 'The Happy Land,' then look out for squalls and stand clear. If 'Scots wha hae,' then there is some grand vision of discovery before his mind. . . . But on all occasions humming of airs is a bad omen." [2]

A little farther on this tolerant and genial observer begins to exhibit alarm at his chief's apparently irrational doggedness, and to find it anything but amusing. "The river gets no better," he writes—"snags and shoals with tortuous windings. . . . Still there is no change in Dr. L.'s plans; he is for going on still, regardless of the return. His

[1] Coupland, op. cit., p. 239.
[2] Ibid., p. 240.

determination seems to amount to infatuation. We go where the boat cannot float at many parts, and where natives can wade across at almost all points." [3] Three days later comes the definite opinion committed to the diary: "I can come to no other conclusion than that Dr. L. is out of his mind." [4] And finally, on September 25th: "Dr. L. is a most unsafe leader. He never thinks of getting back. All he cares for is accomplishing his object at any risk whatever. It is useless making any remark to him." [5] Well may Professor Coupland add the comment: "The most interesting feature of the story is the light it throws again on Livingstone's personality. How strange it is that he should never, save in one sentence, have discussed the question with his companions, of whom Kirk, at any rate, he knew to be a sensible man and trustworthy! How strange that he just gave his orders and went silently on, seemingly careless or unaware of what his subordinates were thinking! Another than Livingstone, more human, if perhaps less great, would surely have talked it over with them, humoured them, if need be, and encouraged them, and, if danger really had to be faced, persuaded them to follow him into it willingly and with a single mind." [6]

This intensity of concentration on an end to be attained to the exclusion of all ordinary human interests may be reckoned a mark of greatness; it has characterized most of the colossal personalities of history, but has not seldom been found in combination with a ruthlessness in regard to the infliction of suffering and the destruction of human life quite alien to Livingstone's character. If, as Dr. William MacDougall would say, we must distinguish between sympathy and compassion, we can rightly credit Livingstone with a moderate amount of the former and a great deal of the latter. Like many strong natures, he was capable of very deep tenderness, especially for the weak and helpless both of the human and subhuman creation, and, as we have had repeated occasion to observe, he could be roused to a fury of moral indignation by the infliction of cruelty and injustice. He dis-

[3] *Ibid.*, p. 241
[4] *Ibid.*, p. 242.
[5] *Ibid.*, p. 244.
[6] *Ibid.*, p. 246.

liked the killing of wild animals and birds for sport, and often went
out of his way to succour wounded creatures in extremity; his trouble
of mind over the loss of his faithful dog is an illustration of the kindly
feeling he ever exhibited towards almost all living creatures. No one
can read his vivid and discerning notes on natural history without
perceiving that he was no mere classifier, but a keenly interested lover
of almost all forms of life; these were to him examples of divine
thought and care, and he never ceased to marvel at their beauty and
variety. If he were less consistently forbearing towards human fault
and frailty, it was not because he was less solicitous for the welfare of
his fellow-men than that of furred and feathered creatures, but because of his moral sensitiveness. In contradistinction to the experience of many other travellers, he never became so accustomed to human
depravity as to be able to view it undisturbed; it shocked and revolted
him as inexpressibly in his last acquaintance with it as when, a young
missionary, he recorded his horror of it in his first journey through the
country of the Bakwains.

Yet he could make more allowance for the shortcomings of savages
in this respect than for the selfishness and meanness of civilized men.
He did not readily enter into the thoughts and feelings of the latter,
and their needs had usually to be thrust upon his attention before he
saw them; but once he did see them he would do far more towards
satisfying them than would many persons whose commiseration was
more easily excited. This is only another way of saying what has been
said above, that with him compassion was stronger than sympathy.
He never had the grace of suffering fools gladly unless the fools happened to be weak, ignorant, and unsophisticated; then indeed his
patience was limitless and his benevolence inexhaustible. But woe to
the proud and powerful who sought to frighten him from the path of
duty or the trail of oppression! Then he was like a bloodhound on
the scent and almost as ferocious. The dread which he inspired in
corrupt Portuguese officials and half-caste slave traders was a very
real thing, though he had no material force wherewith to back it; it
was near akin to that which hypocrites and crafty spoilers of the poor
felt in the presence of Christ.

It says much for the moral elevation of Livingstone's character that the men who admired him most and became his staunchest friends through evil report and good report in his maturity were themselves men of like temper—Sir Bartle Frere, William Oswell, James Young, Sir Roderick Murchison, W. F. Webb, Bishop Mackenzie, Horace Waller. The last named, though much younger than Livingstone, sprang into an intimacy with him during the period of the Zambesi expedition and their mutual association with Bishop Mackenzie which continued to the end of Livingstone's life had important results in the issue to the public of the story of the last days and the closing scene at Ilala. Waller was a man after Livingstone's own heart, manly, frank, and outspoken, independent in judgment, and as honest and disinterested in his desire to benefit Africa and the Africans as the explorer himself. His voluminous and carefully posted manuscript diaries reveal very clearly the attraction which Livingstone possessed for men of his type. As examined by the author, though space forbids quotation, they show that the young, cultured English clergyman conceived a respect for the blunt and somewhat austere veteran missionary which made him proud and willing to execute to the best of his power any directions the latter chose to give. Yet never for a moment in the very considerable correspondence the two had with each other—and Livingstone wrote more to Waller than to anyone in the last half-dozen years of his life—does the older man take the trouble to accommodate his language to the principles and prepossessions of the younger. He is habitually blunt in his criticisms to the point, at times, of positive rudeness, and never professes to agree with or even to condone a practice or a policy he disapproves. This is particularly the case with regard to the withdrawal of the Universities Mission to Zanzibar and the proposed establishment of an episcopate in Madagascar. Livingstone lets himself go on these and other matters in a way that would have offended a smaller man than Waller, but nothing marred their relations; Waller says plainly that it was Livingstone's rugged integrity that first attracted him and led him to discern the simple unfeigned goodness of the man and his rare nobility of spirit.

In bearing witness to the same thing Stanley is a Daniel come to judgment. The former workhouse boy had known none of the earlier advantages of Horace Waller and lacked the latter's fine Christian quality, but he, too, yielded to the spell of Livingstone's moral greatness, and for reasons very similar to those which influenced Waller. In his report to the *New York Herald* on December 26th, 1871, after having been a few weeks in Livingstone's company, he confesses to having been taken by surprise. From what he had previously heard he expected to find in the explorer an eccentric, petulant, fractious individual with whom it would be difficult, if not impossible, to consort for long. On the contrary, he found a man in whose every aim and motive he could detect nothing that was not admirable. He writes:

> In him religion exhibits its loveliest features. It governs his conduct towards his servants, towards the natives and towards the bigoted Mussulmans—all who come in contact with him. Without religion Livingstone, with his ardent temperament, his enthusiastic nature, his high spirit and courage, might have been an uncompanionable man and a hard master. Religion has tamed all these characteristics; nay, if he was ever possessed of them, they have been thoroughly eradicated. Whatever was crude or wilful religion has refined, and made him, to speak the earnest, sober truth, the most agreeable of companions and indulgent of masters.

That the hypothetical traits Stanley enumerates as not unlikely to have detracted from the charm of Livingstone's character were not wholly imaginary may readily be conceded. Waller knew they were there, and did not think the worse of the man for their existence in view of the fact that they were held in subordination to Christian principle. Livingstone was severer with himself than with any one else, and a rigorous censor of his own conduct and spiritual states; his expressions of indignation against other people's unrighteous behaviour were habitually tempered by reminders of his own frailty and imperfection. Nothing is more frequent in his diaries than reflections of this kind subjoined to the bald narration of acts of poltroonery

or pure scoundrelism of which he had been the victim. "The recollection of my own shortcomings makes me charitable," is his comment when faced with suffering and death through the wanton theft of his medical stores. And in the midst of his consternation at the treachery, truculence, and callousness of followers who had abandoned him a thousand miles from the nearest base of supplies and left him to die he meekly observes: "Consciousness of my own defects makes me lenient." Apostolical charity could no further go.

Stanley's perception was accurate; this was not nature but grace. Livingstone had disciplined himself through the consistent exercise of a working faith in Christ until all his natural faculties were co-ordinated therewith. He was a born fighter and came of a fighting stock, and he knew the value of the fighting instinct when harnessed to the service of a consistent moral purpose, as his whole career abundantly illustrates, and never more so than in the closing period. Thus he writes within a few months of his death:

> The pugnacious spirit is one of the necessities of life. When people have little or none of it, they are subjected to indignity and loss. My own men walk into houses where we pass the nights without asking any leave, and steal cassava without shame. I have to threaten and thrash to keep them honest, while if we are at a village where the natives are a little pugnacious they are as meek as sucking doves. The peace plan involves indignity and wrong.[7]

His views on the principles of the Peace Society as applied to primitive conditions we have already noted, but at the same time his own practice was their vindication. What he mainly relied upon was the innate sense of justice of even the worst of men, and was content to appeal thereto with tireless patience while pursuing a wise, unaggressive policy which did not neglect available precautions for self-protection.

His courage was amazing, both moral and physical, and carried him through jeopardies where an instant's failure of nerve would have been fatal. Sir John Kirk gave emphatic testimony to Living-

[7] *Last Journals*, vol. ii., p. 256.

stone's possession of this characteristic in an interview with Mr.
Basil Mathews, published in the L.M.S. *Chronicle* in December, 1912:

> His absolute lack of any sense of fear amounted almost to a weak-
> ness. He would go into the most perilous positions without a
> tremor or a touch of hesitation. I never knew him blench or show
> a sign of timorousness in any circumstances whatever.

If the man of whom this could be said had been other than a consecrated emissary of the Gospel of Christ he might have left a track
of fire and blood behind him, instead of one of hope and peace. He
had no confidence either in the effect of material power or of scientific wizardry to elevate and refine the African people, and is at pains
to say so repeatedly:

> One might imagine that, as mechanical powers are unknown
> to the heathen, the almost magic operations of machinery, the dis-
> coveries of modern science and art, or the presence of the prodigious
> force which, for instance, is associated with the sight of a man-
> of-war, would have the effect which miracles once had of arresting
> the attention and inspiring awe. But, though we have heard the
> natives exclaim in admiration at the sight of even small illustra-
> tions of what science enables us to do—"Ye are gods and not men"
> —the heart is unaffected. In attempting their moral elevation, it
> is always more conducive to the end desired, that the teacher should
> come unaccompanied by any power to cause either jealousy or
> fear. [8]

Again:

> No jugglery or sleight-of-hand, as was recommended to Napoleon
> III., would have any effect in the civilization of the Africans; they
> have too much good sense for that. Nothing brings them to place
> thorough confidence in Europeans but a long course of well-doing.
> They believe readily in the supernatural as effecting any new
> process or feat of skill, for it is part of their original faith to ascribe
> everything above human agency to unseen spirits. Goodness or un-

[8] *Narrative of an Expedition to the Zambesi*, p. 224.

selfishness impresses their minds more than any kind of skill or power. They say, "You have different hearts from ours; all black men's hearts are bad, but yours are good." The prayer to Jesus for a new heart and right spirit at once commends itself as appropriate. [9]

He was the living exemplification of the spirit in which he trusted for the regeneration of savage Africa. No one man before or since has ever impressed the native mind as David Livingstone did. Goddon came nearest to it, and for similar reasons, but in a different part of the continent and in widely different associations. Sir H. H. Johnston, by no means a biographer prepossessed in his subject's favour, acknowledges that this is Livingstone's greatest title to distinction and the principal secret of his lasting influence. Johnston tells that in his own extensive travels he has listed over and over again to native Africans discussing the character of white men with whom they had made acquaintance. They are very shrewd, he says, and as inveterate gossips and lovers of scandal as their more sophisticated European contemporaries, and no man who gives them cause for animadverting on his weaknesses can hope to escape censorious notice, little though he may be aware of it. A trader's or traveller's reputation, or a missionary's for that matter, will spread from village to village over many hundreds of miles, and tales be told of his doings that he imagines could not possibly be known. Being familiar with Bantu dialects, Johnston was able to understand what his bearers were saying among themselves at times when they thought he was paying no heed or was ignorant of the subject under discussion, and his verdict on what he thus learned, so far as it concerns Livingstone, is notable:

> I have, in fact, at different times and in many African experiences, on the hot, weary midday march, by the brookside, in the quiet grey moonlight round the camp fire, in the gloomy forest, under the snows of Kilima-njaro, becalmed on the expense of Tanganyika, or gliding rapidly down the Congo in a canoe, listened half-idly, half-attentively, to the discussions which would arise

[9] *Last Journals,* vol. ii., p. 201.

among the Wa-swahili carriers as to their view of the lives led in
Africa by most great travellers. Of one thing, however, these gossips were all convinced (and among all the scandal they were talk-
ing there was little reason for them to exempt one man more than
another), and that was, that Dr. Livingstone, who, according to
their traditions, was sometimes cross and even peevish, who was
sometimes in their eyes unreasonable and sometimes inexplicable
in his actions, was nevertheless absolutely pure from the least suspicion of immorality. Had he been otherwise, had he been as frail
as are ninety-eight African travellers, and, for the matter of that,
other men, out of a hundred, I should not have alluded to this subject, because it is one which is better left undiscussed; but as I have
heard this foolish slander half-gleefully hinted at by those who
derive some undefined pleasure by belittling great men, I thought
it better to refer to the rumour, and state that, judged by the verdict of Livingstone's native followers, it is absolutely false.[10]

A testimony of another sort, and more recent, comes from the
mouth of an erstwhile heathen, or child of heathen parentage, who
confesses to owing all that he values most in life to the influence of
the greatest missionary Africa ever saw. It is written by Miss Mabel
Shaw, and is extracted from her Journal Letter of June, 1928. Miss
Shaw is Principal of the L.M.S. Livingstone Memorial Boarding
School for Girls at Mbereshi among the Awemba, Cazembe's tribe.
Describing a visit paid by her to a district within her radius, she
gives a brief, unadorned account, memorable in its mingled pathos
and beauty, of a conversation with a man still living who had once
come face to face with Livingstone:

In that village there is a very old man, the last man on the
Luapula who had seen David Livingstone. He had come to the
camp that morning to talk to me, and he and I sat looking over
the river, he once again a boy seeing the white man coming round
the bend in a little dug-out. The people scattered, climbed trees,
the roofs of their houses. He had fallen from the sky, they said.
"He had clothing on his feet," the old man said excitedly. "I was

10 *Op. cit.*, p. 365.

a boy, I went near, I touched, but the head man pulled me back. 'You'll be bewitched by his medicine,' they said." Then he sat long in silence, and at last he said, as if to himself: "And he laughed, there was love in his eyes, he was not fierce."

Again the silence I dare not disturb.

"He made a path through our land, and you his followers have come. God's Light-bringers; and more come to-day."

I was a very little child, seeing a great and high adventure that morning. I have never met David Livingstone as I did then. I, too, saw him coming round the bend in a little canoe, carrying all he possessed. It became holy ground. Then the others came, his followers, with all their innumerable packages. I thought of the array I came out with. He, the great saint and pioneer, God's adventurer, could put all into a little canoe; and he cut the highway of God all across this great continent, and that old man's eyes grew misty and his voice tremulous when he spoke of him, and tears came to me; we seemed to share a wonderful thing, that old African and I on the bank of the great river.

The vignette thus etched illustrates, as perhaps no lengthy dissertation could, the indelible impression produced for good by the impact of Livingstone's personality upon the imagination of benighted Africa. It was an impression entirely unique in that home of blood and terror; yet he himself little realized its extent or the spiritual reactions that followed it. In the *Last Journals,* vol. i., p. 303, appears this entry: "1868, *June 11th.*—Crossed the Mbereze, ten yards broad and thigh deep." This is all; but under the simple memorandum, as we now see, a piece of work was unconsciously done that remains an immortal memory in the mind of at least one negro. Here and there throughout central Africa signs like this abound, pointing to the enlightening and uplifting influence exerted by Livingstone's mere presence upon the Africans he met day by day in his journeys. That he was not altogether unaware of its worth we are led to infer from his observations on the necessity of setting a good example if real ascendancy were to be gained over the susceptible African mind, but he could not have foreseen more than a fragment of the marvels of regeneration to which it would lead. Incidents like this are a sufficient demonstration of the fact that the predominant interest in his life was not that of exploration for its own sake, or that of amassing information about curious and unfamiliar features of natural history, but of bringing to bear upon heathen Africa the fraternal spirit of the Gospel of Christ. The salvability of the African was with him a passionately held article of faith. Like so many of the world's spiritual pioneers, and especially his divine Master Himself, he sacrificed his life for his conviction; the hour of his passing was dark, the forces of evil apparently triumphant; but the victory was won.

Is Miss Shaw right in attributing saintliness to him? At first sight it may seem absurd. David Livingstone was no gentle and gracious spirit of the type of a Fénélon or a Francis of Assisi. There was a touch of austerity about him, as his portraits reveal. He was rough-spoken at times; he could smite, and smite hard, when there was occasion for so doing, and he was not wont to spare the guilty holders of place and power; his denunciations of cruelty and lust disguised as beneficence or legitimate trading were like those of the prophets of old; with his whole soul he hated and abhorred oppression, and hurled himself at it to destroy it. He was a Moses and an Isaiah rather than a Francis de Sales or a George Herbert. But if we have regard to other criteria of saintship, few have better deserved the title. He dwelt in the presence of God and breathed the air of devotion; his was the worshipful attitude to life which forbids making light of opportunity or proving recreant before stern duty. His spiritual insight grew with his years, and was the fruit of his practice. Nothing is more astonishing in his wonderful career than the development of his mind in connection with the fundamental truths of religion, considering how he was shut away from the better part of his life from intercourse with the leading thinkers and teachers of the day, or from more than the slenderest acquaintance with their works. He had to think for himself, and, man of action as he was, his thinking was the concomitant of his constant habit of prayer—prayer that was scarcely ever concerned with the definition of abstract truths, but almost wholly with the practical problems of character and service. Take the follow-

ing paragraph set down in his Journal on August 5th, 1872, while awaiting at Ujiji the coming of the new bearers and supplies Stanley had promised to send him:

> What is the atonement of Christ? It is Himself; it is the inherent and everlasting mercy of God made apparent to human eyes and ears. The everlasting love was disclosed by our Lord's life and death. It showed that God forgives because He loves to forgive. He works by smiles if possible; if not, by frowns; pain is only a means of enforcing love.[11]

The man capable of writing these words and believing them must rank with the foremost of spiritual seers; they pierce right to the heart of the greatest of the Christian mysteries. When we remember that they were written nearly sixty years ago they are the more remarkable, for this is not the way in which the evangelicalism to which Livingstone owed his spiritual training was in the habit of expressing itself at that period. He had outgrown most of the limitations and prejudices of his religious upbringing without shedding in the process any of his confidence in the beauty and imperishableness of the revelation they enshrined. His very handwriting changed in the interval with the expansion and refinement of his views, and the acquirement of a broader outlook upon life. At the author's hand lies Livingstone's first letter of application to the London Missionary Society. He was then a young man of twenty-four, and had for some time been in regular attendance at the winter sessions of Glasgow University; nevertheless, the style is stilted and awkward, and the handwriting cramped and unformed, like that of an ill-educated schoolboy. To place this jejune document alongside of the mass of correspondence and notes proceeding from the same hand between thirty and forty years later, and from which most of the citations in the foregoing pages have been taken, is to be struck by the contrast. The latter is as free, flowing, and unrestrained in form and expression as the former is the opposite; it might be esteemed the work of another man if one did not know the contrary. In a sense it is another man who writes, a man of rich and ripe experi-

[11] *Last Journals*, vol. ii., p. 228.

ence and amplitude of soul. The genius was doubtless there from the first, but it needed the strenuous wrestlings with titanic obstacles in an august cause through three decades packed with adventure to call it forth and give efflorescence.

On Livingstone's greatness as a missionary and an explorer all men are now agreed. Of the outstanding importance of his contributions to geology, botany, ethnology there is no need to argue, subsidiary though these were to his geographical discoveries; their value is now universally acknowledged. The dynamic he communicated to commercial enterprise was in itself enough to establish his claim to eminence during his lifetime and immeasurably more since. But far and away beyond all these is the heritage of his faith in righteousness and brotherly-kindness. The nineteenth century produced no greater moral force than he, and its propulsive energies show no sign of diminution. He has been the means of evoking more zeal for human welfare, more honest belief in the capacities of human nature, more unselfish willingness to labour in the cause of human emancipation from the shackles of hatred, and fear, and hoary antipathies than almost any single personal influence that could be named; certainly none other has been more fecund in operation. And the work goes on, and will go on till the race of man has reached that inconceivably distant goal towards which all the men of vision of all generations have raised their eyes and led the way.

ITINERARY OF DR. LIVINGSTONE'S TRAVELS IN AFRICA FROM 1841 TO 1873

FROM " 'NYAKA,' THE DOCTOR," BY W. A. ELLIOTT

Depart	Date	Arrive	Date	Miles	Notes
England	December 8, 1840	Cape Town	February 28, 1841		
Cape Town		Algoa Bay	May 19, 1841	530	With Edwards.
Algoa Bay		Kuruman	July 31, 1841	700	With Edwards.
Kuruman	September, 1841	Lepelole		250	Alone.
Kuruman	December 8, 1841	Kuruman	February 10, 1842	250	Bamangwato, and on.
Lepelole		Lepelole	June, 1842	250	Exploratory.
Kuruman		Shoshong		200	Bakoa.
Lepelole		Kuruman		750	And return.
Kuruman	February, 1843	Sebehwe's		?	Lion adventure.
Kuruman	August, 1843	Shoshong		800	Evangelizing.
Kuruman	September, 1843	Mabotsa		250	To meet Moffats.
Mabotsa	? 1844	Kuruman		250	Evangelizing.
Kuruman		Mabotsa		300	Betrothal.
Mabotsa		Kuruman		250	Evangelizing.
Kuruman	1845	Mabotsa		250	Marriage.
Mabotsa	1845	Kuruman		250	Honeymoon.
Kuruman		Mabotsa		250	
Mabotsa	February, 1846	Chonuane			
Chonuane	1846	Magaliesburg and back		1,000	Two journeys.
Chonuane	February, 1847	Kolobeng		50	And return home.
Kolobeng	June 6, 1849	Ngami Lake	August 1, 1849	800	And return home.
Kolobeng	April, 1850	Ngami Lake	July 8, 1850	800	With Oswell.
Kolobeng	April 8, 1851	Linyanti	July, 1851	500	With Oswell.
Linyanti		Zambesi R.	August 3, 1851	150	Kolobeng destroyed.
Zambesi		Kuruman		750	Mrs. L. to England.
Kuruman		Cape Town	April 16, 1852	600	
Cape Town	June 8, 1852	Kuruman	August 29, 1852	600	By desert route.
Kuruman	June 20, 1853	Linyanti	December, 1852	800	Upper Zambesi.
Linyanti		Naliele	February, 1853	300	With Sekeletu.
Naliele		Linyanti			
Linyanti	November 11, 1853	Loanda	May 31, 1854	1,500	
Loanda	September 20, 1854	Linyanti	September 11, 1855	1,500	
Linyanti	November 3, 1855	Quilimane	May 20, 1856	1,300	Thence to Mauritius and England (arrive December, 1856).

From	Departure	To	Arrival	Distance	Remarks
Liverpool	March 10, 1858	Zambesi	May 16, 1858	300	With *Ma-Robert*.
Kongone		Tette	September 8, 1858	450	Three double journeys.
Tette	January, 1859	Kebrabasa		700	And return.
Tette	March, 1859	Shire R.		750	And return.
Tette	August 25, 1859	Shire		} 1,000	Lake Nyassa discovered.
Shire R.		Shire			
Kongone	December 16, 1859	Kongone		650	And return.
Shesheke		Shesheke	August 18, 1860	200	*Ma-Robert* sank.
Shesheke	September 17, 1860	Linyanti	August 31, 1860	650	Double journey.
Kongone	February 25, 1861	Kongone	January 4, 1861	150	With U.M.C.A.
Kongone		Rovuma R.		800	Mrs. L. died April 27, 1862.
Nyassa (north)		Nyassa	November 8, 1861	800	And return.
Kongone	August 6, 1862	Up Rovuma R.	January 31, 1862	300	And return; recalled.
Kongone	January 10, 1863	Nyassa and N.W.		1,700	
Kongone		Zanzibar, Bombay, and England			
England	August, 1865	Rovuma		500	*Via* Bombay, Zanzibar, depart Bombay March 9, 1866.
Rovuma	April 4, 1866	Nyassa	August 8, 1866	750	Deserted, exhausted.
Nyassa		Tanganyika	April 1, 1867	400	
Tanganyika	May 1, 1867	Mweru and Bangweolo	July 18, 1868	450	With slave caravan.
Bangweolo	December 11, 1868	Ujiji	March 14, 1869	650	A journey of intolerable suffering.
Ujiji	July 12, 1869	Bambarre and Nyangwe	March 29, 1871	650	"A ruckle of bones."
Nyangwe	July 20, 1871	Ujiji	October 23, 1871	200	Stanley arrived October 28, 1871.
Ujiji		North end Tanganyika		650	And return with H. M. Stanley.
Ujiji	December 27, 1871	Unyanyembe	February 18, 1872	350	"Good-bye."
Unyanyembe	June 24, 1872	Bangweolo		600	Died May 1, 1873.

The distances are estimates carefully measured on the map. Were pedometric distances available, these distances would almost certainly be considerably increased. Livingstone's travels probably covered twenty thousand miles.

RELIEF PARTIES

1867. E. D. Young's Expedition. Proved D. L. was not dead.

1869. Kirk sent fourteen men to Ujiji. Seven died of cholera. The other seven having consumed their provisions, had, with the concurrence of the Governor of Unyanyembe, drawn upon the stores intended for D. L. Remnant of stores reached D. L. in 1871.

1870. Consul Churchill sent (November 18) seven men with beads, clothes and provisions. (See Appendix to *How I Found Livingstone*.)

1871. Stanley left Zanzibar February 5. Returned May, 1872. Kirk found (February 18) that Churchill's seven men sent in November were still at Bagamoyo on the mainland opposite Zanzibar. Started them off inland.

1872. Lieutenant Dawson's expedition arrived Zanzibar April 19 on way out. Started but turned back.

1872. Jacob Wainwright and fifty-seven men left Zanzibar in May. In August D. L. started on tramp again with this escort. D. L. died May, 1873.

1873. Lieutenant Cameron left Zanzibar February 27. Met porters who told of D. L.'s death.

1873. Lieutenant Grandy took a boat expedition up Congo from West Coast. Recalled.

LIST OF BOOKS

Adams, H. G. The Weaver Boy who Became a Missionary. 1867.

Adams, H. G. The Life and Adventures of Dr. Livingstone in the Interior of Africa. 1868.

Adams, H. G. David Livingstone. Hodder and Stoughton. 1881.

Arthur, Grace. David Livingstone. 64 pp. Morgan and Scott. 1919.

Batty, J. A. S. Livingstone, the Empire Builder. S.P.C.K. 1913.

Bedford, C. J. Livingstone of Africa. (For Children.) Seeley. 1924.

Beeton, S. O., and Smith, R. M. Livingstone and Stanley. 1872.

Bitton, Nelson. The Liberator of Africa. 64 pp. L.M.S. 1912.

Blaikie, W. G. Six Heroic Men. 1906.

Blaikie, W. G. David Livingstone: Missionary and Explorer. 32 pp. Religious Tract Society. 1908.

Blaikie, Rev. W. G., D.D. The Personal Life of David Livingstone. John Murray. 1910.

Charles, Elizabeth. Three Martyrs of the Nineteenth Century: Livingstone, Gordon, and Patteson. S.P.C.K. 1885. (Abridged edition, 1927.)

Cooley, W. D. Dr. Livingstone and the Royal Geographical Society. 1874.

Coster, G. T. Dr. Livingstone: His Work and Character. A Funeral Sermon. South Norwood. 1874.

Crawford, Daniel. Back to the Long Grass: My Link with Livingstone. Hodder and Stoughton. 1922.

David Livingstone Film Expedition. (A prospectus.) Ward, Lock and Co. 1924.

Dawson, R. B. Livingstone: The Hero of Africa. Seeley, Service and Co. 1918.

Devereux, W. C. A Cruise in H.M.S. *Gordon* and Up the Zambesi with Dr. Livingstone. 1869.

Elliott, W. A. "Nyaka": The Doctor. L.M.S. 1s. 1908.

Ellis, Jas. Jos. David Livingstone, etc. 64 pp. Pickering and Inglis. 1928.

Entwistle, Mary. The Child's Livingstone. Henry Frowde. 1913.

Finger, Charles J. David Livingstone. Allen and Unwin. 1927.

Fraser, Mrs. A. Z. Livingstone and Newstead. John Murray. 1913.

Galt, Alex. The Livingstone Centenary Loan Exhibition at the Royal Scottish Museum. 1913. (Reprinted from the *Scottish Geographical Magazine*.)

GARDINER, ALFONZO. Livingstone's Travels in South Africa. Adapted from the Original of D. L. "Masterpieces of Standard Literature." 1908.

GOLDING, V. The Story of David Livingstone. (Children's Hero Series.) Nelson and Son. 1906.

GOODWIN, HARVEY, D.D. Memoir of Bishop Mackenzie. Deighton, Bell and Co., Cambridge. 1864.

GREGORY, B. K. The Story of Livingstone, Weaver Boy, Missionary and Explorer. Nat. S.S.U. 1896.

GREGORY, J. W. Livingstone as an Explorer. J. Maclehose and Sons. 1913.

GRIFFITH, ROBERT. David Livingstone: Cyfaill y Caethwas. (Welsh.) Maps by J. Sibree. 1925.

HARRIS, W. MELVILLE. David Livingstone: A Hero of Peace. Congregational Union of England and Wales. 1912.

HAWEIS, H. R. Travels of Dr. Livingstone. (Routledge's "Wonder Library.") Routledge and Son. 1886.

HORNE, SILVESTER. Life of Livingstone. Macmillan. 1912.

HUGHES, THOMAS. David Livingstone. (A Biography.) ("English Men of Action" series.) Macmillan. 1889.

HUME, EDWARD. David Livingstone: The Man, the Missionary, and the Explorer. Andrew Melrose. 1904.

JOHNSTON, SIR H. H. Livingstone and the Exploration of Central Africa. 1891 and 1912.

KELTIE, SIR J. K. The World's Great Explorers and Exploration. 7 vols. George Philip and Son. 1889 to 1892.

KINGSTON, W. H. G., and Low, C. R. Great African Travellers from Mungo Park to Livingstone. Routledge and Sons. 1890.

LACIRDA, ALMEIDA DE. Reply to Dr. Livingstone's Accusations and Misrepresentations. 1867.

LACIRDA, ALMEIDA DE. Examen das Vinagens de Douter Livingstone. 1867.

LINCOLN, ARTHUR. David Livingstone: Missionary, Explorer, and Philanthropist. ("World's Hero" Series.) 1907.

Livingstone, David, and Cambridge. (A Record of Three Meetings in the Senate House.) Cambridge University Press. 1908.

LIVINGSTONE, DAVID and CHARLES. Narrative of an Expedition to the Zambesi and its Tributaries. John Murray. 1865.

Livingstone, David: A Missionary Poem in Memoriam. 1874.

LIVINGSTONE, DAVID. Dr. Livingstone's Cambridge Lectures. Cambridge. 1858.

Livingstone, David, Last Journals of. See WALLER.

LIVINGSTONE, DAVID. Missionary Travels and Researches in South Africa. (Several editions and adaptations.) John Murray. 1857.

Livingstone, David: The Story of his Life and Travels. T. Nelson and Sons. 1887.

Livingstone and Stanley: Opening Up of the Dark Continent. W. and R. Chambers. 1895.

LIVINGSTONE, W. P. The Story of David Livingstone. Livingstone Press. 1929.

LUNT, T. R. W. Talks on David Livingstone. 1911, 1920.

MACAULAY, J. Livingstone Anecdotes: A Sketch of His Career. Religious Tract Society. 1886, 1887.

MACGILCHRIST, J. The Life of the Great African Traveller, Dr. Livingstone. Haughton and Co. 1872.

MACLACHLAN, T. B. David Livingstone. ("Famous Scots" series.) Oliphant, Anderson and Ferrier. 1901.

MANNING, MISS A. Heroes of the Desert: Moffat and Livingstone. 1875.

MARRAT, J. David Livingstone: Missionary and Discoverer. Wesleyan Conference Office. 1877.

MATHEWS, BASIL. Livingstone: The Pathfinder. (Pathfinder Series.) Livingstone Press. 1912.

MAXWELL, GORDON. The Life and Travels of David Livingstone. (Selected from his own Narrative.) Brodie Books. 1927.

MOIR, F. L. M. After Livingstone. Hodder and Stoughton. 1926.

MONTEFIORE, BRICE. David Livingstone: His Labours and His Legacy. ("All About" Series.) Partridge. 2s. 6d.

MOSSMAN, SAMUEL. Heroes of Discovery: From Magellan to Livingstone. Edinburgh. 1868.

NEW, CHARLES. Life, Wanderings and Labours in Eastern Africa. Hodder and Stoughton. 1873.

NOEL, HON. R. B. W. Livingstone in Africa: A Poem. Ward and Downey. 1874.

OSWELL, W. E. William Cotton Oswell, Hunter and Explorer: Story of His Life, with Extracts from the Private Journal of David Livingstone. 2 vols. Heinemann. 1900.

PALGRAVE, MARY E. David Livingstone: The Best Friend of Africa. 1902.

PICKERING, HENRY. Scotia's Noblest Son: Concise Account of the Life and Labours of David Livingstone. 1916.

RITCHIE, J. E. A Pictorial Edition of the Life of Livingstone. (A big album.)

ROBERTS, J. S. The Life and Explorations of D. Livingstone. (Compiled from reliable sources.) 1874.

SHARP, JOHN A. David Livingstone. 1920.

Sketches of Dr. Livingstone's Missionary Journeys and Discoveries in Central Africa. 1857.

SMILES, R. David Livingstone. ("World's Workers" Series.) 1885.

SMITH, GEORGE B. Heroes of the Nineteenth Century: David Livingstone. 1899.

SMITH, RONALD M. Stanley in Tropical Africa: A Narrative of the Livingstone Search Expedition.

SMITH, GEORGE WATT. David Livingstone. 1913.

STANLEY, H. M. How I Found Livingstone. 1872.

STANLEY, H. M. Life and Finding of Dr. Livingstone. (With original letters.) Dean and Son. 1874.

STARRITT, S. S. Livingstone the Pioneer. R.T.S. 2s. 6d. 1927.

STODDART, JANE T. David Livingstone as Bible Christian. 1913.

The Travellers: Sir J. Maundevell to Livingstone. 1883.

THOMAS, R. Hanes Bywydd Dr. David Livingstone. 1912.

WALKER, ELSIE B. Livingstone the Pioneer. Congregational Union of England and Wales. 1925.

WALKER, VERA E. Four Lessons on David Livingstone. 1928.

WALLER, REV. HORACE. Last Journals of David Livingstone in Central Africa: 1868-1873. 2 vols. 1874.

WILSON, HUBERT LIVINGSTONE. Livingstone the Master Missionary. Hodder and Stoughton. 1923.

Wonders of Africa: Life History of Dr. Livingstone. Philadelphia. 1874.

YOUNG, E. D. Livingstone's Adventures in Exploring Lake Nyassa. John Murray. 7s. 6d.

YOUNG, E. D. The Search After Livingstone. 1868.

INDEX

Abreu, Cypriano di, Portuguese officer, befriends L., 146

Africa, world's debt to, 1; appeal to, by Pope Gregory the Great on behalf of heathen England, 1; early Church in northern, 2; centre and south untouched by north of, 2; indigenous races of, 2; isolation of interior of before L., 3; reasons for backward state of, 4; baleful effect of European contact with, 4; natives of, erroneously believed incapable of culture, 5; British anti-slavery policy in, 5; L.'s influence in giving world a new view of inhabitants of, 5, 6; Treveleyan on danger of establishment of slave states in, 34 f.; permanence of L.'s moral effect on, 6 ff., 273 ff.; decision of L.M.S. directors to send L. to, 6; L.'s desire to remain in, 43 n., 225, 244; L.'s conversation with Moffat on, 43; L. lands in, 49; state of missions in south, 49 f.; L.'s policy of colonizing, 55; L. urges penetration to interior of, 62 ff.; moral problems of missionaries in, 77 ff.; British and Dutch rivalry in, 80 ff.; Dutch missions in, 83; early Boer hostility to missions in, 83; early belief in aridity of interior of, 86; L.'s initial discoveries in, 86 f.; attempts to encourage commerce with interior of, 91, 115; L.'s resolve to open to world, 97 f., 114 f.; his protest against Boer raids on natives of, 107 ff.; treaty protecting native rights in, 112; L.'s first great journey in, 116 ff.; L. on heathenism in, 120 f.; fever greatest drawback to development of, 121 f., 155; L.'s route to West Coast of, 125; his preaching in, 129 f., 131, 161 f., 162; L.'s first experience of slave trade in, 132; former Jesuit influence in, 151, 170; Portuguese failure in, 152; conformation of centre of, 163; L.'s intention in crossing, 163 f.; new missionary operations begun in, 180; L.'s appeal for, 184; L.'s first book on, 186 f.; L. appointed British consul for East Coast of, 188; prophesies his own death in, 189; begins second great exploration in, 192 ff.; his prayer for, 195 f.; Portuguese countenance of slave trade in, 190; agitation for suppressing slave trade on East Coast of, 230, 236; L. commissioned to ascertain Nile sources in, 231; his desire for a grave in, 244; effect of his death in stimulating interest in, 262; statistics of missionary enterprise in, 264 f.; L.'s predominant purpose for, 256

Africans, races of, 2 f.; backwardness of central, 4; oppression of, 4; regarded as inferior type, better view of due to L., 5, 51; respect for L. among, 7 f., 273 ff.; "cattle-lifting" habits of, 19; protests against exploitation of, 48, 51 f., 82 ff., 107 ff.; Moffat's views on needs of, 43; L.'s views on methods of evangelizing, 50, 54, 62 f., 66 f.; conflicting opinions concerning capacity of, 51; Philip's work for, 51 f., 112 ff.; L. on conversion of, 54 f., 186; L.'s first experience of uncivilized, 57 ff., 120-121; desire to place native teachers among, 50, 57, 62, 64 ff.; L.'s appeals for, 64, 184, 189; danger of Europeans deteriorating among, 69; moral lapses of, after conversion, 76 ff.; harried by Boers, 83 ff., 104 ff.; L. seeks to encourage trade with, 91, 115; sojourn among heathen undesirable for European children, 101; L.'s first acquaintance with slave trade among, 132; childishness of, 128; means of gaining influence over, 130 f.; bad traits of savage, 132 f.; Portuguese failure to raise, 151 f.; L.'s good name among, 157, 247, 273 ff.; difficulty of establishing missions among, 179; L.'s disappointment at proposal to neglect central, 180 n.; his endeavours to awaken public sympathy for, 184, 190; his hope to promote cultivation by free, 196; Portuguese connivance at enslaving, 216; British action for suppression of slave traffic among, on East Coast, 221, 230, 263; L.'s resolve to stand by, 225; success of missions among, 263 ff.; L.'s patience with, 268; respect of, for L.'s memory, 273 ff.

Agar-Hamilton, J. A., on L. and arming of natives, 111 f.   [222

Ajawa, native tribe engaged in slave trade, Ambaca, Portuguese outpost, 126, 147

America, primitive inhabitants of, 3

Anderson, Arthur, perceptor of L., 33, 34

Angola, Portuguese West African province, 125, 147, 153, 157, 170, 171

Appin, Stewarts of, 18

Argyll and the Isles, Bishopric of, 11
Campbells of, 15

Asthmatic, nickname of the *Ma-Robert*, 197

Augustine, St., 2

Bachuill, Barons of, 11, 15, 16, 18 f.

Baines, Thomas, member of Zambesi expedition, 189; dismissed, 199, 202

287